NPDP Certification Exam Prep

A 24-HOUR STUDY GUIDE

Teresa Jurgens-Kowal, PhD, NPDP

GNPS Press, Houston, Texas USA

NPDP CERTIFICATION EXAM: *a 24-hour study guide*

ISBN: 1515191346

ISBN-13: 978-1515191346

Table of Contents

A Brief Introduction to this Guide 1

  Why Take the NPDP Certification Exam?...1

    On-Line Resources 1

An Overview of the NPDP Certification Exam 2

  Qualifications to Take the Exam 2

    Application and Fees 2

  Overview of the NPDP Certification Exam...3

    The Exam..3

Chapter 1 – NPD Strategy 7

  Learning Objectives...7

    Strategy Differentiates the Best from the Rest 7

    The Role of Senior Management in NPD Strategy.........................8

    Six Key Elements of Strategy 9

    Mission, Vision, and Values Statements 10

    Strategy Frameworks... 12

    Innovation Strategies 21

  Summary 32

Chapter 2 – Applying Innovation Strategy 35

  Learning Objectives... 35

  Business Model Innovation 35

    Product Innovation Charter 36

  Disruptive Innovation 41

    The Disk Drive Industry 41

    The Airplane Industry 42

    Comparing Sustaining and Disruptive Innovation 43

  Open Innovation 43

  Summary 45

Chapter 3 – Portfolio Management 47

  Learning Objectives... 47

  Portfolio Management Defined 47

Benefits of Portfolio Management...49

Role of Senior Management in Portfolio Management 49

Goals of Portfolio Management..54

    Maximize Portfolio Value 55

    Balance the Portfolio..62

    Ensure Strategic Alignment...67

Resource Allocation 69

    Resource Productivity 70

Summary 71

Chapter 4 - NPD Processes **73**

Learning Objectives 73

Brief History of NPD Processes 73

Structured NPD Process Definition 74

    Disciplined and Defined..74

    Normal and Repetitive 75

    Embryonic Ideas and Salable Products 75

Standard NPD Process..75

    NPD Process Overview...76

    NPD Process Gates 76

    NPD Process Stages 79

    Management Roles in the NPD Process 92

Summary 95

Chapter 5 - Market Research..**97**

Learning Objectives 97

Importance of Market Research in NPD 98

Fundamental Market Research Definitions 98

    Secondary Market Research 99

    Primary Market Research 102

    Market Research Tests 112

Summary 126

Chapter 6 - Teams and Organization **129**

Learning Objectives 129

Teams in New Product Development 129

    A Small Number of People...129

    Complementary Skills 130

    A Common Purpose 130

    Performance Goals 130

    Team Members are Mutually Accountable 130

    Functional Departments are Not Teams 131

    New Product Development Teams 131

    Team Leader...131

Organizational Structure for NPD Teams 131

    Functional Work Teams 132

    Lightweight Teams 134

    Heavyweight Teams 135

    Venture Teams 136

Choosing an NPD Team Structure 138

    Pros and Cons of a Functional Work Team..138

    Pros and Cons of a Lightweight Team 138

    Pros and Cons of a Heavyweight Team 139

    Pros and Cons of a Venture Team..139

    Choosing an Organizational Structure 140

Building an NPD Team 141

    Organizational Culture 143

Senior Management Roles and Responsibilities 159

    Champion 160

    Sponsor 160

    Facilitator...161

    Other Senior Management Roles..161

Summary 162

Chapter 7 - Tools and Metrics **165**

Idea Generation...165

    Divergent Thinking Methods...166

    Problem-Based Ideation 169

Convergent Thinking 171

Quality Function Deployment (QFD) 172

Benefits of QFD 172

Conducting a QFD 173

Additional Considerations for QFD 175

Engineering Design and Analysis Tools 176

Engineering Design Tools 176

Engineering Analysis Tools 178

Project Management Tools 180

Scope of Work 181

Schedule 182

Budget 184

Risk Management 186

The Risk Management Process 187

Quantifying Risk 187

Contingency Plans 189

Monitoring and Controlling Projects 190

Project Reports 191

Project Reviews 191

Financial Analysis for NPD 192

Net Present Value 192

Return on Investment 194

Economic Profit 194

Project Payoff 195

Sales Forecasting in NPD 196

Diffusion of Innovation 197

ATAR Forecasting Model 198

Summary of Innovation Tools 200

Innovation Metrics 201

Designing a Metrics Program 201

Pitfalls of Innovation Metrics 214

Summary of Innovation Metrics 214

Chapter 8 – Hints and Tips for the Exam 217

Preparing for the NPDP Exam..217

Eight Tips for Taking the NPDP Certification Exam 218

Final Words 219

Appendix A – NPV Example 221

NPV Calculation Basics...221

Simple Project Comparison 222

   Extension Project 222

   Platform Project 222

   Project Comparison 223

Life Cycle Project Comparison 223

   Derivative Project Example 223

   Standalone New Product Example 224

   Project Comparison 225

Benefits of NPV 225

Appendix B – ROI Example 227

Benefits of ROI 228

Related Metrics 228

   Return on Assets (ROA) 228

   Return on Capital Employed (ROCE) 229

References 231

Index 235

A Brief Introduction to this Guide

Congratulations on taking this step toward innovation success! New Product Development Professional (NPDP) Certification recognizes your comprehension and expertise within six best practice areas of new product development. The New Product Development Professional certification leads to career advancement and is recognized around the world. This guide will provide specific information on what you need to know in order to pass the exam.

The benefits of NPDP certification are numerous. First, NPDP certification demonstrates that the practitioner can confidently demonstrate knowledge of industry best practices. Note that these best practices apply across a wide variety of technologies and businesses. For example, the best practices for new product development and innovation can be applied to the food and beverage industry, to the medical devices industry, to software and IT, as well as to drilling equipment and chemical materials. Moreover, best practices extend to the service industry, such as health insurance, education and non-profit organizations as well.

One of the reasons that the NPDP best practices apply to so many industries is that practitioners are able to understand a common language and vocabulary. In fact, terminology is quite important for the NPDP certification process, thus a significant portion of each subject matter area will include defining terms that are commonly used in the world of new product development.

Why Take the NPDP Certification Exam?

Today, more than ever, organizations hire professionals for more than just experience. They want to know that you have mastered the fundamentals and standards of new product development. NPDP certification is the most renowned innovation credential around the world. The NPDP certificate demonstrates that you are part of an elite group of practitioners that have been trained and credentialed in globally-recognized new product development best practices.

On-Line Resources

With the purchase of this guide, you have access to many additional on-line study tools. For example, an NPD Glossary, describing innovation terms and linking to additional knowledge and study information, can be found conveniently on-line at the Global NP Solutions website (www.globalnpsolutions.com/services/npd-reference).

An Overview of the NPDP Certification Exam

Qualifications to Take the Exam

To qualify for NPDP certification exam, you will need to meet criteria in three different areas: *education*, *experience*, and *knowledge*.

For those with a bachelor's degree or higher from an accredited university, you must have accrued at least two years of professional experience working in the new product development field, of which the required experience must have been accumulated within the past four years. You will also need to achieve a passing score on the NPDP certification exam as explained below.

If you do not have a bachelor's degree and have come to the field of innovation through another route, you will need to hold the equivalent of a high school degree or GED, and have accrued at least five years of professional experience working in new product development during the previous eight years. Of course, you will also need a passing score on the NPDP certification exam.

Table 1 - NPDP Certification Exam Qualification			
Category	Education	Experience	Knowledge
Type One	Bachelor's Degree	Two years within prior four years	Passing score on NPDP certification exam
Type Two	High School Graduate	Five years within prior eight years	Passing score on NPDP certification exam

It is quite possible to take the NPDP certification exam without the requisite experience and be granted *provisional status* by the Product Development and Management Association (PDMA). This is a popular option for recent college graduates and MBA students. PDMA will grant up to five years to gain the experience as specified and you will NOT have to retake the exam.

Application and Fees

PDMA waives the application fee for all members. You are still responsible for an examination fee paid to cover the facilities cost. Membership fees vary depending on the region in which you are located, but are typically less than the application fee, so it is recommended to become a PDMA member in order to sit for the NPDP exam. You will also benefit from the PDMA community and resources, such as the Journal of Product Innovation Management and PDMA Visions magazine. Also available are discount membership fees for students and those working in academia.

At the time of publication, the application fee ranges from $100 for student members to $200 for non-members, and the exam fee is $250. The current application and exam fees can be found at the pdma.org website.

Overview of the NPDP Certification Exam

The NPDP certification exam includes 200 multiple choice questions. Each question will have four answer choices. You will have three and a half (3-½) hours to complete the exam. A passing score is 75%, equivalent to answering 150 of the 200 questions correctly.

It is important to try to answer every question, since unanswered questions are considered wrong answers. Your score will be calculated and provided to you upon completing the exam at the testing facility.

The Exam

There are six key areas of new product development knowledge that are covered by the NPDP certification exam. These are:

1. NPD Strategy,
2. Portfolio Management,
3. New Products (NPD) Processes,
4. Teams and Organization,
5. Market Research, and
6. Tools and Metrics.

Questions on the exam are not necessarily presented in this order. However, the number of questions in each subject area is fixed based upon the percentages shown in Figure 1 below. The following table shows the number of questions in each subject matter area as well.

Table 2- NPDP Certification Exam Content	
NPDP Subject Area	Number of Questions
NPD Strategy	30
Portfolio Management	20
NPD Process	40
Teams & Organization	40
Market Research	30
Tools and Metrics	40
NPDP Certification Exam	200

Note that the section on Tools and Metrics accounts for 20% of the NPDP certification exam, or 40 questions. These questions are split to emphasize tools somewhat more than metrics, with 24 questions on NPD tools and 16 questions on metrics.

It is a good practice to know how many questions are included in each subject matter area, since questions on the NPDP certification exam are grouped according to subject matter area. However, there is no formal indication of the subject matter given on the exam.

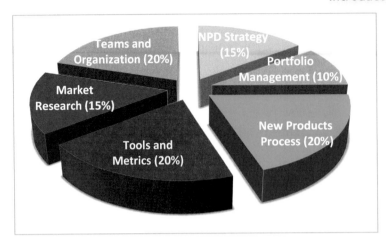

Figure 1 - NPDP Certification Exam Subject Areas

PDMA does make periodic changes to the exam, the application process, and qualifications required. You should always check for the latest information from PDMA at www.pdma.org.

NPD Strategy

First and foremost, the **NPD Strategy** guides all aspects of a new product development program. Strategy is overarching above all other elements in the NPDP framework (see Figure 2). In this guide we will discuss why strategy is important and some basic strategy statements and philosophies. Note that senior management is responsible for the innovation strategy. Get started learning about NPD Strategy in Chapter 1.

Applying Innovation Strategy

Strategy is the key link between a successfully planned innovation program and the active implementation of new product development. Different techniques, such as open innovation and business model innovation, drive success in the execution of NPD projects. In Chapter 2, learn about the application of innovation strategy through these techniques and threats to existing products via disruptive innovation. The product innovation charter (PIC is a tool to link the innovation strategy to efficient product development work and is presented in Chapter 2 as well.

Questions on the NPDP certification exam regarding the application of innovation strategy fall within the NPD Strategy category. **Applying Innovation Strategy** involves emerging practices and evolving theories, therefore, these topics are discussed separately in this guide in Chapter 2.

Portfolio Management

Next, senior management is also primarily responsible for **Portfolio Management** (Chapter 3). Portfolio management is a tool that allows New Product Development Professionals to select the most attractive projects from the entire suite of available projects. Effective portfolio management leads to selecting NPD projects that are the most clearly aligned with the innovation strategy.

In the section on portfolio management in this guide, we will discuss why and how new product portfolios are constructed and managed. We will also discuss some typical tools that are used to analyze portfolios through a series of different charts and graphs.

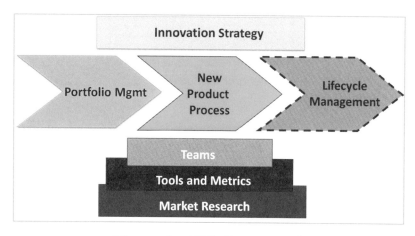

Figure 2 - NPD Framework

NPD Process

As projects are selected and implemented in support of the innovation strategy, each project will flow through a series of checkpoints in the New Product Development process, sometimes called a Stage-Gate™ system. The **NPD Process** is a structured process to validate individual NPD projects against a checklist of success criteria and to ensure alignment with the innovation strategy. Unlike portfolio management where all projects are evaluated simultaneously, the NPD process forces each project to be compared against an independent set of success measures. You can start learning about NPD processes in Chapter 4.

Life Cycle Management

Another segment of the NPDP framework is *life cycle management*. This is an important part of the new product development framework in that commercialization of any new product should also consider the obsolescence, or eventual retirement, of that product. Life cycle management should address, for example, how parts and services will be delivered to support the products that customers have already purchased, as well as how the next generation products will be developed and commercialized. We will introduce the concept of product roadmaps, a tool used for life cycle planning, when we discuss platform strategies (see Chapter 1). Note that while PDMA has acknowledged the importance of life cycle management within the NPD framework, this topic is not currently included on the NPDP certification exam.

Market Research

Market Research and business development are entire fields of study by themselves. Many NPD practitioners are introduced to new product development from a marketing perspective and will be familiar with the techniques we discuss in the section on Market Research. However, many others are led to NPDP certification from a technical, engineering, or scientific background – these individuals may not have the same degree of familiarity with market research techniques. Outcomes

---

Stage-Gate is a registered trademark of Stage-Gate International, Inc. in the United States.

of market research studies will be invaluable to senior management as they lay out an innovation strategy, thus leading full circle through the NPD framework as shown above in Figure 2.

Teams and Organization

The strategy, portfolio, and projects are, of course, implemented by the people in the firm and the organization. In Chapter 6 of this guide, recommended **Team and Organization** are discussed which support various types of NPD projects.

You will find that much of the information presented as organizational structure models is fairly intuitive since most of us currently work within team structures on an on-going basis. Much of the information regarding team structure and innovation project leadership roles is specific to the NPD framework, however.

Tools and Metrics

Of course, teams and management both use a variety of **Tools and Metrics** to effectively develop new products. For example, the charts and graphs used to present data for decision-making in portfolio management are examples of NPD tools. In this guide (Chapter 7), we'll also discuss commonly used tools in project management and specific success metrics linked to the various strategies typically followed for innovation.

Hints and Tips for Passing the NPDP Exam

In Chapter 8, we wrap up the study materials for the NPDP certification exam with some recommended test-taking tips. Many candidates for NPDP certification are familiar with electronic, computer-based exams; however, for those with less familiarity, we offer a few pointers to successfully prepare the exam.

Chapter 1 – NPD Strategy

In this chapter, we will introduce some basic definitions that are important for understanding innovation strategy. Best practices for innovation strategy are described as well as several theories and frameworks for outlining business strategies for new product development.

As indicated in the introduction and overview section, NPD strategy accounts for 15% of the NPDP certification exam, or 30 questions.

Learning Objectives

After studying this chapter you will be able to:

1. Explain the role of senior management in developing an effective strategy;

2. Define strategy and the mission, vision, and values statements;

3. Identify different strategy frameworks, including the Miles and Snow responses to change;

4. Define specific innovation strategies, such as the platform, marketing, and technology strategies;

Strategy Differentiates the Best from the Rest

Strategy is important, not only to outline which technologies, markets, and products in which a firm will invest, but also to understand which arenas are "out of bounds." If the strategy for *new product development (NPD)* is not well-defined, the company and organization will underperform when compared to their competition.

Product strategies must also include planning for the entire life cycle, sometimes called *life cycle management*. As new products are developed, senior management must also consider plans to replace the product line and how to service obsolete products as they are discontinued from the firm's portfolio. This is sometimes called the *exit strategy*.

> *"Strategy 101 is about choices: You can't be all things to all people."*
>
> - Michael Porter
>   (Harvard Business School)

Periodic benchmark studies are conducted by various organizations on the status of innovation in different firms and industries. Particularly interesting are the trends in innovation best practices over time, demonstrating processes and systems that are becoming institutionalized as well as some emerging practices intriguing in the field of innovation.

For example, 58% of new products introduced in the previous five years were considered successful (Barczak, et al., 2009). Firms labeled *"the best"* are either in the top one-third of their industry or are above the mean in sales and profit success for new product development. On average, the firms that are *best* at successful innovation are significantly more likely to guide their new product development efforts through an innovation strategy (86%) as compared to the rest (just 69%) (Barczak, et al., 2009). These companies are also most likely to initiate a new product development project with a strategy alignment and product planning activity. Additionally, the innovation strategy is applied to about three-quarters of projects in the portfolios of firms with the best innovation success rates, as compared to only about half of those in the rest of the organizations (Barczak, et al., 2009).

Furthermore, it is interesting to note that one-third of new product development teams are working on projects that do *not* have goals and objectives clearly related to the business strategy (Barczak, et al., 2009). As a trend, the gap is growing between the best and the rest in utilizing strategy as a guide to new product development efforts. In fact, strategy, not ideas, initiates the most successful new product development processes.

The Role of Senior Management in NPD Strategy

Of course, determining technologies, markets and products is the responsibility of senior management. Moreover, while having good technologies, great research and development (R&D), and superior marketing campaigns are all important to profitable innovation, the two key elements for successful new product development are:

Figure 3 - Senior Management's Role in Strategy

1. Developing product ideas that deliver a clear solution to a customer's problem, and
2. Designing products for delivery to the marketplace with flawless execution.

Fundamentally, any business strategy must address a key set of decisions, and senior management is responsible for making decisions about the direction of the business and market segments, as well as which projects should be pursued. Thus, senior management defines strategy through the markets, technologies, and products that the company will develop and which projects in its portfolio that it will commercialize.

Senior management also has control of the strategy by answering the question of "*What should we do?*" The NPD teams, on the other hand, are responsible for executing the process by answering "*How can we do it?*" and to deliver new products to the market in a timely fashion.

What is Strategy?

Strategy is a company's game plan to achieve long term goals and objectives in light of the firm's position in the industry, new opportunities, and available resources. Strategy sets the direction for both business growth and related product development efforts. Growth includes creating shareholder value in most companies. (Non-profit organizations will focus on optimum utilization of available resources and service for their clients, also a measure of shareholder value.)

There are three common ways to create shareholder value. First, merger and acquisition involves two companies becoming one. According to a study by Bain & Company (Voigt, 2009), as many as 70%

of mergers and acquisitions fail. Often failure is due to an inability of the firms to effectively consolidate disparate cultures and product lines.

The second way to increase shareholder value is by re-engineering the manufacturing processes that produce existing products. Unfortunately, creating value through cost-cutting alone is limited because it often includes decreased quality of products and/or service delivery.

Finally, the best way to create shareholder value is by developing new products. As an example, research from the University of Rhode Island (Dugal & Morbey, 1995) has shown that firms investing in innovation during a recession will outperform their competitors when the economy later recovers. Additionally, companies that institute NPDP best practices, such as following a well-planned innovation strategy, achieve greater success in new product commercialization than the rest of profits coming from sales of new products over the previous five years (50% as compared to just 21%) (Barczak, et al., 2009)).

Six Key Elements of Strategy

Strategy should include several key elements in order to construct a successful and innovative business. Senior management must address these elements and make effective decisions for the firm to sustain new product development over the long run. These six foundational features are (Markides, 1999):

1. Deciding what the business is,
2. Deciding who the customers are and what you have to offer them,
3. Deciding how you will play the game,
4. Identifying strategic assets and capabilities,
5. Creating the right organizational environment, and
6. Identifying and analyzing the impact of trends, competition, and market demand.

As indicated, the first element of defining a business and innovation strategy is *deciding what the business is*. It is also important to understand what areas of the market are in and out of bounds. For example, many restaurants are very successful offering only breakfast and lunch. Perhaps the restaurant is located in a business district or downtown office complex with few people living in the area, so offering dinner would drive little traffic to the restaurant. Therefore, offering only breakfast and lunch will maximize the restaurant's profitability by minimizing expenses associated with a low revenue period (dinner). This reflects a decision of what the strategy is and is not.

The next key decision in developing a strategy is to fully understand *who your customers are and what products and services you will offer them*. Gaining such customer insights is discussed later in Chapter 5 on Market Research. However, it is important within the context of strategy to understand that identifying a target market segment and fully understanding the customer needs will lead to a more effective outcome in new product development.

Next, the firm has to decide *"how they will play the game."* Recall that strategy is, in part, defined as a game plan for achieving the firm's long term objectives. How you will play the game includes the firm's decisions regarding in which markets it will participate, how to deliver services, and whether or not to bundle products and services, for example. Other decisions reflecting how to play the game will include in-house or open source technology and R&D, patent and legal protection in an intellectual property plan, partners and relationships with suppliers and vendors, and/or core decisions for product categories and branding schemes.

As a part of *"how to play the game,"* the firm will also need to identify those strategic assets and capabilities that are unique, distinctive, and value-added for the firm. Many small businesses and start-up companies, for instance, will perform all services in-house, including bookkeeping. However, it is often more cost-effective and allows better use of the key entrepreneurial resources to outsource the bookkeeping service. For a new product development strategy, the firm will need to identify specific capital assets and technical or marketing capabilities that are unique to the company and allow them to offer increased value in the marketplace.

Strategic capabilities are more than just special technical knowledge within a firm. These core competencies are typically interwoven and sustainable beyond the current set of employees. Core capabilities both fit with and reinforce one another while supporting the overall strategy. For instance, Procter and Gamble (P&G) uses ethnographic research as a core capability to gain novel customer insights for new product development. P&G's ability to conduct market research is unique among its competitors and is intricately linked to the company's product development processes and branded consumer packaged goods.

With a full inventory of the firm's core capabilities in hand, senior management plays a key role in *creating the proper organizational environment* for innovation to flourish. Senior management sets the tone and culture for innovation within the firm, as we'll discuss in Chapter 6 on Teams and Organization. Likewise, senior management sets the direction for the firm by owning the strategy and enabling new products to be efficiently developed utilizing core assets and resource capabilities. It is important to recognize that only senior management can develop and design the strategy for the business. Senior management must acknowledge ownership of the innovation strategy and put in place policies and procedures which allow the firm to acquire and grow the core capabilities for new product development.

Finally, senior management is responsible to *identify and analyze market trends* which may indicate opportunities in the market, including emerging technologies, pace and strength of competition, and market demand. For example, the smartphone industry has experienced tremendous growth in technical capabilities over the past several years.

Smartphone manufacturers needed to be aware of trends in how the device is used (such as for social media updates and in place of a full-sized camera) in order to acquire and develop the technical capabilities for success. Similarly, senior management at these firms need to understand the specific market segments, what features to offer customers, and how to address the high level of competition on a global basis. It is the responsibility of senior management to keep abreast of trends in the market and with competitors in order to connect the organization's long-term objectives with the specific new product development initiatives to achieve success.

Mission, Vision, and Values Statements

Strategy connects all activities in new product development. Many firms will separate the overall corporate business strategy from the innovation strategy since the overall business strategy focuses on growth goals, which may include ways to increase shareholder value such as mergers, acquisitions, re-engineering, and/or cost reduction projects. The innovation strategy is separated from the overall business strategy due to the higher risk involved in successfully deploying new technologies or developing a new market for emerging customer needs. A corporation's overall objective - their reason for being in business in the first place - is captured in its *mission*, *vision*, and *values* statements.

Mission

The mission of a firm is defined as a statement of the company's creed, philosophy, purpose, business principles, and/or corporate beliefs. The purpose of a mission statement is to focus the energy of the employees around a common set of objectives. The mission statement explains why the company is doing business and what it hopes to accomplish. It describes the company's central purpose, direction, and scope. Another description of the mission statement is an expression of the company's ultimate objectives, declaring the company's core purpose.

A mission statement should be simple and concise in order to convey the company's purpose. Simple and directly worded mission statements allow communication throughout all levels of the organization. When all staff and employees can identify the company's mission statement, they are more likely to develop ideas and products that will further the firm's growth initiatives.

> *"Make people happy."*
>
> - Disney's Vision Statement

Vision

The vision statement is the second element of an overall corporate strategy. A vision statement will paint a picture of the future for the company – how the firm sees its future position with employees, consumers, the marketplace, and the communities in which it operates. The vision statement should be used in conjunction with product and technology roadmaps to help the firm outline specific tactics to achieve its strategy into the future.

Typically business strategies are outlined for the next three to five years. The vision statement and product roadmap may look farther into the future, even eight to ten years in some cases. For example, Toyota outlined a vision for the luxury Lexus automobile in 1989 (Smith, 2007). After researching top competitors, such as Mercedes Benz, BMW, and Jaguar, Toyota's vision included the following product benefits: great high-speed handling; fast and smooth ride with low fuel consumption; super-quiet yet lightweight, elegant styling and great aerodynamics; and warm yet functional interior. These statements eventually served as a filter for the project leader during the product design stages so that the new product would closely align with the corporate strategy.

Sometimes, there is confusion between the vision and mission statements. To clarify, the vision statement details *"what"* the company plans to do, while the mission statement explains *"how"* they will do it. In many cases, the vision is not actually achieved because it looks far into the future, and as the company grows, it may achieve success in different arenas as it continually monitors and adjusts the vision of the company in that future state.

Values

Values are the code of ethics that guides a firm. We have heard a lot about ethics in the last several years, starting with the Enron scandal in the United States in 2001. Since then, governments have legislated additional rules and regulations to prevent ethics violations, such as the Sarbanes-Oxley rule in the U.S. However, the only true way that a company can uphold strong values is through exemplary leadership.

The top executives of a firm must always demonstrate high ethical behavior, inspiring and modeling ethical behavior for the organization. Values describe the code of conduct and the behavior expected of employees to carry out the firm's business. Many firms will include values statements regarding employee safety and regulatory compliance. Collectively, the code of conduct (values), vision, and mission comprise the corporate strategy.

Strategy Frameworks

Researchers have studied effective business strategy for decades. One of the earliest researchers to identify successful strategies was Michael Porter of the Harvard Business School. Perhaps Porter is most famous for his five forces model which describes the intensity of competition for a company, and therefore, the degree of market attractiveness. In this case, market attractiveness refers to the overall industry profitability.

Porter's Strategy Framework

Porter later refined the five forces model to include three general strategic approaches to addressing

market attractiveness in a classical framework (Porter, 1985). The three most successful strategies are shown in Figure 4, categorized by the breadth of the market (industry) and the core competencies of the firm (unique focus or cost leadership).

Porter's classical work on strategic frameworks laid the groundwork for later researchers to identify specific innovation strategies. You will see that the basic themes in Porter's classic strategy framework are reflected in Cooper's Five Technology Strategies (Cooper, 2013) and in

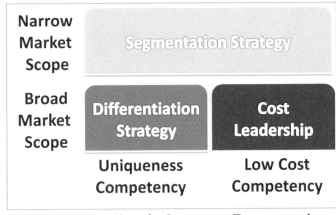

Figure 4 - Classic Strategy Framework

Miles and Snow's response to change (Miles & Snow, 1978), which are described later in this chapter.

Note that the NPDP certification exam will test the new product practitioner's knowledge of and experience with the different strategy frameworks. However, the exam will not focus on the researchers of the various strategic themes. It is convenient, though, to reference the strategy schema by the original researcher since some of the strategies have similar or identical naming conventions. For example, both Porter and Cooper identify a "differentiation" strategy framework for business and innovation. While many of the elements of the two strategies are the same, the basis for the frameworks varies from their research perspectives. Thus, in this guide, we will frequently utilize a naming convention that identifies a specific strategy framework with the lead researcher, such as "Porter's differentiation strategy" or "Cooper's technology push strategy".

Porter's Cost Leadership Strategy

As shown above in Figure 4, Porter's cost leadership strategy has a broad market focus in conjunction with expertise at minimizing operating and distribution costs. This strategy framework involves growing the firm's market share by appealing to cost-conscious customers or so-called "price buyers". Often, only a small percentage of customers will purchase a product based only on the price of a good or service. Buyers perceive value in the use of the product, loyalty to a brand, or social status exhibited by using a particular product. Companies that manufacture commodity products often follow a cost leadership strategy, for example, since the products offered to consumers are not uniquely differentiated nor perceived by the customer to offer special value.

A firm following a *cost leadership strategy* will strive to offer the lowest price to customers among all competitors. To succeed at the cost leadership strategy, a firm must be successful at operating at a lower cost than its competitors and maintain the lowest distribution costs as well. Cost leadership can be successful over the short-term; however, lower cost competitors can enter the market at any time, often utilizing modern technology to manufacture and distribute products at an even lower cost than existing producers.

Typically, there are three ways to accomplish a cost leadership strategy. First, the firm can manufacture higher levels of output. Generally, this means taking advantage of the scale of operations and operating at the low end of the experience curve. Fixed costs within the manufacturing facility decline on a per-unit basis, thus lowering the overall cost of production for the company. The firm hopes to take advantage of these effects to have the lowest cost of production in the market, thereby achieving a scale necessary to match or better the lowest prices in the marketplace while still maintaining a profit. Profit margins in the cost leadership strategy thus tend to be quite thin.

Next, the firm can maintain low production costs by offering "no frills" or "value" products. Products with few features can also help to maintain low manufacturing costs. The firm will follow low-cost advertising and distribution schemes as well, with minimal investment in R&D. While this formula is attractive in the short-run, competition can win against this strategy by adding attractive features to their products, resulting in higher profit margins and/or greater market share.

Finally, the firm can optimize the supply chain. A good example of optimized, low-cost distribution is Walmart, the big box retailer of consumer packaged goods. Walmart demands standardized products from its suppliers and just-in-time ordering, such that overall inventory costs are exceptionally low compared to the competition. Thus, the company is able to sell products cheaper than many competitors taking advantage of a cost leadership position.

The biggest disadvantage of a cost leadership strategy is that the product and service quality often decline over time, creating an opportunity for competitors to enter the market. For example, a restaurant following a cost leadership strategy will encourage high turnover of tables. This strategy would not be conducive to long business meetings over lunch, or couples lingering over coffee and dessert. Thus, the quality of service may be perceived as low by customers in these market segments.

However, many restaurants are quite successful offering high table turnover rates. For instance, those that serve lunch in a high traffic shopping mall succeed by providing standard quality items with extremely fast service.

Companies operating with a cost leadership strategy openly accept low profit margins. Another shortcoming of the cost leadership strategy is that price buyers are not brand-loyal consumers. If a competitor offers a similar product or service at a lower price, the cost-conscious customer will instead buy the competitor's product. Firms following the cost leadership strategy are often perceived as offering lower quality goods and services, and since these companies operate on low profit margins, innovation is often focused on manufacturing and distribution optimization.

Porter's Differentiation Strategy

Porter's *differentiation strategy* focuses on a broad market base (see Figure 4 above), just as the cost leadership strategy does. However, in this case, the firm gains market share and loyal customers by delivering a superior and unique customer experience. Products and services are perceived by customers to be of excellent value, and the products are differentiated from the nearest competitors in one or more ways.

Examples of differentiated products include Nike athletic shoes, the Lexus automobile, and Starbucks coffee. These products are not targeted toward cost-conscious consumers. In many cases, products are differentiated by the perceived status that a customer gains by using the product. Firms, such as Nike, are able to focus on market segments that are not highly competitive and on customers that have very specific needs that are not already met in the marketplace. In other cases, differentiated products gain a foothold within emerging markets, as a first-to-market product or service.

Consider Starbucks, for example. Delivering a unique customer experience is the hallmark of Starbucks since just about anyone could sell a cup of coffee. Starbucks focuses on the unique customer experience delivered via baristas that are trained in specific customer service models. Starbucks serves a target market segment that values the status of the brand (Vishwanath & Harding, 2000). Often companies, like Starbucks, follow a differentiated strategy with a business model or product concept that is difficult to replicate. Such elements of a business model may include intellectual property protection, unique technical experience, or innovative processes.

A primary disadvantage of the differentiation strategy is that a firm must convince customers of its unique value proposition. Time-to-market is therefore critical so that brand loyalty is built-in early as the new product or service is delivered to an emerging market. Note that a firm risks maintaining only a short-term advantage if it fails to continue to innovate and deliver new products or services to back up the original innovation.

Another weakness of the differentiation strategy is that if the proper customer value is not selected, the product may not be successful in the marketplace. For example, Apple had made a big bet on the Newton personal data assistant with handwriting recognition in the late 1990s. The product failed to gain traction because consumers did not accept the value proposition advertised by Apple (Honan, 2013). The device was too big, too expensive, and the handwriting capability was inadequate.

Differentiation as a strategy, however, remains one of the most successful ways in which to win over the long run with new product development. A differentiated strategy focuses on a broad market base and delivers a unique customer experience.

Porter's Segmentation Strategy

Porter's *segmentation strategy* is also called a "focus strategy" or "strategic scope". Rather than concentrating on the broad market, as in the cost leadership and differentiated strategies, the segmentation strategy adopts a narrow market focus (see Figure 4 above). It is this limited focus that leads to a successful business strategy.

With a narrow focus, the firm maintains intimate knowledge of a key market. That is, the company understands a target set of customers in a market better than any of their direct competitors. These target market segments are distinct groups of customers with very specialized needs. The firm competes successfully under Porter's segmentation strategy by focusing their marketing efforts on just one or two of these specialized markets. A clear advantage is that the business can gain in-depth understanding of these target customers, divining their needs better than any competitor thus leading to highly customized product development.

The focus of the company, in a segmentation strategy, is on delivering a competitive advantage through exceptional product innovation or brand marketing. Note how this contrasts with the cost leadership strategy, for example, where operational and supply chain efficiency are at the forefront. With a focused strategy, the firm may offer a unique capability to its customers or it may offer a significant cost advantage as compared to competitors (see Figure 4). The degree and level of focus on a distinct market segment inspires high degrees of customer loyalty.

A disadvantage of the segmentation strategy is that the business is dependent upon the health of a narrow target market. If this market begins to decline, the business cannot sustain its long term advantage. Sometimes, new technologies will replace existing technologies, causing a general decline in an industry. For instance, both Kodak and Fuji excelled at manufacturing photography film. With niche markets for professional photographers and low ISO film speeds, the manufacturers were able to focus on target market segments with high-profit product lines. However, as digital photography took over the industry, the health of the film market declined and a segmentation strategy was no longer valid for Kodak or Fuji. In essence, the benefit of knowing the customer better than the competition dissolved when confronted with new technologies.

Another example of a firm using a focus strategy is Tata Motors (India) that manufactures the Nano automobile. Tata well understood the need for an inexpensive, safe vehicle that could transport the typical Indian family. Tata also innovated the business process around selling cars – offering driving lessons and driver licensing at the point of sale for the Nano as many new customers did not already hold a permit.

Cooper's Strategy Framework

Another framework for innovation strategies is attributed to Robert Cooper (Cooper, 2013). Whereas the framework of the classic Porter strategies are categorized by the scale of the market and competency of the firm, Cooper's strategic framework is modelled on parameters of technology and market fit. You will note similarities between these strategies and those identified above.

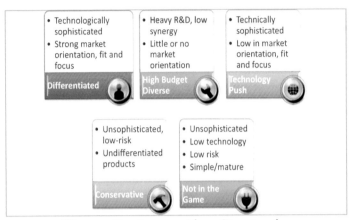

Cooper's work identified strategic themes among businesses that outperform their competitors. Again, the approach examines both technology and market dimensions for strategic alignment. These strategic themes include:

Figure 5 - Innovation Strategies

1. A focus on one or only a few key areas,
2. Strong technology and a strategy driven by technology,
3. Strong market focus with a fit and focus to customer needs, and
4. An offensive orientation (that is, a position aimed at growth in market share instead of a defensive stance to simply protect a market position).

Cooper's Differentiated Strategy

In this strategy, a firm targets attractive, high-growth and high potential markets with premium-priced, superior products. New products are closely related to one another and the company focuses on delivering high quality products that meet customer needs by offering unique features and benefits to the consumer. The focus is to deliver unique products that are superior, offering a compelling customer value proposition. Note that this strategy is similar to Porter's differentiation strategy described previously.

Not surprisingly, Cooper's *differentiated strategy* leads to the most success in innovation as measured by the sales of new products, success rate at launch, and profitability. Firms that are successful implementing a differentiated strategy will sustain deep understanding of the customer base and only begin to develop new products after customer needs are fully identified.

Cooper's differentiated strategy involves a high fit with customer needs and a high focus on the customer before, during, and after development. The technology dimension is also highly focused on the strategic opportunities introduced by a given set of customer needs. Technical research and product development efforts are sophisticated, using the latest technological advances to deliver innovations targeted to the needs of the market.

Cooper's High Budget Diverse Strategy

Continuing with a focus on technology development is the *high budget diverse strategy*. Cooper calls this the "bull in a china shop" strategy (Cooper, 2013), since the R&D efforts are numerous but unfocused. The high budget diverse strategy is nearly opposite that of the differentiated strategy with heavy spending in research and development, yet with no strong focus in these R&D efforts. Probability of success is low for new products, while development costs are high. With little attention paid to the market or customer needs during development work, this strategy often results in the worse innovation performance among competitors.

Cooper's Technology Push Strategy

Technology push is the most popular strategy with over a quarter of businesses employing this strategy either consciously or unconsciously (Cooper, 2013). These firms have a technologically sophisticated new product development effort with highly innovative ideas, similar to the differentiated strategy. New products are technically complex, however the overall innovation effort is dominated by the technical side of the business. Like the high budget diverse strategy, market focus is lacking.

Customers may not adopt the new technology and the new products may be unsuccessful in dispersed, unattractive markets. Consider that the technology push strategy first develops the new product without understanding consumer needs. It is an expensive proposition to later mount an extensive marketing and advertising campaign to convince consumers that they need, want, and desire a new product that is already manufactured. Firms that follow a technology push strategy are likely to experience average innovation performance.

Cooper's Conservative Strategy

A low-risk strategy that follows a theme of limited R&D spending is called the conservative strategy. Product development efforts are closely related to existing product lines and research is focused within familiar territory for the firm. Many of the resulting products are copycat or "me-too" products, offering little advantage among competitors.

Cooper's conservative strategy shares traits with Porter's segmentation strategy. For instance, the business has intimate familiarity with the technology of the new products offered and the market focus is narrow. New products will demonstrate strong synergy with the existing manufacturing, distribution, and marketing components. Thus, the returns from a conservative strategy are reasonable, yet because the strategy lacks a long-term vision for innovation, profitability is not optimized.

Cooper's Not in the Game Strategy

Finally, we take a look at Cooper's *not in the game strategy*. This strategy is similar to the reactor strategy in the Miles and Snow framework discussed later in this chapter. The not in the game strategy tends to result in copycat and "me-too" products (similar to the conservative strategy), yet also fails to develop linkages between new products and existing manufacturing processes. Technology developments are unsophisticated and similar to competitor positions.

From a market perspective, the not in the game strategy fails to capitalize on the firm's known customer base and may result in products that deviate significantly from the core business. Thus, while the technical development efforts are lower risk, the market approach is high risk, because in many cases, the company is entering unfamiliar territory.

A not in the game strategy take a defensive stance and does not actively pursue new product innovations. As would be expected, the performance of firms following a not in the game strategy can be quite poor since a high number of the new products are likely to fail in the commercial marketplace.

Miles and Snow Strategy Framework

Raymond Miles and Charles Snow studied how organizations respond to environmental change in the late 1970s. Their research initially focused on hospitals (in light of the new U.S. Medicare regulations), college textbook publishing (in light of industry adjustments), and food processing (in light of wide variation in the application of technology) (Miles & Snow, 1978). Miles and Snow's research led to a process of categorizing how different firms within an industry will adapt to large-scale changes. As such, the Miles and Snow strategy framework focuses on how firms adapt to change, as shown in Figure 6.

How a business responds to change includes how the business responds to aggressiveness in the market and how much risk it is willing to accept. Thus, the Miles and Snow framework is also useful to describe a strategic approach for new product development. The key problems and changes that a business faces are the administrative problem and the engineering problem. The former includes markets and distribution, while the latter includes manufacturing and technology developments.

You will notice many similarities between the Miles and Snow strategic framework and those of Porter and Cooper, discussed previously. Note that firms may employ one strategic framework in one business unit and another strategic outlook in another business unit that has different products or markets. This is not uncommon, so it is important to understand the various innovation and business strategies, as well as the fact that these strategic approaches may overlap in some instances.

The four Miles and Snow adaptations to environmental change are identified as prospectors, analyzers, defenders, and reactors. Within this guide, we will use the terms "prospector strategy" interchangeably with "prospector," meaning a firm that is following a prospector strategy.

Miles and Snow Prospector Strategy

A firm following a Miles and Snow *prospector strategy* is risk tolerant and is anxious to exploit new market opportunities. From a technology perspective, a prospector company will be flexible, developing prototypical technologies with multiple thrusts. This strategy, thus, shares similarities with Cooper's high budget diverse and technology push strategies.

In short, a prospector strategy is followed by firms that value being first to market with a new technology above all other elements. A prospector firm highly values speed,

Figure 6 - Response to Change

and, as such, will actively seek out new opportunities, new markets, and new technologies. The firm is not afraid to take risks and often introduces new products first to fringe customers that are willing to pay more just for the privilege of having the newest technology.

This can be a very successful strategy since first-to-market products tend to garner a high market share over the entire life cycle of the product. However, nearly half of first-to-market products fail upon commercialization. Because the technology is new for products developed by a prospector firm, the company must be prepared to educate customers on how to use the new product. As with the technology push strategy, marketing and advertising a new product without a defined customer need can be very expensive.

Further, as the business begins to understand customer needs for the new technology, each new product launch will cannibalize the previous product. Cannibalization is defines as taking sales from the last product version and replacing them with sales of the newest version. In fact, it may take as many as four generations of a "new" product for it to become accepted and successful in the marketplace. For example, the first Apple iPad® was launched through a prospector strategy since consumers did not previously express a need for a tablet computer and much of the technology was new for the product.

Prospector strategies can be effective for innovation, especially with disruptive or breakthrough ideas. On the other hand, a prospector may find it difficult to maximize profitability due to unfocused development efforts leading to organizational inefficiencies. Over the long run, prospector strategies can be profitable for a company, as long as the firm recognizes the risks involved with this methodology.

Miles and Snow Defender Strategy

Companies that follow a *defender strategy* focus on a narrow and stable domain. They are cost efficient and tend to utilize vertical integration in their operations to maximize profitability. Defenders maintain focus on core capabilities, perhaps even a single technology. Overall, defenders will resist radical development efforts, but will respond swiftly and strongly to competitive threats. You will note that the defender strategy resembles Porter's segmentation and cost leadership strategies, and shares characteristics with Cooper's conservative strategy.

Within the marketplace, a defender firm will market full and complete product lines, offering all possible colors, sizes, and add-on features. Because the firm is risk averse, especially with regard to its operations, it will rarely compete outside of a familiar market. Note how this strategy contrasts with the Miles and Snow prospector strategy in regard to risk tolerance and R&D activities.

Innovation for new products within a defender firm is focused on product enhancements and, typically, is not highly sophisticated from a technical standpoint. This strategy can be successful as the firm may have near monopoly market share, producing very specific products for a very specific target market. Product and service packages are often linked for the business, establishing superiority in serving a particular market. The defender firm is also above average in manufacturing excellence, for example, and values the steady state operations at its factories.

For example, GM, Chevy, and Dodge pickup trucks in the United States are primarily defender products in that there are few breakthrough innovations, the target market changes very little, and new products are generally simple line extensions of existing products. Development work often focuses on adding features without a great deal of fundamental research geared toward game-changing efforts.

A defender strategy can be successful over the long run due to the stability of the market (e.g. a steady market demand for pickup trucks in the United States). Much of the success of a defender strategy results from careful financial and operational planning.

Miles and Snow Analyzer Strategy

An *analyzer strategy* balances the priorities of a prospector and a defender strategy. This line of attack is a somewhat more conservative than a prospector strategy, yet is more risk tolerant than a defender. Analyzers will work within a hybrid domain, developing technical solutions that support existing product lines as well as focusing on new market opportunities.

Analyzer firms will often quickly follow the prospector's first product introduction with an imitator product. This is sometimes called a "fast-follower" strategy. In comparison to the prospector strategy, the analyzer's lower risk tolerance and higher focus on manufacturing quality can result in significant market share. Moreover, profitability in the long run can be high, since the analyzer may find less expensive ways to manufacture the new product or may be able to eliminate flaws that were identified by consumers in the first-to-market product originally introduced by the prospector company. Normally, new products introduced by the fast-follower strategy have at least one competitive advantage that is valued by consumers, and for which they are willing to pay, over the first-to-market product.

The analyzer strategy can be successful from a long-term perspective since the firm carefully balances risk of new product development with high quality manufacturing and stable business processes. It is important to carefully monitor the competition in order to be successful with an analyzer strategy. Honda and Nissan's hybrid vehicles are examples of analyzer products since they were introduced in response to the Toyota Prius®, yet offered new features that consumers wanted and desired.

Miles and Snow Reactor Strategy

Finally, the Miles and Snow *reactor strategy* is one that is not very successful long term. Firms that engage in a reactor strategy are usually undergoing significant change in their industry, markets, or internal business leadership. Thus, the firm fails to articulate strategic goals and objectives, and will find itself responding to market changes with a scattered approach to technology development and market entry. A reactor firm will typically begin developing new products when it observes a decline in sales of existing products, or for a variety of other reasons, such as perceived competitive advantage and management preference.

Frequently, a reactor firm will offer a lot of products that are not closely related, and will have a somewhat random approach to R&D and market development activities. Sometimes, it is said that the reactor strategy is not really a strategy at all. The Chevrolet Volt car is a product example from a business employing a reactor strategy. General Motors, the American automobile giant, recognized the sales of the Prius and other electric hybrid vehicles and responded with the Chevy Volt.

Unfortunately, the Volt suffered from poor technical design, leading to vehicle recalls and thus, very low sales compared to the more aggressive competitors. Reactors often fail because they move too slowly in response to market changes and are reluctant to destabilize the base business (pickup trucks for Chevy) for the new product lines (hybrid vehicles like the Volt). In addition, a firm may perceive a competitive threat, as Chevy did with hybrid vehicles, yet have little expertise to participate in a new market. Offering products in a new market without appropriate background studies or setting clear business objectives can lead a firm to dismal results.

Because of the scattered approach to business goals and objectives, the reactor strategy is not successful long-term. As discussed previously, a firm that is only reacting to market and environment changes is often a firm undergoing significant change in leadership. Merged companies often experience a period in which they follow a reactor strategy until the new corporation evolves to deliver strong, clear, and concise business goals. However, if the firm cannot do so quickly, it is not likely to remain an active and competitive business participant in its industry.

Innovation Strategies

While the strategy frameworks described above encompass the entire business, there are several strategies that should be evaluated specifically for innovation. These include the platform strategy, the marketing strategy, and the technology strategy. Often specific innovation strategies are incorporated through business plans or project charters; however, the decisions required of senior management for innovation must be clearly communicated for long-term, sustainable success in new product development.

Product Platform Strategy

Long-term success of a business depends not on a single product launch, but on a continuous stream of products developed and commercialized for growth markets. Developing products from core technologies to place in new markets allows the firm to continually profit from their innovations.

A *product platform* is defined as a set of subsystems and interfaces that form a common structure from which a stream of derivative products can be efficiently developed and produced. The term "product family" is often used interchangeably with product platform, since the platform of core technologies will yield an outcome of many interrelated products (the product family). Another definition of the product platform is the underlying structure or basic architectures that are common across a group of products that will be the basis of a future series of products commercialized over a number of years.

Thus, a platform may encompass a tangible, core technology, such as an ingredient used throughout a family of food products, or may be intangible, such as a set of programming codes and architectures or a database management protocol used for a family of cloud based software products. A key to understanding a platform is that the basic technical invention is re-used, re-purposed, and manipulated for leverage across many products, product lines, and markets.

One benefit of using a product platform for innovation is that it allows optimum use of manufacturing capabilities and other company resources. Additionally, these core product building blocks can offer strategic advantages. The platform is managed as an evolving entity in which the design components are shared among a set of products. New product launches within this product family are planned so that a number of derivative products can be efficiently created from the foundation of the core technology.

An example of a platform product are M&M® candies. The original candies were simply candy coated milk chocolate. Other products derived from the core technology include peanut M&Ms, almond M&Ms, and seasonally colored M&Ms for spring and fall, for instance.

Another example of platform products is demonstrated in the automobile industry. Overall changes in a car's engine, transmission, and chassis are infrequent, perhaps every five to ten years. However, new models are released annually, built upon the basic technology of the engine, transmission, and chassis. Car models may even experience significant body style changes, but the core technology of the engine, transmission, and chassis (the platform) will be updated infrequently, though on a routine basis. This simplifies the manufacturing process and saves capital investment as well.

Advantages of using a platform approach for new product development include the following:

1. Underlying elements of the product platform are clearly understood by the firm and the customer;
2. The defining, core technology of the product platform is unmistakably distinguished from other platforms in the firm or among competitors;
3. A product platform offers a medium- to long-term, sustainable advantage over other competitors; and
4. Single markets or market segments can be served by a single platform product.

Furthermore, the product platform is utilized to define the product platform strategy, to identify the core technical building blocks, to design the platform architecture, and to develop a roadmap of potential derivative products within the product family.

Principles of a Product Platform

Because there are many advantages to using a product platform within an innovation effort, companies can efficiently plan and manage new product development on the basis of a product family. Cross-functional product development teams are better aligned around a platform effort, developing specific expertise, and market growth activities are directed toward well-defined and well-known segments of customers.

As indicated above, the manufacturing process is streamlined by using a product platform since derivative products will not require significant capital investments. Manufacturing considerations are integrated into the planning process so that the product platform allows for simultaneous design of production systems. The resulting integrated manufacturing design allows new products to reach the market faster.

Moreover, markets are often identified from a global basis when viewed from a platform perspective. Whereas a single new product may focus on a narrow target market, perhaps even one that is geographically restricted, a platform product must address the largest available market to optimize profits. The new product development team will necessarily incorporate a global outlook to source the technology and to drive market growth activities.

Because platform products are subsequently introduced to several, broad markets, the feedback from customers is important for next generation, derivative product development, often aiding the development team to identify latent, unmet customer needs. Features can be added and tested easily by derivative products within the product family or within particular market segments. A product development effort following a platform strategy will need to carefully monitor market trends since the success of many products depends upon meeting customer needs built upon a high-quality core technology.

A firm's product portfolio can be simplified by the introduction of platform products. As discussed in Chapter 3 (Portfolio Management), most companies find they are working on too many low-value projects and will stretch their scarce development resources too far. The platform product approach results in simplified designs and, ultimately, better use of scarce product development resources.

Finally, product platforms allow for modular construction, another simplification for both manufacturer and the consumer. An example of modular construction is the HP® inkjet printer – many different printer models are sold, but one replacement ink cartridge can be used in a variety of printers. This allows the ink delivery systems, for example, to be designed and installed in a modular fashion. Again, the manufacturing costs and capital investment for the products within a product family are minimized by using and re-using the core technology building blocks.

Product Roadmaps
It is often helpful to communicate a product platform visually, through the use of product roadmaps. Figure 7 shows an example of a product roadmap for the Kodak Fun Saver® product family of single use cameras. A roadmap is a graphical process that identifies multiple steps necessary to meet future technical and market demands. Roadmaps may represent products for external parties, such as customers and suppliers. Alternatively, roadmaps may be internal documents, laying out the strategic development plans for product development teams.

Kodak, a major manufacturer of photography film, had long recognized the need for a lightweight, compact camera. Following a Porter segmentation strategy, Kodak held a deep understanding of amateur and professional photographers. In the 1980s, Kodak invented a technology (polycarbonate camera lens) that allowed the development of the much desired, lightweight camera (Wheelwright & Clark, 1992). Coupled with the company's expertise in manufacturing photography film, the new technology was positioned for a groundbreaking product introduction.

Originally dubbed "the Fling", Kodak finalized development of the single use camera in 1987 and released the Fun Saver product in 1988. Using a variant of the product platform strategy called "secondary wave strategy," Kodak assigned the original team that developed the Fun Saver camera to design and develop two derivative projects: the Weekend and Panoramic models. The former (now called a Sport version) was best suited as a waterproof camera, and the latter derivate was adapted for a double-wide image, normally used for landscape photos. As this example shows, it can be a strong technical advantage to use the same development team for derivative products that designed the original product platform.

Within a very short period of time (one year), Kodak had thus released a new platform, the single-use or disposable camera, along with two derivative products, the waterproof and panoramic versions.

Again using a secondary wave strategy, the development team was assigned to develop another core technology building block and a feature much desired by customers. The next generation platform product was designed to incorporate a flash in the single use camera to meet customer needs for low light and indoor photography. Because the technology required advanced electronic controls for the flash, the manufacturing process needed to be designed and adapted for the next generation platform camera. Without the need for significant technical development, the single use flash camera could have been released as yet another derivative product in the first wave product launch.

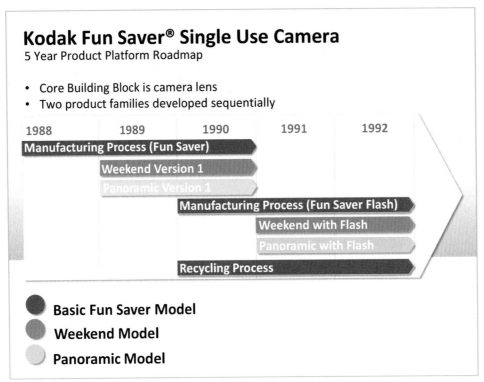

Figure 7 - Example Product Family Roadmap

Thus, the second platform of products for the single-use camera, incorporating a flash feature with an improved and refined manufacturing process, was released in 1990. Rapid deployment of derivative products followed, including the waterproof, weekend version, and the panoramic versions of the single use camera with flash.

Figure 7 shows one model of a roadmap for the Kodak single use camera. Recall that roadmaps are visual representations of the product strategy and may illustrate the product, the market, or the technology approach over a three to ten year period. Roadmaps are especially useful for technology and market planning within the initial platform product and subsequent derivative products. The product roadmap can also be a useful tool for the sales staff to share with customers or distributors to leverage brand loyalty. Moreover, the product roadmap is an essential tool for the development team to plan their work and stay on track with technical advances within the industry.

In summary, the benefits of employing a product platform strategy for new product development can be very efficient. Again, the defining technology is a core building block that reinforces the core capabilities of the firm.   Similarly, a single product's unique differentiation is derived from the *platform*, not the individual products within that platform.   The common architecture is a constant theme woven throughout the entire product family.

Advantages of a Product Platform

Because the platform is developed with a specific plan and the derivative products are deliberately planned within a given time frame, management can focus on the key decisions at the right time.   For example, management must make decisions regarding product functions and market segments.   Additionally, derivative products are focused within a time frame that is appropriate to that individual product, while the underlying platform can remain unchanged within other profit-producing markets.   In the Kodak example shown in Figure 7, the manufacturing process for the single use camera with a flash was planned well in advance of the commercial launch.   Thus, capital investment, sales, and distribution decisions were made in a timely and logical fashion.

Also, as illustrated with the Kodak Fun Saver camera, derivative products can be deployed both consistently and rapidly.   Kodak launched the two derivative products – the panoramic camera and the waterproof version – within one year of launching the initial platform product.   Further benefits result from brand leverage throughout the next generation product launches, as illustrated by the Fun Saver II flash camera and its derivative products.

Another benefit from a platform strategy is that the product planning process is viewed from a long-term perspective through the product roadmap.   A long-term focus provides the best overall innovation and profitability results for a company.   Utilizing the product roadmap to outline future derivative product launches in line with platform development work will also result in the optimum use of company resources.

Finally, the product roadmap clearly outlines when management must consider replacing a major platform.   For Kodak, the roadmap distinctly laid out the time frame in which the flash version of the single use camera needed to be commercialized.   This led to better planning for the manufacturing facilities and for the development team.

An Alternative View of the Platform Strategy

There are many advantages to using a platform strategy as discussed above.   Normally, a company will focus one product platform within one, single market.   However, there is an argument to supplying *multiple* platforms within a single market.   It is possible that competing with only a single platform in any given market may leave opportunities open to competitors.   For instance, a single platform product may be inadequate to address multiple segments or customer bases within a target market.

However, working on multiple platforms can retard development and hinder competitiveness as well.   The effects of stretching resources needed to update original platform products can result in lengthy development times and delayed derivative product launches.   An additional argument against multiple platforms within a single market is that customers may be confused when offered too many products that share many similarities among features and benefits.

Overall, however, the product platform strategy approach has proven effective for new product development efforts. The product platform strategy utilizes both horizontal and vertical market leveraging with highly effective R&D, manufacturing investment, and operational efficiencies.

Steps to Building a Platform Strategy
The five steps to build a platform strategy include the following.

1. Segment markets,
2. Identify growth areas,
3. Define current platforms,
4. Analyze competing products, and
5. Consider future platform initiatives.

Segment the Markets
As you will recall, Porter's segmentation strategy involved identifying a narrow market focus and building customer loyalty within that target group. In simple terms, market segments are groups of customers or potential customers who have common purchasing patterns or characteristics. For example, children who are interested in photography but are not yet mature enough to handle an expensive camera would be one target market for the Kodak single use camera. Another market segment includes people who snorkel or scuba-dive and want to take photos underwater but cannot afford the expensive equipment required to protect their normal camera gear in those conditions.

It is important to also look "down-market" at lower cost, lower quality customer segments in addition to the higher margin, higher quality markets. In some industries, the low-end market provides such a large volume that the profitability is greater than the high-end segment. For example, customers may prefer the simplicity or convenience of a product with fewer features. Additionally, a product with fewer features can be priced more attractively to encourage a larger volume of customers to purchase it.

Identify the Growth Areas
There are three considerations for identifying the growth areas. First, what are the current sales volumes in the target market segments for existing product lines? Next, what is your firm's market share in this segment and in the overall market? Finally, what is the projected five-year growth rate for this market? If the long-term growth rate is not attractive, another product family may prove to be more suitable for development.

Define the Current Product Platforms
Next, management needs to understand and define the company's current product platforms. Many firms employ platform strategies without a conscious plan since the common technologies often result from the firm's strongest capabilities and manufacturing advantages. Listing these building block technologies can help to identify the firm's current platforms.

Understanding the current platform offerings allows the firm to consider adding derivative products to a product family. Additionally, management can choose to further advance the existing platforms. Another consideration for the platform strategy should address the alternatives discussed previously. For example, is it advantageous for the firm to offer multiple platforms within a single market?

Analyze Competing Products

As always, monitoring competition is an important part of any strategy development activity. As discussed earlier, senior management is responsible for understanding the competitive trends applicable to a new product development effort. This information is sometimes called *competitive intelligence* and will assist the management team in understanding the competitive landscape for a new product platform under consideration. For example, senior management can gain information on whether there are few or many competitors, whether the technology is simple or advanced, and whether demand is light or heavy for these new products.

Consider Future Platform Initiatives

Finally, utilizing an assessment of the firm's core capabilities, existing product platforms, and trends in the industry, management will be able to consider future platform initiatives. In the case of Kodak, this led to extending the single use camera platform with a flash version of the single use camera. For the case of M&M candies, the platform has been extended with specialized marketing by offering customized printing on the chocolate candies for birthdays, weddings, and graduations.

Product platform strategies can be very successful in developing new products and should be considered for continuous integration of new products for the firm. An innovation strategy should examine the potential benefits of utilizing a platform strategy to meet overall goals and objectives.

Market Strategy

While the *market strategy* is similar to the fundamental business strategy, the focus is narrowed to just the markets and consumers of the products and services being developed and improved by the firm. As with each individual strategy framework, there are overlaps between the market strategy and the six key elements of the business strategy (above).

Sometimes the market strategy is called the *market vision*, yielding a long term perspective of the innovation. It is especially important to lay out and plan a market strategy for projects that are in the early stages of the NPD process. Market strategies are also beneficial in planning radical innovations that will introduce new technologies to customers.

Critical issues in the market strategy include the number of platforms, the number of derivative products, and the frequency of new product introductions. Of course, these decisions will provide feedback to the technology strategy (see below) so that new developments are timed appropriately. In particular, the market strategy should address fundamental what, who, how, and why questions.

- First, *what products will be offered?* This includes determining the breadth and depth of the product line and products within a product family.
- Next, *the target customer segment must be identified.* Again, it is important to understand the boundaries of the market. This involves not only understanding the markets and segments in which firm will participate, but also those markets in which the company chooses to *not* participate. Again, the market strategy can take advantage of the platform product by offering different features from a common technology basis to a luxury market segment, to a commodity market segment, and to a value, or price-buyer, market segment.
- The market strategy should also include consideration of *how the product will reach the customer.* For example, Apple's iTunes™ and Amazon's Kindle™ e-books use an internet

platform for immediate product delivery. On the other hand, food and beverage products may require special handling to reach the consumer while maintaining freshness and quality. In some cases, government regulations may restrict or limit product distribution by requiring additional special handling of the product.

- Finally, the market strategy must *define why the company believes a customer will prefer their product over a competitor's product.* This piece of the market vision will describe the distinctive benefits that a consumer will receive by using the product and which attributes are most important to the customer in order to gain the perceived value. Often, for comparable products, the benefits are communicated through catchy advertising slogans in order to differentiate one product from a competitor's product. Such benefits may not derive from the use of the product or the specific feature set but can be imparted based upon status. For example, luxury automobiles serve the primary purpose of transportation, yet convey a benefit message of wealth and prestige to the buyer.

One tool that is used to help define the market strategy is called the product/market matrix or Ansoff matrix (Ansoff, 1957). An often used, but incorrect, assumption in new product development is that every product is either employing a new technology or addressing new markets. In fact, the new product strategy is much broader and can address many dimensions of technology or markets. One of the strategic decisions that senior management must take involves the growth vector: the direction that the company chooses to take from its existing position when it attempts to serve an identified market with its products or services. The product/market matrix is a tool to assist management in understanding the growth strategy from a marketing perspective, as shown in Figure 8.

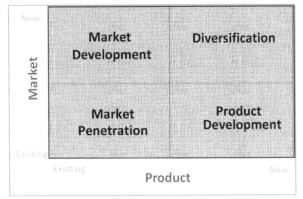

Figure 8 - Product/Market Matrix

Furthermore, existing or current markets do not necessarily mean that the firm has immediate customers, but instead it represents customers that are already identified within a target market segment as well as non-customers that may purchase the product in the future. In the same vein, a new market is one that the company is not currently serving. Existing products are those that the company is currently selling, while new products are those that still need to be created and introduced commercially by the firm. Depending on the market orientation and newness of the product, there are four growth alternatives a company may pursue:

- Market penetration,
- Market development,
- Product development, and
- Diversification.

Market Penetration

A firm may pursue a marketing strategy that leads to growth through increased sales volumes. Increases in sales can occur by selling additional units being sold to existing customers or by selling units to consumers who previously did not purchase the product. The market penetration strategy, illustrated in the lower left hand corner of the product/market matrix, focuses on existing products or services that the firm already sells and on familiar markets in which the firm already participates.

For instance, Pepsi™ and Coca-Cola™ are similar products, each with a large market share. As Pepsi targets Coca-Cola drinkers and converts them to purchasing Pepsi instead, they are employing a market penetration strategy. In this case, Pepsi targets non-consumers (Coke drinkers) and increases sales volumes. Alternatively, Pepsi could encourage existing customers to drink more soda and likewise increase sales volumes. Sodas have been re-packaged from cans in six-packs to two-liter bottles under this market penetration strategy, for example.

A *market penetration strategy* can be profitable in the short- to medium-term. It is generally the least costly of the four product planning strategies since it utilizes existing technologies and pathways to the target market, building off existing customer and product knowledge. The cost and risk of failure are relatively small.

Market Development
Next, as shown in the upper left hand corner of the product/market matrix in Figure 8, the *market development strategy* utilizes existing product technologies while trying to develop new markets and customer bases for sales. In this case, the firm seeks to open new markets for the existing product line in order to achieve growth. The company capitalizes on the existing product technology to fend off competitors.

For example, a company may be able to open new geographic market areas or attract additional customer segments to use the product. This strategy requires finding new uses and applications for the existing product or identifying existing applications within new industries. The advantage of this product planning strategy is that it builds on the technical know-how of the firm and on the existing product-related knowledge available within the organization.

An example of a market development strategy is introducing an existing food product into new markets, such as Chex® cereal. Traditionally, Chex cereal is a breakfast food in North America. However, the company has moved the product into a new market – snack foods – by packaging the cereal with pretzels, crackers, and nuts sold as Chex Party Mix™. In some cases, the new markets can be as valuable as the traditional markets, as Chex Party Mix is widely available wherever snack foods are sold (such as service stations and quick stop shops), while the traditional cereal product is primarily sold through existing channels (such as supermarkets and grocery stores).

Product Development
Shown in the lower right hand corner of the product/market matrix of Figure 8 is the *product development strategy*. This strategy seeks to develop new products to better satisfy the needs of an existing market. As the firm adds new features to products, it can fend off competition with a more diverse product line. Other examples of a product development strategy involve developing quality variations of the product line (going up-market and down-market, for example, with luxury and value-priced versions). Product development strategies may involve developing different grades, models, or sizes of the product as well.

The product development market planning strategy addresses the question of "What do our customers buy that we can supply and they do not currently purchase from us?" The firm's growth occurs by expanding the customer base and building on the knowledge of existing customers' needs and behaviors.

Many new products fall into the product development strategy, such as derivative products within a product platform. The iPhone® 6 is a new product, for example, that offers new features to existing customers. Customers in the existing market who previously used an iPhone 5, for example, are eager to adapt the new features and will purchase the new product.

Diversification

Finally, a *diversification strategy* is represented in the upper right hand corner of Figure 8, illustrating the product/market matrix. Because this approach to business growth involves both new technology development for new products and entry into uncharted markets pathways, this strategy may be of higher risk for a firm. However, depending upon the current economic and industry trends, a diversification strategy can be very profitable as well.

A diversification strategy is long-term and should include planning for transition periods as the firm begins to manufacture new products and enter new marketplaces. Diversification is an attractive strategy for firms that are facing aging or obsolete technologies, experiencing declining sales, or managing complex industry risks. Firms can choose to follow a vertical, horizontal, or lateral diversification strategy.

In a vertical diversification strategy, the firm may acquire other companies within the value chain. For example, Samsung not only manufactures smartphones, but they also produce the primary integrated circuit for the smartphone. A horizontal diversification strategy, on the other hand, will yield new products within a new market but will also capitalize on the firm's highest capabilities. For example, a company that sells ice cream will have insights into customers who purchase seasonal products. Following a horizontal diversification strategy and by focusing on their deep customer understanding, the company may begin selling peppermint candy canes. Internal development of such new products will require significant resources and a transition period to ensure a strong market presence.

Finally, lateral diversification involves entering an entirely new industry. For example, a corporation that has excelled at manufacturing airplane engines may enter the waterski market in order to hedge against weaknesses in the airline industry. For a successful diversification strategy, the company must have a clear and defined understanding of the firm's core capabilities, as well as significant data forecasting industry and market trends.

Technology Strategy

In addition to the overall business and market strategies, a separate technology strategy is often necessary to address the higher risk of technology development. For instance, if a new technology is required for a platform extension (such as the flash feature in the previously discussed Kodak Fun Saver single use camera), the risk of failure is greater than technical failure of an independent product. Sales for the entire product line can be lost if the technical advances cannot be met and new features do not deliver benefits to customers.

Additionally, technology strategies are often segregated from the overall business strategy due to the scope of the R&D efforts. Many corporations invest in fundamental research programs, either internally or externally (via universities, partnerships, or alliances). The strategy for these fundamental research efforts needs to be captured so that the work is properly aligned and will position the firm for future product launches consistent with the business strategy. In fact, many companies will specifically segregate their NPD processes into two distinct systems, one covering the fundamental technology research and another identifying the traditional product development phases (see Chapter 4).

Moreover, a technology strategy needs to address the underlying reasons in developing new technical applications in addition to understanding how to convert the technology to a useful product or service. This is sometimes called the "know-why" of technology development. Much of the technical know-why is tacit knowledge possessed by senior technical experts within the firm. Correspondingly, by defining specific capabilities of the firm, know-why can help to focus the technology strategy thus giving it a competitive advantage.

A key question for the technology strategy involves sourcing of the new technical applications. New technologies may be researched in-house, or they may be acquired through licensing activities. Technologies may also be acquired through university partnerships and open source or co-creation initiatives. While a new product may use several sources of technology acquisition, both in-house and external, it is important to frame the technology strategy so that the firm can establish a consistent approach aligned with the overall business and innovation strategy frameworks.

Furthermore, senior management must establish the timing and frequency of technology implementations. At the extremes are the *rapid inch-up* and *great leap forward* philosophies. In the rapid inch-up strategy, the firm adopts small, frequent changes in the technology leading to cumulative and continuous performance improvement. The great leap forward philosophy in technical development yields infrequent, but large-scale, changes to the technology in order to advance the state of the art.

The mobile phone industry provides an example of the rapid inch-up strategy. New features and new technologies are launched for cell phones on a very frequent basis with small feature enhancements over previous models. On the other hand, the Apple iPad® is an example of a product with a great leap forward technology strategy. The nearest product in the company's portfolio was the iPhone, yet the iPad required significant technology development to bridge the gap between a smartphone and the new tablet computer. A technology strategy can position the firm to be a market leader, as in Apple's case.

Finally, senior management must address resource utilization through the technology strategy since new product ideas always outnumber the available development resources. At least one recent case study of a company providing electric power generation equipment found that aligning the organization's resources and activities with the stated technology strategy resulted in stronger financial performance (Bergek, et al., 2009).

Technology strategies are therefore an important element of an overall innovation strategy. A technology strategy helps to address the inherent risk in research activities while maintaining alignment with the new product portfolio goals and objectives.

Summary

Strategy is an overarching theme throughout all of new product development. Companies that dedicate up-front effort to laying out a strong and achievable innovation strategy are the most successful with long-term new product development.

In this chapter, we have described the foundations of innovation strategy. Senior management plays a key role in making the formal decisions for new product development strategy. Moreover, increased attention and dedication from senior management directly impacts the quality of an innovation program. Senior management must determine the direction for the firm by identifying opportunities based upon the market, technology, and product orientations, as well as managing all of the necessary resources for a new product development effort.

Strategy is defined as the company's game plan for reaching its long-term growth goals. Composed of the firm's mission, vision, and values statements, the corporate business strategy defines objectives that can be met by innovation and new product development for specific markets by utilizing the company's core technical capabilities.

Several strategic frameworks were discussed in this chapter. These strategic frameworks overlap in many cases and are associated with various elements of the market, technology, and product.

- Porter's classical strategic framework identifies the breadth of the market segment and the core competency of the firm. A broad market segment coupled with effective operations leads to a *cost leadership strategy*, while a focus on a unique customer value proposition leads to a *differentiation strategy*. A narrow market focus defines the *segmentation strategy*.
- Cooper's strategic framework is defined by the scope of the market and technical development effort. A *differentiated strategy* focuses on a well-defined market segment and highly sophisticated technical research efforts. The *technology push* and *high-budget, diverse* strategies also invest heavily in technical research but lack market focus. In contrast, the low-budget, *conservative strategy* limits technical investment, while the *not in the game strategy* lacks both market and technology focus.
- Miles and Snow's strategic framework addresses how a firm will respond to environmental changes. *Prospectors* enjoy being first to market and will focus their strategy on developing new-to-the-world products. *Analyzer* firms will recognize the need for new product development, often following the prospector firm quickly to the market with new technologies. Yet, the analyzer strategy values steady operations and long-term objectives. A *defender* prefers to focus on efficient operations but will innovate to protect the boundaries of its market. Each of these strategies can be successful in the long run. On the other hand, a *reactor* firm is often undergoing significant internal change and fails to lay out a cohesive strategy. Without identifying business goals and objectives, reactor firms are unlikely to remain in business for the long-term.

Finally, specific strategies for the platform, marketing, and technology elements of new product development were defined. *Platform strategies* take advantage of a core technology building block to develop a series of products over an extended period of time. The *product/market matrix* helps a firm to identify opportunities and competitive threats in existing and new product arenas. A separate *technology strategy* is important for a firm since technical development involves more risk and should inform the company regarding technology acquisition. Firms that are successful in designing and implementing innovation strategies, including platforms, markets, and technology, are the most successful with new product development.

Chapter 2 - Applying Innovation Strategy

In this chapter, we continue the discussion of new product development strategies. While Chapter 1 lays out the common philosophies and frameworks for innovation strategy, this chapter will focus on application and implementation of a new product development (NPD) strategy through techniques such as open innovation. Threats to an innovation program that should be addressed through strategic planning, such as disruptive innovation, are defined and described.

Many of these practices are emerging and are evolving more rapidly than other areas of NPD. Content in this section is contained within the NPD Strategy category on the NPDP certification exam.

Learning Objectives

After studying this chapter, you will be able to:

1. Describe the business model approach to NPD using the product innovation charter, or PIC,

2. Identify the four main sections of the PIC,

3. Define and give examples of disruptive innovations, and

4. Contrast and compare traditional and open innovation.

Business Model Innovation

Business model innovation is an emerging strategy to identify new market opportunities. In short, a unique business model innovation offers a new value proposition to the customer, whether through a new technology or a new market interface.

For example, Apple took an existing technology in the MP3 player and coupled it with new hardware (the iPod™) and new software (the iTunes™ stores) to offer a new service model. This business model even allows customers to listen to an entire song before requiring a purchase. Apple offered unique value to customers by offering previews and downloads of only songs that were of interest to them, and offered a new value to the music industry which had been fighting pirating issues for some time.

Apple has continued to overturn business models through the Apple store, which delivers significant profits to the enterprise. The Apple store allows customers to try computer products in a non-threatening environment before purchasing them. Service is also delivered in a new way through the Genius Bar, where training and learning are the key goals in order to emphasize the "user-friendly" aspect of all Apple products.

Generally, business models offer a unique value to customers through a new interface, as with iTunes, or by delivering a product via a new distribution channel. In all cases, the company profits by identifying a novel value to direct customers and/or intermediaries. New business models typically go hand-in-hand with the innovation strategy. For instance, the Miles and Snow strategies (Chapter 1) represent a company's response to changes in the marketplace. Business model innovation parallels this methodology with radical innovations introducing technical changes to the marketplace or with new pricing models offering unique value to the distributors.

There are four fundamental aspects to a business model (Johnson, et al., 2008): customer value proposition, profit formula, key resources, and fundamental processes. First, and most important, is

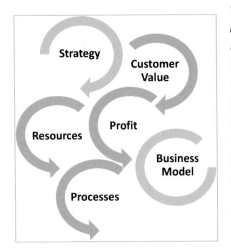

the customer value proposition. As an example, let's consider Minute Clinic. These clinics are staffed by nurse practitioners and physician assistants inside of CVS pharmacy stores in the United States. Nurses and trained medical staff can treat minor illnesses, like the common cold or ear ache, at these neighborhood clinics. Minute Clinics are "walk-up" and significantly reduce the patient's time spent to receive treatment. Patients have a short wait time to see the medical staff and avoid the hassle of having to make an appointment with a doctor. Traditionally, a sick person must make an appointment with their primary care physician, wait in the reception room with other ill people, and pay excessive amounts for simple prescriptions which are filled at a separate location.

Figure 9 - Business Model Innovation

Thus, the Minute Clinic offers a true business model disruption to the traditional delivery of medical services. Customers perceive new value through reduced wait times and quick filling of prescriptions at reduced cost. Importantly, the consumers perceive no quality impact by visiting a nurse at the Minute Clinic as compared to the traditional service delivery model.

Next, business model innovation must focus on the profit formula. For a Minute Clinic, the profit formula relies on less expensive staff (a nurse practitioner as compared to a primary care physician) and the use of retail space in existing CVS shops. Similarly, competitors may offer reduced features on a product and accept lower profit margins to enter the marketplace and deliver new value to price-focused consumers.

In order for a business model innovation to be successful, key resources must be identified. In the Minute Clinic example, the key resources are the nurse practitioners and physician assistants who evaluate, diagnose, and provide treatment and patient education. Additionally, relationships with physicians and on-call doctors (available through a technology-driven network) assists in keeping costs for medical care low in this new business model.

Finally, key processes are a differentiating cultural factor for all companies. Minute Clinics use a proprietary software program to follow evidence-based diagnoses and rely upon a network of on-call physicians for additional consultation. Patients appreciate the quick service and value the convenience of one-stop shopping to obtain a diagnosis and to fill any necessary prescriptions.

Business model innovation creates a strategic advantage for a firm by creating new customer value. It is important in innovation to recognize new ways to deliver products through technology and market opportunities.

Product Innovation Charter

The *product innovation charter*, or *PIC*, is a written strategy document that links the key elements of strategy (see Chapter 1) with the competencies and capabilities of the innovation team to successfully implement the NPD project. Ultimately, the PIC defines the relationship between the business strategy and the product policy, laying out the boundaries and interdependencies of each innovation project.

At the project level, the PIC will focus on product improvements and enhancements, as well as exploiting the firm's existing capabilities. Other projects will use the PIC to focus the development team's efforts around radical innovations and higher risk, disruptive business models. At an organizational level, the PIC will reflect the overall innovation strategy and how management should view these opportunities for new product development and future business growth.

The PIC is composed of four primary sections, which are somewhat similar to the sections of a business plan, as follows.

1. Background,
2. Focus arena,
3. Goals and objectives, and
4. Special guidelines.

Normally, the product innovation charter is a relatively short summary document. Additional project documents, such as the product protocol and team charter, may be appended to the PIC as the new product development project progresses through the various stages of work.

PIC: Background

First, the primary element of the product innovation charter is the background section. The purpose of this section is to validate the strategy and the purpose of the project. Each new product development project should document alignment with the strategy in the charter.

Moreover, this section should address any key ideas resulting from a situation analysis or the product roadmapping exercises. Assumptions regarding the validity of the project to inform the strategy are recorded in the charter background. In general, the background section is answering the question "Why is the firm pursuing this project in the first instance?"

The background section provides a link between the work of the project with the overall corporate strategy and goals of the business unit. It clarifies the role of the team in developing a particular product or service in alignment with the strategy. Further, the logic of why the project is being pursued should be clearly outlined. The team will return to this section of the PIC frequently to clarify the scope of the new product development effort and to understand constraints of the project. Frequently, throughout the later execution phases of a project, additional scope items will be suggested, and the PIC is used to limit these attempts at scope creep by carefully outlining the boundaries of the development effort.

Additionally, the background section of the PIC is useful to document project assumptions. For example, if the firm is pursuing a first-to-market strategy, the PIC documents the importance of speed for the project team. Likewise, if a company is pursuing a fast follower or analyzer strategy (see Chapter 1), product imitation and competitive intelligence will provide important strategic assumptions for the project to maintain alignment with overall business plans.

PIC: Focus Arena

In contrast to why the project is being pursued in the first instance, focus arenas for the project describe the market and technology within the product innovation charter. In essence, this section will address the strategic questions of "where the game is played" (a target market) and "how the game is played" (the technology).

A key area for each new product development effort is to link the technology and product with the market (see the section on Market Strategy in Chapter 1). Technology without a market, or a pure technology push strategy, often results in a product that is feature heavy. Such products force high price points to accommodate development costs and may be too expensive for many consumers. Likewise, a pure marketing push without technology development may result in fancy advertising campaigns with no new market penetration. Thus, it is important to ensure that the new product development effort demonstrates focus on both markets and technologies.

Thus, to improve the odds of success for a new product development effort, the PIC should document *at least* one technology dimension and one market dimension that will be addressed by the project. Suggested technology dimensions are, for example, core competencies or existing technologies. Market drivers, on the other hand, include arenas such as the target consumer segment, customer benefits, and/or the distribution channel. Identifying at least one market driver aligns the project with the overall business strategy and addresses the market strategy elements, as described in Chapter 1.

In addition to market and technology drivers, it is useful to document the competition's profile and the industry trends in the focus arena section of the product innovation charter. An open market will have little, if any, existing competition. For example, if the target market segment is relatively open at the time the project is initiated but competition is expected to increase quickly, these assumption must be documented in the PIC to clarify the impact of competitive responses on the NPD effort. Impinging competition is a key component for the project team to understand as the new product development effort progresses. In addition, senior and mid-level management need to formally recognize such project constraints to effectively align the project with the overall business strategy.

Product development boundaries may include competition, brand leverage, and manufacturing or operational constraints. Additional considerations for the PIC should document whether the technology is developed in-house or using open sources as well as the degree of innovativeness that is sought. Again, a product pushing known technical limits with state-of-the-art breakthrough technology will require a different strategic outlook than will an incremental improvement to an existing product. Moreover, the tactics necessary to execute an aggressive technology development will also vary and should be documented in the PIC.

PIC: Goals and Objectives

The third section of the PIC details goals and objectives particular to the new product development project. In this section, the purpose of the project, as described in the background section, is elaborated to include specific operational outcomes. Critical success factors of the project are described in measurable terms and performance metrics for the project, and the team, are documented as realistic targets.

In particular, both short-term and long-term goals and objectives of the project should be described. For instance, a new technology may be developed for a specific product that will be utilized in the long-term as a core building block in a new platform for the company. Project team accomplishments may include a rough timeline of milestones for the project that will be linked to the NPD process (see Chapter 4). Team performance measures should be included to motivate and inspire cross-functional relationships throughout the project execution stages.

It is crucial to detail the specific and measurable success criteria for the project in the PIC document. Normally, it is best if the project team members themselves contribute to defining these metrics. When the team bears responsibility in identifying the success metrics, they will be better equipped to work toward these measures during the project execution stage. Team members will also be motivated to accomplish the project goals collaboratively, rather than working solely as individual contributors.

Some metrics that are commonly included in a project charter are profit or sales volume, growth (as an income statement variable, such as increased revenue or decreased operational costs), and market share or market penetration for the new technology. Team metrics should include overall success of the project and achieving milestones throughout the project in addition to individual performance improvement. Be aware that particular strategies lend themselves to specific sets of metrics that can be linked to the product development effort through the PIC (see Chapter 7).

As an example, consider a firm that is pursuing a first-to-market strategy. This firm will normally include metrics, such as market penetration or market share as key measures of success. Aiming for first-to-market capabilities, the firm will also track the trend of units sold over time as an important gauge of their success. Alternatively, a company that is following a defender strategy (see Chapter 1) may be most concerned with project metrics regarding quality and customer satisfaction while maintaining a given market share. Loss of market to competitors would be particularly devastating to a defender company.

Goals and objectives of the NPD effort must tie the overall innovation strategy to the expected project work. Senior management and the innovation teams will agree upon the most critical deliverables for the new product project. Team members will document specific technical and group objectives in the PIC to ensure success of the project.

PIC: Special Guidelines

The final section of the PIC describes any special considerations for the innovation effort. In some cases, the innovation team will also document their established working procedures in this section of the PIC. In the goals and objectives section, for example, the team documents the metrics of success that are aligned with management expectations for the project. Additionally, the team will document any special "rules of the road" necessary for them to accomplish the goals and objectives for the project.

As an example, a team that is globally dispersed may wish to document basic working rules in the PIC, such as how and when meetings will be held, frequency of face-to-face meetings, and shared file handling.

Management will include special project guidelines, such as the high-level budget and schedule, required for the new product effort. Again, the primary purpose of the PIC is to align the strategy of the business with the specific innovation effort, so the comprehensive budget and schedule will be developed later during the project's detailed planning stages. However, high-level project boundaries and constraints should include any special considerations that may influence how the new technology and product will be developed.

For instance, product development constraints may include target market or customer limitations, manufacturing requirements (such as no new plant or equipment to be purchased), and technical acquisition (patents or licenses). Again, these constraints are documented in the PIC to link the overall innovation strategy, market strategy, and technology strategy to the specific product development effort.

Other special requirements that should be described in the PIC often involve legal and regulatory requirements. An example can be found in the pharmaceutical industry, where product development involves FDA testing and approval in the United States. These tests are lengthy, covering several years of time, and include extremely detailed and specific data. Any product development effort must include these tests and the requirements for FDA testing should be clearly outlined in the PIC.

PIC: Additional Considerations

Both senior management and the NPD teams should consider some additional elements in preparing the product innovation charter.

First, who is responsible for writing the product innovation charter? Generally, the project team should retain the primary responsibility for documenting the project guidelines. Personal input from team members is important since they will be executing the development work. Team performance metrics and stretch goals that are designed by team members will tend to result in higher levels of achievement of project objectives.

On the other hand, management should also be represented throughout the development of the product innovation charter, since the primary purpose of the PIC is to align the strategic direction of the firm with the specific new product development effort. Documenting the background, constraints, and boundaries for the PIC at a project kick-off meeting is a typical practice for new product development efforts. This allows the project team to interact with senior management to fully understand the expected outcomes for the NPD effort.

Finally, whether the PIC can be changed over time is often a cultural element of an organization. For example, some firms demand that once a charter is written it cannot be changed. Other companies are comfortable with updating the PIC as the project progresses and new market or technical information comes to light. Of course, if the PIC is changed too frequently, the team will have difficulty executing a project against a moving target. Other documents, such as the product protocol (see Chapter 4) may be appended to the original product innovation charter in order to capture refinements as the project advances from idea to commercialization.

Because the PIC is a charter or contract, some teams feel that a signature by the team members increases their commitment to the project. Many studies have shown that when a person physically adds his or her signature to a document, motivation and commitment to the project will increase.

In summary, the product innovation charter documents a shared basis of understanding of strategic objectives determined by senior management and the specific new product development work effort. The PIC provides a common framework that outlines expectations and limitations, allows sharing of information across the organization, and increases the odds of success for a given innovation project.

Disruptive Innovation

Like the product innovation charter, disruptive innovation is an emerging practice. The concept of *disruptive innovation* is somewhat new and can be difficult to understand or apply to innovation in the real world. Clayton Christensen first described the idea of disruptive innovation in his seminal book, *The Innovator's Dilemma* (1997).

In his study of why some businesses fail and why others succeed, Christensen conducted extensive research in the computer disk drive industry. When personal computers (PCs) first became popular in the 1980s and 1990s, computer memory was primarily managed by disk drives. Disk drives migrated from applications in mainframe computers with 14" drives, to mini-computers with 8" drives, to desktop computers with 5-¼" drives, and finally, to laptop computers with 3-½" drives over the time period from 1976 to 1994.

Christensen noted an apparent trend demonstrating that as a firm gained industry experience and a larger customer base, the firm's technology tended to move up-market adding product performance and new features. These firms would follow Cooper's technology push strategy (see Chapter 1), for example, as they added performance capabilities to a product, such as the disk drive, packing more and more bytes onto a platform, such as the 14" disk or the 5 ¼" disk. As the firms added features requested by their very best customers, they tended to increase performance beyond the level required by less sophisticated customers. On the other hand, less sophisticated customers were willing to sacrifice performance for other features, such as reduced cost or increased convenience.

The Disk Drive Industry

In the disk drive industry, for example, as the lead companies refined the performance for 5-¼" floppy disks (called *sustaining innovations*), they failed to recognize that a smaller, less fragile disk, such as the 3-½" disk, was more desirable to laptop customers. Even though the 3-½" disk initially had lower performance, held less information, and had a lower capacity than the 5 ¼" floppy disk, it offered convenience to a new set of customers (Christensen, 1997).

Thus, as the mainstream companies continued to improve the capacity of the primary product, small start-up firms were able to displace the mainstream companies with an initially lower-performing product. The new product offered features that were beneficial only to a smaller volume, fringe market. In the case of computer disk drives, the emerging laptop market embraced the product with more convenient features, whereas the much larger and more established desktop market continued to press for improved performance in existing products. Eventually, as the start-up firms gained a foothold in the emerging markets, the technology improved and they were able to expand market share. Eventually, these start-up firms were able to overtake the established firms in terms of profitability and sales revenues, while the mainstream companies tended to fade away.

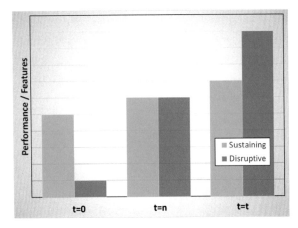

These trends are illustrated in Figure 10, where the sustaining technology is shown as the left column (green bar) with the customer's desired level of performance and the number of features shown on the left axis. Early in the innovation cycle (t=0), the established firms offer a product with a level of performance that meets customer demands. The sustaining innovation continues to build upon the known technology, slowly increasing performance over time (shown by the green bar at times t=n and t=t in Figure 10).

Figure 10 - Disruptive Innovation

Alternatively, as the disruptive technology emerges and offers convenience or other novel features to fringe customers, a new product is released with lower performance and fewer features than is desired by the average consumer. This disruptive technology is shown by the second column (blue bar) in Figure 10, illustrating much lower performance at an early time in the innovation cycle (t=0). However, as the technology improves and more customers begin to purchase the disruptive product, its performance meets that of the established firms (t=n in Figure 10). Finally, as the disruptive technology gains a larger market share and acquires traditional customers, the technology develops to a point at which the performance and number of features exceed that of the established firms (shown by the blue bar at time t=t in Figure 10, for example).

Interestingly, Christensen concluded (1997) that *good corporate management practices* helped the firms develop these sustaining innovations, yet these were the very *same* practices that forced the established firms away from accepting the risk of the disruptive technologies. Such practices include: querying existing customers, investing aggressively in technologies that deliver solutions to known customer problems, seeking higher profit margins (e.g. through cost reduction projects), and targeting large markets instead of smaller, emerging markets.

The Airplane Industry

Another example illustrating the difference between sustaining and disruptive innovation is the airplane industry. Boeing has been a sustaining innovator for decades, starting with the DC-3 model appearing in the 1930s. Better products, appealing to the largest airlines, were offered to attract existing customers with features such to deliver longer travel routes or lower cost per plane (e.g. B-747, B-777, and B-787 models).

On the other hand, Embraer, a Brazilian company, recently entered the market for airplanes. This smaller firm recognized that they could not compete with major manufacturers like Boeing and Airbus directly. Therefore, Embraer decided to manufacture smaller, simpler jets to appeal to a less attractive set of customers, down-market of the Boeing customers. Typically, these aircraft are used in local and regional service for discount airlines and are displacing propeller planes in this service. While Boeing pursues sustaining innovations in aircraft designs, Embraer is disrupting the market with its smaller jets.

Comparing Sustaining and Disruptive Innovation

A firm that practices sustaining innovation will continue to develop products that increase performance over time. Product performance can be measured with small step changes in performance with gradual increases, or the performance improvement can take large leaps between existing and next generation products. In the latter case, the innovation may be considered "radical" since it has taken a great leap in performance, yet the product is still addressing existing markets with existing technologies.

Working on product improvements through sustaining innovations for a well-known customer base is a good strategy for an established company. Customers account for a large market share and are sophisticated in applying the product solution to their problems. Typically, companies that are successful with sustaining innovations are working in arenas with slow technology changes and few outside competitive threats.

However, a firm that recognizes a down-market opportunity can compete with the established companies by utilizing disruptive technologies. Again, these firms will address fringe customers with less attractive or smaller markets, often operating with tighter profit margins. The pace of change of the technology, or the rate that the performance of the disruptive technology improves, can be similar to the sustaining technologies or may advance much more rapidly. A key concept of the disruptive innovation is that the initial performance of the product is lower than the established products in the market, yet the disruptive technology offers other benefits to emerging markets, such as convenience or lower cost, as trade-offs for the lower performance.

A disruptive strategy is well-suited to firms that are seeking to create new growth and are willing to accept lower profit margins today in exchange for future revenues. Often, the disruptive technology requires a high degree of trial and error to address the needs of a new market, so the business plan and operational teams need to be flexible. Organizational structures for sustaining and disruptive innovations are described in Chapter 6. In short, the disruptive technology introduces a new customer value proposition and the firm implements a different business model than is typical for the established industry.

Open Innovation

Before concluding the discussion on applying innovation strategy, it is important to emphasize the differences between traditional and open innovation. In short, open innovation uses external ideas as well as internal ideas for new product development. The term "*open innovation*" was coined by Henry Chesbrough (2003).

In essence, open innovation contrasts with traditional, or closed, innovation in that the firm actively seeks outside ideas as well as internal sources for innovation. The firm may use external paths to market instead of their own single channel distribution systems. For example, Dr. Pepper™, a popular soda in the United States, is bottled by large manufacturers, Coca-Cola and Pepsi. To a degree, these manufacturers are direct competitors with Dr. Pepper. Though Coca-Cola and Pepsi control the vast majority of market share for sodas in the U.S., Dr. Pepper utilizes the distribution channels of Coke and Pepsi to get its product to market without having to

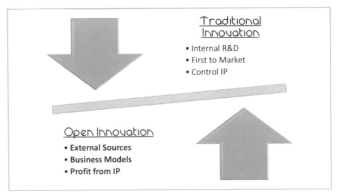

Figure 11 - Contrasting Traditional and Open Innovation

invest in trucks and related resources. Thus, the boundaries between the firm (Dr. Pepper in this case) and the outside sources (Coca-Cola and Pepsi's distribution channels) become more permeable. Improved technologies and business models may then transfer into and out of a company by using open innovation.

Additionally, a broader base of knowledge is accessible to a firm practicing open innovation. Encapsys, a division of Appleton Paper Inc. (now known as Appvion, Inc.), develops and manufactures micro-encapsulation solutions for a variety of industries. While Encapsys maintains the industry's expert knowledge of encapsulation, their partners introduce the capability into wide-ranging industries such as detergents, perfumes, and colorants. Open innovation allows many firms to take advantage of technologies through shared and/or licensed intellectual property.

This leads to the final point regarding open innovation. Many companies hold patents that may not support the core business capabilities. Open innovation offers a new pathway to license technologies that are not core to the business, allowing the firm to capitalize on a unique profit stream that can offset development costs that have already been incurred. Internal inventions can be taken outside of the company through partnerships, joint ventures, spin-offs, licensing, and other opportunities.

In a traditional innovation model, a company assumes that they have the ability to hire and retain all of the subject matter experts in the field. Moreover, traditional innovation follows a model that intellectual property should be controlled by the company and that products introduced to the market first are the most profitable. In short, firms employing traditional innovation practices assume that if they have the most and the best ideas, they will win in the marketplace.

Conversely, an open innovation model recognizes that talent exists both inside and outside of the firm. External R&D can generate significant value for the company, especially when coupled with internal development efforts. Open innovation recognizes that the firm does not have to create or own all of the intellectual property in order to profit from it, and it is better to build a successful business model to market new products than be first to commercialization. Winning with open innovation is the result of advancing both internal *and* external pathways to market.

Summary

This chapter has provided a review of some of the emerging practices to effectively apply open innovation strategies. Recalling that strategy provides the overarching goals and objectives for successful new product development, the practices of business model innovation, disruptive innovation, and open innovation are making an impact in today's competitive world.

First, *business model innovation* involves changing the customer value proposition to address new market opportunities. A business model involves creating a profitable new technology or opening new markets with a unique perspective. The four key elements of a business model innovation are:

1. Customer value proposition,
2. Profit formula,
3. Key resources, and
4. Fundamental business processes.

A new business model strategy for a particular program or service can be implemented through the *product innovation charter*, or PIC. The PIC is a guidance document that aligns management expectations and their perspective of the business strategy with the specific goals, objectives, and measures for the NPD project. Four sections should be included in any PIC: background, focus arena, goals and objectives, and special considerations. A product innovation charter should be utilized for all types of innovation projects, whether they are radical or incremental improvements.

Companies that continually improve known technologies for existing customers are actively pursuing sustaining innovation programs. Sustaining technologies often result in feature-heavy products with increased performance measured by existing product standards and customer satisfaction. In contrast, disruptive innovators pursue fringe customers with an initially lower performance product that offers a unique value proposition, such as convenience or reduced price. As the performance of the disruptive innovation improves over time, the market share of firms concentrating on sustaining innovations is eroded.

Finally, open innovation is an emerging practice in which firms adopt ideas and distribution channels from external sources as well as internal resources. Traditional innovation focuses on internal R&D, being first to market, and owning intellectual property. Open innovation may involve new pathways to the market as well as optimizing intellectual property through licensing or other partnerships leading to improved profitability.

Chapter 3 - Portfolio Management

A primary responsibility of senior leaders, *portfolio management* is an important tool that helps to identify and differentiate new product projects with the highest potential to add value to the firm. Sometimes called *product portfolio management*, there is some overlap with project management (discussed in Chapter 7, Tools and Metrics). However, portfolio management focuses on the entire suite of available projects instead of individual new product efforts.

As indicated in the Introduction and Overview section, portfolio management accounts for 10% of the questions on the NPDP certification exam. Like strategy, portfolio management may be a lower scoring area since many individuals may not have actively worked in the field. Portfolio management is primarily the responsibility of senior management because it is a tool that ensures effective implementation of the innovation strategy.

Learning Objectives

After studying this chapter, you will be able to:

1. Define portfolio management,

2. Outline the roles of senior management in portfolio planning,

3. Name the three goals of portfolio management,

4. Describe financial and non-financial scoring models,

5. Understand basic trade-off charts to balance the portfolio, and

6. Explain the resource allocation processes used for portfolio management.

Portfolio Management Defined

Portfolio management is a decision-making process to select the best new product development projects for the firm to actively work while optimizing the use of scarce resources. In contrast, project management (see Chapter 7) involves planning and executing specific steps to conduct the work of an individual new product project, such as administering the project budget and schedule within the defined scope of work. For new product development efforts, project management involves tactical execution of the project, mostly occurring during the development stage of the structured NPD process (see Chapter 4), while portfolio management evaluates the best mix of projects, from the overall pool of available projects, to move forward yielding the highest potential value to the firm.

> *Portfolio Management is inextricably linked to the innovation strategy.*

The formal definition of portfolio management is a *decision-making process* where a business' *list of active projects* is *continually reviewed and revised*. Each of these phrases in the definition is important in describing the role of portfolio management in an organization.

A Decision-Making Process

First, portfolio management is a process to help senior management evaluate the myriad of new product ideas and make decisions on which projects should be advanced consistent with the firm's strategic objectives. Portfolio management provides information to aid executives in making decisions about which new product development projects are suitable for investment, which ones should be abandoned, and which ones may be put on hold for later consideration. Those projects in which senior management invests resources are considered "*active*" and will be assigned resources and priority for completion.

Continual Revision of the Portfolio

Next, continual review and revision is a unique characteristic to the portfolio management process. NPD projects that are actively being pursued by the firm will span a range of maturity from idea to commercial products ready to launch. Recall within the framework of innovation, the term *product* can refer to tangible goods, intangible goods (like software), as well as services, and specific programs coupling goods and services for a new customer value proposition.

Generally, the scope of portfolio management is limited only to new products and will not include process improvement initiatives, such as efficiency in the supply chain or manufacturing upgrades. However, when any business process has the potential to directly impact a customer's perspective of the quality, delivery, or functionality of a product, the project should be included in the portfolio management review. For those firms that utilize a project management office (PMO), the definition of a new product development project is explicitly and clearly stated. In other cases, it is better to err on the side of caution and include projects in the portfolio planning process if there is any chance of the customer seeing a change in the product.

Dealing with Future Events

Finally, it should be noted that portfolio management deals with future events in a very dynamic environment. A firm cannot identify *a priori* which projects will be successful technically or commercially. There is, of course, always an element of risk or uncertainty when dealing with new product development and innovation.

To be sure, an organization is constantly learning new information about the technical aspects of a potential product as well as new information about the target market. Additionally, as the portfolio management process contrasts projects worthy of investment with those of lower priority, each project may be at a different stage of completion or maturity. Thus, portfolio decisions are made comparing projects that are at the idea stage with projects that are at the prototype stage, for example. Moreover, the slate of projects is constantly changing, as projects may enter or exit the portfolio on a daily basis due to advances in technical knowledge and/or shifts in the marketplace.

While it is difficult for NPD leaders and senior management to predict the future, the purpose of portfolio management is to help decision makers improve the odds of success. Senior management must also recognize that part of the decision-making process that strategically identifies which projects to *not* advance for further development.

Resources

A key responsibility of senior management in the portfolio planning process includes managing scarce and limited resources. While the senior leadership may choose to expand idea generation processes by using open innovation (see Chapter 2), internal development resources must be aligned with the highest value projects.

Resources should account for time, money, people, and equipment. Naturally, these resources are shared with other business functions and need to be properly allocated to the best use for the firm overall. For example, pilot plant equipment often is shared among business functions within a corporation to perform testing and troubleshooting for factory production tests as well as to produce prototypes for new product development efforts. If equipment is not available, NPD efforts may be delayed or stalled. Additionally, time itself can also be a limiting resource when a firm relies upon open innovation or extensive co-creation efforts with target customers. These customers, for instance, may not sense the same urgency as the firm for the new product development effort. Time, then, can become a limiting resource for testing and must be managed to maintain a competitive position in the market.

Benefits of Portfolio Management

Studies have shown that firms using portfolio management tools perform the best, meeting their new product profit goals 75% of the time as compared to others (Barczak, et al., 2009). Portfolio management techniques provide a structure for companies to identify and select the most valuable innovation projects out of the entire suite of available projects. Other studies (Cooper, 2013) demonstrate higher return on investment for an NPD program when utilizing portfolio management tools. In part, this is due to the better decision-making framework available to senior managers by comparing each project to all other new product projects available, thus prioritizing the highest value projects to move forward in the development process. Moreover, firms employing product portfolio management realize a better balance among the projects in the portfolio from both a risk and return basis.

Role of Senior Management in Portfolio Management

As described in Chapter 1, NPD Strategy, senior management plays a vital role in determining which, markets, technologies, and products are pursued for new product development success. Senior management links the strategy to implementation by identifying the types of projects included in the portfolio to achieve a balance between risk and profitability. Balance in the portfolio also reflects the time frame (short-term vs. long-term) for return on investment (ROI) that is acceptable to the firm and establishes appropriate growth opportunities. In particular, senior management must assess the amount of funding that will be provided for projects that are cost reductions, incremental improvements, line extensions or enhancements, and radical innovations (including new-to-the-world or new-to-the-company products).

Direction Setter

Thus, the first role of senior management is to set the direction for the organization in terms of risk tolerance for innovation projects. Again, some businesses are willing to accept more risk or are willing to wait for a longer time period for return on the innovation investment. Meanwhile other firms are focused on short-term returns and may be far less risk tolerant. Choosing to invest in particular types of NPD projects determines how well the new product portfolio is aligned with the overall business strategy.

For instance, a firm that is actively tracking a prospector strategy will deploy a new product development portfolio with more radical innovations, demonstrating a high risk tolerance. In contrast, the new product portfolio of a defender company will be populated with less risky, shorter term projects producing incremental improvements to existing products.

Product Line Architect

Another role in portfolio management for which senior management has primary responsibility is the product line architect. The product line architect reflects senior management's critical responsibility to ensure the organization works on the *right* products and the *right* group of projects. Additionally, these products must be commercialized in a time frame and sequence that is attractive within the marketplace. Project selection techniques, balance of the portfolio, and mix of NPD project types are all part of the portfolio management role.

In this case, *right* means that the projects are strategically aligned with both the overall business objectives as well as the particular innovation strategy. Senior management will use the framework of portfolio management to draw the requirements for active new product development projects and will select the set of projects that collectively deliver the most strategic value to the firm. Thus, as the product line architect, senior management plans, designs, and oversees the construction of an active innovation portfolio aligned with the NPD strategy.

Additionally, as the product line architect, senior management defines the product types. Common new product development project types include:

- Breakthrough,
- Platform,
- Derivative, and
- Support.

Other project types may include new-to-the-world, new-to-the-company, product enhancements, and cost reductions. Of course, within each organization, a set of standard project types should be defined by senior management to describe the level of innovation from both technical complexity and market orientation perspectives. Standard project types are described as below in reference to portfolio management.

Breakthrough Projects

For portfolio management purposes, a breakthrough project is one that strives to bring a new product to a new market with new technologies. Breakthrough products involve deep and wide innovations that depart significantly from existing practices. The product will serve a unique, emerging market segment and utilize a new business model. Often breakthrough projects will be staffed by a venture team (see Chapter 6) that is more accepting of risk while simultaneously understanding the size and significance of the new market opportunity.

In short, a breakthrough project is one that involves something very new. Sometimes this type of project is called a radical innovation, and certainly, disruptive innovations fall into the category of breakthrough projects. Both terms describe new products that intrinsically alter customer choices with new applications of technology.

A firm may be extending its reach through the development of a breakthrough project. For example, a company that manufactures carbonated sodas may venture into a new product line of flavored, vitamin-enhanced bottled water products. This is a significant departure for the organization because it not only involves new technologies and new target markets, but also new distribution channels and new business models for the vitamin-enhanced water.

Platform Projects

As described in Chapter 1, a platform strategy takes advantage of a common core technology to develop and commercialize a series of products over a long period of time. Product derivatives (see below) may be launched into existing markets or new markets, depending upon the specific technology captured in the platform product. Together the platform and derivative products make up a product family.

New platforms are included in an active product portfolio to help achieve long-term growth consistent with the NPD strategy. Developing a new platform typically involves more risk than a product enhancement or incremental improvement and will often use a heavyweight team to execute the development and commercial launch (see Chapter 6).

Platform projects are not typically as radically innovative as breakthrough products, yet can introduce risk to the firm since many future product efforts will be initiated based on the common set of architectures developed for the platform product. Often the product platform allows a firm to enter multiple markets with a single technology and this strategy can yield a substantial boost to the firm's new product portfolio value.

A classic example of a platform product is the X86 microprocessor chip series by Intel®. The original computer chip was manufactured and utilized in 286 computers; later, the architecture was upgraded for performance enhancements. Intel thus developed and marketed the 386, 486, and Pentium™ (586) microprocessor computer chips. Much of the core architecture in the X86 series remained constant throughout the subsequent development efforts, until a new platform using dual core processing was designed to replace the X86 platform.

Derivative Projects

Compared to breakthrough and platform projects, a derivative project yields relatively lower risk. Derivative products may be spin-offs from a platform, offering enhancements and features based on the common architecture of the core technology.

Derivative products may also fill a gap in a product line or offer a cost competitive method of production. Extension of a product line may be accomplished by development of derivative products as well. Many derivative projects are designed, developed, and executed by lightweight development teams (see Chapter 6).

Normally, an organization will consider a derivative project to be less complex than either breakthrough or platform projects. As indicated, a derivative project may represent a next generation product within a given product family. For example, an automobile manufacturer may introduce a convertible version of a coupe car which was originally based on a successful sedan design. For this reason, derivative products may also be called "enhancements" or "derivatives".

Derivative projects normally make up a significant portion of a firm's new product portfolio. Many derivative projects offer only modest enhancements to existing products. For instance, consider adding a smartphone to the product line that adds buttons to automatically call up Facebook or Twitter. Application additions such as this are considered modest enhancements to the product design, yet can fill a gap to meet or exceed the features offered by competitors.

Support Projects

Least risky of all new product development projects are the support products. These projects will address manufacturing efficiencies and incremental improvements for the product. In the unfortunate case that a previously commercialized product has a defect or other performance issue, the support projects will be undertaken to reintroduce the product without flaws.

Consider the case where a product requires the buyer to assemble it, such as popular do-it-yourself furniture. After the product is commercialized, the company may observe that many customers complain about needing to use a particular tool (e.g. an Allen wrench) that is not readily available to them. A support project can be undertaken to include a cheap, disposable Allen wrench in the product box and the self-assembly instructions would be updated appropriately by the NPD team.

Minor improvements in the product line and extending the range of applications are the primary purposes of support projects in new product development. As such, a functional work team within a single department or division may be assigned to accomplish the project (see Chapter 6).

Role of Product Line Architect

Thus, the role of senior management as the product line architect involves determining appropriate investment levels for each project type. Moreover, the product line architect role includes assessing the balance of the project types to ensure alignment of new product development efforts with the firm's strategy.

Senior management may approve research and development budgets in line with the project type balance (e.g. 20% breakthrough, 30% platform, 25% derivative, and 25% support) in order to force strategic alignment. In other cases, business unit spending will reflect the project type balance in conjunction with the growth arenas established for the company in its business and innovation strategies.

Portfolio Manager

A key point regarding portfolio management is that the decision-making process must be *owned* by senior management. Normally, the portfolio decisions in which new product development projects are included in the active project set will be made by a team of executives responsible for research and development, technology growth, marketing, operations, and business strategies of the firm.

As the portfolio management team, these individuals will routinely review the set of projects that are actively being pursued, those that are on hold, and any new ideas created since the last review. In this way, the team of senior executives in the firm serves as the portfolio manager – making the key decisions to define the active set of NPD projects.

Additionally, because of their intimate knowledge of the business strategy and growth initiatives for the future, these senior managers are also responsible to match resource capabilities with project execution. The project types and balance have already been determined by senior management within their capacity as the product line architect.

As an example, consider a firm that is developing a cloud computing solution with strong demand from a specific target market. The firm itself already has significant capabilities in the area of software coding, but the company has little experience with internet application development. Through portfolio management aligned with strategic direction, senior management will establish a set of technology programs to be developed in order to launch a product platform for the cloud computing solution. With a deep understanding of the business strategy, senior management recognizes through portfolio management that the firm will need to recruit and hire individuals with a skill set in internet applications. Another alternative that senior management may consider is to acquire a start-up company that has demonstrated this skill set and will easily integrate with the existing culture of the firm. Regardless of their final choice, the portfolio managers are responsible to identify and fill resource gaps that can impact the strategic execution of new product development projects.

Likewise, if the firm is tackling several parallel new product development efforts at the same time, senior management will need to ensure that skilled technical and marketing teams have enough capacity to handle the numerous projects. So, it is apparent that senior management has a role as a portfolio manager to match the skill sets of resources with the required capabilities for new product development.

Again, senior management must *own* the process for portfolio planning. Senior management must describe the processes and frequency for review of the portfolio. Which projects are included? Are reviews held weekly, monthly or quarterly? Do new ideas go through the same ranking and prioritization as products near commercialization? Are there separate NPD processes for the fuzzy front end and for development?

Of course, these decisions establishing how and when projects will be reviewed for inclusion or exclusion from the active new product portfolio will be closely integrated with the structured NPD process, or staged and gated process, where each project is *individually* reviewed against a set of given criteria (see Chapter 4). Firms with a robust NPD process to review individual projects may hold less frequent portfolio review sessions, for example.

Not surprisingly, communication is very important for effective portfolio management. Senior management may be most familiar with the strategic plans and directions for the firm, yet personnel "on the ground" may have the closest interactions with customers and potential new product users. Therefore, as a part of integration under the role of process owner and portfolio manager, the senior management team must integrate customer needs and wants into the strategic direction of the firm by selecting those projects which will most closely match the risk tolerance and profit objectives of the firm.

Portfolio management is a planning and decision-making technique used to select the best innovation projects for the firm to pursue. Senior management selects this set of most valuable projects from all those available to the firm at any given time, thus the portfolio decision-making environment is continually changing and is very dynamic.

Goals of Portfolio Management

Recall that the definition of portfolio management is a decision-making process where a business' list of active projects is continually reviewed and revised. Therefore, the aim of portfolio management is to achieve a set of active new product development projects that will align with the firm's strategy and will deliver the most value. There are three primary goals of portfolio management.

1. Maximize new product portfolio value,
2. Optimize projects with business objectives (balance the portfolio), and
3. Ensure strategic alignment.

The first goal, maximize new product portfolio value, is designed to attain maximum financial return on the innovation investments. Common ways to evaluate projects within the suite of all available projects will utilize both financial and non-financial methods. Early stage projects are most likely to benefit from a non-financial analysis (scoring methods) to be able to rank and prioritize the projects within the portfolio.

Second, portfolio management should ensure a good balance of projects within the active portfolio. Consider an analogy with personal financial planning for retirement. You will want to have a certain mix of stocks, bonds, real estate, and money market funds in order to achieve your objectives. Moreover, the balance of these investments may change over your lifetime as you might be more accepting of risk when you first enter the workforce. Later, when you are married with children, your financial goals include saving for your kids' college education. Finally, your risk tolerance and financial investments will adjust to meet the circumstances as finally you attain your goal to retire at age 62, for example.

Portfolio managers will similarly strive to balance the types of projects in the new product development portfolio according to risk and reward, thus making it possible to achieve the firm's strategic objectives. However, just like in your personal financial portfolio, the balance of projects will vary from company to company, among industries, and over time.

Finally, the third goal of portfolio management is to ensure that the projects actively being worked are aligned with the strategic plans previously determined by senior management. Because of the strong linkage between product portfolio decisions and innovation strategy, senior management's role is critical in portfolio management, as described above. Strategic alignment includes not only the balance and mix of project types in the portfolio, but also resource allocation to deliver the projects within the desired timeframe.

Maximize Portfolio Value

In order to rank and prioritize projects within an active new product development portfolio, senior management will need to compare each project against the other available projects in the portfolio. The most common way to assess product portfolios uses financial methods, such as net present value (NPV) or return on investment (ROI). Some firms use other financial valuation methods, such as return on capital employed, income before taxes, or expected commercial value[*].

In short, NPV is a financial method that allows dissimilar future investments to be compared at the present. Any future revenues and costs are discounted to today's value by using an expected interest rate and expected life cycle of the commercialized product. The expected interest rate is sometimes called the cost of capital and will vary depending on company standards. A common estimate for the expected interest rate is the rate that banks pay for savings, for instance.

Similarly, ROI is a standard measure of profitability for a project in which the discounted profits are indicated as a percentage of the initial investment in the project. Like the cost of capital, many firms have a "hurdle rate," reflecting a minimum ROI leading to project approval. For example, a firm may set the hurdle rate at 15%, such that any new product development project estimating a higher return on investment may be approved but any NPD project falling below the hurdle rate will be rejected.

Financial Scoring – NPV

In order to prioritize the projects within the new product portfolio using the net present value method, there are just a few simple steps.

First, the NPV is calculated for each available new product development project. This includes projects that are actively being worked and may include projects on hold as well as projects that are still in the idea stage and have not yet been initiated. Financial scoring models for portfolio management do not take project type into consideration and will force project prioritization solely along the financial metric (NPV or ROI) alone. Thus, each project that is under consideration within the firm or division is included on the list, regardless if the project is a breakthrough project with higher risk longer-term rewards, or an incremental improvement with lower risk smaller near-term rewards.

Next, all projects are listed in rank-order from highest NPV to the lowest. Recall that the NPV includes an estimate of future sales revenues and expenses for development and distribution of the new product.

Finally, because every firm is restricted by limited NPD resources, projects that are selected for the active portfolio should only those that can be fully staffed. Adequate resource allocation is a very important point and will be discussed in more detail later in this chapter.

[**] While the NPDP certification exam will not test whether a candidate can calculate financial metrics such as NPV and ROI, it is prudent for a new product development practitioner to be familiar with the basis of these calculations (see Appendix A and B, for example). Many introductory financial accounting and business management textbooks describe the basis of the *time value of money*. An additional resource to learn about these financial calculations is a blog series by the author called *Talking to Your Bo$$*, available at http://chenected.aiche.org/series/talking-to-your-boss-economics-of-engineering/.

Example of Financial Portfolio Management Method

Suppose the firm has a business in snack foods, including products like cookies, cakes, and popcorn. Several new product ideas have been submitted and senior management is undergoing a portfolio evaluation. Potential new products include those shown in Figure 12 below and address existing markets (donuts and popcorn) as well as new markets (cookies and potato chips).

Revenue and cost estimates for these sample projects have already been prepared by NPD team leaders, yielding a net present value as indicated in millions of dollars. For reference, the data also includes the number of required resources to bring the project to commercialization and the remaining development cost (also in millions of dollars).

Project Name	Net Present Value	Project Type	Resources	Development Cost
Cookies	112	Breakthrough	12	2
Cake	100	Derivative	7	2.5
Donuts	84	Support	3	1
Popcorn	68	Support	2	0.75
Peanuts	63	Derivative	6	3
Potato Chips	53	Platform	10	0.5

Figure 12 - Financial Rank Order Example

The projects are ranked from highest to lowest NPV, with the Cookies project having a net present value of $112M and Potato Chips having an expected net present value of only $53M. Because the firm has only 25 engineers, designers, and marketers available to work on new product development efforts, the active portfolio list includes the Cookies, Cake, Donuts, and Popcorn projects, but excludes the Peanuts and Potato Chips projects.

Financial rank-ordering is the very simplest and crudest method of resource allocation to choose an active product portfolio. Management has other choices, for example to acquire and assign 15 more development staff in order to work all of the projects. Instead, many firms choose to keep all of the NPD projects on the active list with just the available resources resulting in understaffing of the active projects. A common failure of innovation programs results from too many projects with too few resources, leading to poor project execution and missed commercialization deadlines. Thus, resource allocation to the highest value projects can help to ensure more focused development efforts.

In addition, as management considers the portfolio presented in Figure 12, they should question whether the NPV of the Cookies project is truly $112M. Likewise, the discussion should consider whether the Donut project is accurately predicted to yield less value than the Cake project. One of the biggest drawbacks of financial rank ordering projects for portfolio management is that the method fails to take account of all available information, including risk, technology capabilities, and market analysis.

Problems with Financial Methods for Portfolio Management

As suggested above, there are several problems with a financial-only method for prioritizing the available projects in a new product portfolio. Financial calculations are easily manipulated by small changes in opportunity costs, expected sales volumes, and the time period used in the analysis.

First, because NPV and ROI require calculating cash inflows and outflows over the life of the product, it is very difficult to obtain accurate numbers. A project that is very early in the development cycle, say the idea stage, is likely to yield an inaccurate sales forecast several years into the future. This inaccuracy increases as the technology and markets require more development, as is the case for more radical innovations such as breakthrough projects. Because of less precise estimates for both new product sales and costs of more radical innovation, NPV and ROI calculations are more suitable for products near commercialization.

Financial analysis alone, therefore, generally leads to a new product portfolio with a shorter term focus that includes new products ready for commercialization in favor of those that require longer term development. Unfortunately, packing a portfolio with a lot of incremental product improvements can dilute the overall innovation effort and lead to lower quality new products. With this approach, companies will find themselves lacking strategic new product growth and lower market share over the long run if they fail to also consider radical innovations with higher risk and longer-term payout.

Moreover, NPV and most other financial tools do not adequately account for development risk from a technical or market perspective. Sometimes, firms will use different interest rates or adjust the final valuation (NPV or ROI) by probabilities of technical and/or market success. Nonetheless, these adjustments remain subjective and will not necessarily prevent skewing the active portfolio toward projects nearer commercialization in the short term.

Finally, financial methods account for revenue and cost only without necessarily reflecting the business strategy. Occasionally, an organization is willing to take a calculated financial loss on a particular product in order to gain market share or other strategic objectives. For instance, consider firms that design and market system applications – any single product within the system may not be profitable on a standalone basis, but the entire system cannot be sold successfully without the full set of components and derivative products.

As an example, computer printers and razor handles are often sold at or below cost. This is a fair strategy for the companies that manufacture these products as they also sell parts and supplies (toner cartridges and razor blades) at a substantial profit, covering any losses on sales of the hardware. A new product project to develop a new printer or razor handle may be strategically attractive to the firm, yet the financial rank order within the new product portfolio would eliminate these projects from a net present value perspective alone.

Financial metrics are a necessary consideration in evaluating a new product portfolio; however, organizations should be cautious in applying only financial ranking to determine an active portfolio. Senior management will also consider alternative methods to rank and prioritize projects, such as scoring methods, to ensure strategic alignment.

Portfolio Management Scoring Methods

As discussed above, pure financial methods may distort the product portfolio with too many shorter term, incremental innovations. One of the reasons is that early stage ideas often do not have sales or expense figures available with an acceptable level of accuracy. Additionally, these longer-term projects may require significant technology and market development with largely unknown costs, while revenues that are expected farther into the future will be discounted more significantly by a time value of money analysis, such as NPV or ROI.

One way to address the problems of financial analysis with early stage projects is to use a non-financial scoring model. Such models also help to address project risk in a structured way. With financial-only metrics, a portfolio may be skewed to shorter term lower risk projects leaving the firm vulnerable to competition pursuing more radical innovations. Thus, scoring models will use a set of value metrics to supplement the financial metrics in assuring strategic alignment of the project with the firm's overall business and innovation goals. Non-financial scoring methods will also determine the technical and market feasibility of the product in general terms to assess whether further investment in the new product development effort is warranted.

Step 1 - Select Scoring Criteria

In the scoring method, the senior executive team responsible for new product development and portfolio management ranks each project against a set of well-defined criteria. Often these criteria are very similar, or perhaps identical, to those included on gate pass checklists for individual projects to progress from stage to stage (see Chapter 4). Each member of the review team will evaluate the project attractiveness versus these criteria. Typically, a ranking scale ranges from strong agreement to strong disagreement, for example, correlating to a score of one to five. In other cases, the project criteria is simply ranked as high, medium, or low. Since the scoring method is not meant to be analyzed with rigorous statistics, the ranking method should be simple to implement and result in consistent project evaluations over a wide range of project types.

Table 3 (below) indicates some suggested scoring method criteria for portfolio management. Some of these criteria may include strategic alignment, attractiveness of the market (e.g. few or many competitors), product advantage offered to customers, risks and uncertainties, the degree of technical feasibility, and relative reward. Other common portfolio scoring standards consider capital investment and intellectual property. Each organization should adopt a consistent set of scoring criteria for all new product development projects.

Step 2 - Assess Scores

Next, the scores are compiled from each of the portfolio evaluators and summed. Recall that the portfolio reviewers will comprise senior management, business unit leaders, and functional managers, as appropriate. As indicated above, scores may range from one to five, where a higher score indicates greater agreement with the evaluation criteria. Note that instead of summing the scores of all evaluators, some firms use an *average* of scores. From a portfolio prioritization perspective, there is no fundamental difference in choosing sums or averages. It is more important to use a consistent approach to compare NPD projects to one another and over time.

Table 3 - Product Portfolio Scoring Criteria			
Strategic Alignment	**Market Attractiveness**	**Product Advantage**	**Technical Feasibility**
• Fit with business strategy	• Meets minimum market size criteria	• Addresses customer needs	• Possess or can acquire knowledge/expertise
• Fit with innovation strategy	• Growth opportunities	• Provides unique value proposition	• Technical complexity and risk manageable
• Leverages skills and core competencies	• Offers competitive advantage	**Risk**	**Reward**
• Supports global business unit needs	• Meets existing market or customer need	• No killer variables	• Return on investment in line with risk
• Renders balance	• No regulatory or environmental hurdles	• Uncertainties can be managed	• Overall life cycle profitability is acceptable

In some cases, the portfolio team will deem one or two of the criteria to be of higher significance. These "must have" criteria are weighted by a factor to emphasize the importance of that element. For example, a firm can multiply all of the strategic alignment scores by a factor of 150% to stress this as a foundational consideration to include a project in the active new product portfolio.

Step 3 – Prioritize the Projects

After summing the weighted scores for all potential new product projects, the project list is sorted. As in the financial method, projects are rank ordered from high to low and active projects are selected until resources are fully consumed. A simple example of the scoring methodology is shown in Figure 13.

Project	Strategic Alignment	Product Advantage	Market Attractiveness	Core Competency	Technical Feasibility	Reward	Points	Normalized Score	Number Resources	Status
Thorium	5	5	5	5	4	5	29	97%	16	Active
Helium	2	5	5	5	4	5	26	87%	20	Active
Neon	5	4	4	4	5	4	26	87%	15	Active
Hydrogen	5	4	3	4	3	3	22	73%	20	Active
Oxygen	5	3	4	3	4	2	21	70%	15	Hold
Nitrogen	2	2	5	2	5	4	20	67%	30	Hold
Fluoride	4	4	2	4	2	4	20	67%	20	Hold
Radium	3	5	5	1	1	4	19	63%	25	Hold

Figure 13 - Portfolio Scoring Method

For this sample portfolio, six criteria have been evaluated: strategic alignment, product advantage, market attractiveness, core competency, technical feasibility, and relative reward. Each project has been scored by the portfolio management review team. A score of five means that the project ranks high in that category, while a score of one indicates a low ranking. As indicated above, an alternative scoring method is to have each portfolio manager score the criteria and calculate an *average score* for each category.

In Figure 13, each category is considered equally important, and the scores are summed across each row to establish an overall score for the individual project. This is illustrated in the column titled "Points". For example, project Thorium has 29 total points, while projects Nitrogen and Fluoride have been scored across the portfolio criteria for a total of 20 points each. The normalized score represents the total points of the individual project relative to the maximum points available for a project. In this case, a new product development project that matches each criteria at the highest level would receive a score of 30 points. Projects Helium and Neon both have normalized scores of 87%, for example.

As in the NPV methodology (see above), the number of full-time equivalent resources required to complete the product development effort to the point of commercialization are also indicated. The company in the example portfolio has 75 resources available for new product development initiatives, so projects that can be fully staffed are considered *active* in the portfolio. All other projects are put on hold. Therefore, projects Thorium, Helium, Neon, and Hydrogen are active in the new product development portfolio. Meanwhile projects Oxygen, Nitrogen, Fluoride, and Radium are put on hold and remain inactive.

Alternative Scoring Method

In the above example, projects were scored with a balanced approach, assuming that each criteria was equally important. However, many firms will stress one or more of the scoring categories as critical to new product development success. For instance, assume that the firm is pursuing radical innovations for which the technology is not fully understood. Therefore, the portfolio management team has decided that the *Technical Feasibility* criterion is of utmost importance. The scoring method is easily adapted to accommodate this situation.

In the analysis of the portfolio, the category of *Technical Feasibility* is assigned a factor of 200%, indicating the importance of this criteria. A project with a perfect score in this case has a total of 35 points. Figure 14 shows the outcome of the alternative rank ordering in which the projects are ranked first by *Normalized Score* (or *Adjusted Points*) and then by *Technical Feasibility*.

Project	Strategic Alignment	Product Advantage	Market Attractiveness	Core Competency	Technical Feasibility	Reward	Adjusted Points	Normalized Score	Number Resources	Status
Thorium	5	5	5	5	4	5	33	94%	16	Active
Neon	5	4	4	4	5	4	31	89%	15	Active
Helium	2	5	5	5	4	5	30	86%	20	Active
Nitrogen	2	2	5	2	5	4	25	71%	30	Active
Oxygen	5	3	4	3	4	2	25	71%	15	Hold
Hydrogen	5	4	3	4	3	3	25	71%	20	Hold
Fluoride	4	4	2	4	2	4	22	63%	20	Hold
Radium	3	5	5	1	1	4	20	57%	25	Hold

Figure 14 - Alternative Scoring Method for Portfolio Analysis

Notice that the project ranking has changed to include projects Thorium, Neon, and Helium in the active portfolio. Assuming there are still only 75 full-time equivalent resources for new product development efforts, the portfolio management team is faced with a decision regarding the active portfolio. Project Nitrogen is now the next attractive project to work within the active portfolio. However, fully staffing projects Thorium, Neon, Helium, and Nitrogen will require 81 full-time equivalent resources. The portfolio management team may choose to assign additional resources so that project Nitrogen can be fully staffed or they may choose to put project Nitrogen on hold and assign additional resources to the three active projects.

A Dynamic Portfolio

Assuming that the firm has rank ordered all of the potential new product projects, the portfolio management team is responsible for continual changes in the dynamic portfolio as new information is learned regarding each project, the technology, and markets. For example, during the next portfolio review meeting, new information regarding competitors and customers has come to light affecting project Hydrogen. The active portfolio, as shown in Figure 13, will need to be adjusted.

Based on the new information, the portfolio management team re-scores the *Market Attractiveness* of project Hydrogen at the lowest level (one) and the potential *Reward* at a reduced score (two) as well. This changes the overall score of project Hydrogen to just 19 out of the potential 30 points, as shown in Figure 15.

Project	Strategic Alignment	Product Advantage	Market Attractiveness	Core Competency	Technical Feasibility	Reward	Points	Normalized Score	Number Resources	Status
Thorium	5	5	5	5	4	5	29	97%	16	Active
Helium	2	5	5	5	4	5	26	87%	20	Active
Neon	5	4	4	4	5	4	26	87%	15	Active
Oxygen	5	3	4	3	4	2	21	70%	15	Active
Nitrogen	2	2	5	2	5	4	20	67%	30	Hold
Fluoride	4	4	2	4	2	4	20	67%	20	Hold
Hydrogen	**5**	**4**	**1**	**4**	**3**	**2**	**19**	**63%**	**20**	**Hold**
Radium	3	5	5	1	1	4	19	63%	25	Hold

Figure 15 - A Future Portfolio by Scoring Method

The project list is again rank ordered, assuming all of the information regarding the other projects has remained constant. As indicated in Figure 15, project Hydrogen has dropped from the active list, while project Oxygen has moved up to become an active project in the portfolio. Because project Oxygen only requires 15 full-time equivalent resources to commercialize the new product, the portfolio management team does not face any significant staffing challenges for this new portfolio.

Scoring methods are effective for new product portfolios that involve a lot of early stage projects. Most firms will balance the portfolio information between financial and scoring methods in order to select the innovation projects of highest strategic value.

Selecting the Portfolio with Maximum Value

One of the primary goals of portfolio management is to identify an active set of innovation projects that will maximize the value of the portfolio. As indicated, there are two methods commonly used to rank order the portfolio of new product development projects. The first, a financial scoring method, is best suited for later stage projects that have adequate sales estimates available to calculate net present value (NPV) or return on investment (ROI) of the projects.

Secondly, the scoring methodology is designed to prioritize all active projects in the portfolio. Scoring methodologies are particularly useful for early stage projects and those still in the idea generation phases that may not have fully defined financial estimates available.

In either case, NPD projects are prioritized so that each project is fully staffed. Balancing the limited resources is an outcome of effective portfolio management.

Balance the Portfolio

As described above, one of the key activities in which the portfolio management team is engaged is aligning the portfolio with the risk profile established by the innovation and business strategies. Higher risk projects may have a higher return on investment, yet may take longer to achieve. Lower risk projects may have immediate returns, yet these profits might not be sustaining over the long term in comparison to more radical innovations.

Thus, the second goal in portfolio management ensures that the selected set of new product development projects is balanced with risk and strategic objectives of the firm. Again, this is similar to balancing a personal retirement portfolio among stocks, bonds, real estate, and cash, for instance.

In addition to project type, companies frequently seek balance in the portfolio among additional parameters. Most often these characteristics involve trade-offs such as:

- Cost vs. benefit,
- Risk vs. reward,
- Ease of product development vs. market attractiveness,
- Technical feasibility vs. time-to-market, and/or
- Strategic fit vs. new industry opportunities.

Other information used in the decision-making process involves the stage of the project within the NPD structured process (see Chapter 4). The size of the projects is also considered for resource allocation purposes along with the size of the prize - the return on the investment - as well as percent of R&D investment and other parameters which are important to the decision-making authority of the senior management team.

Balance in the portfolio will reflect each business's specific goals and objectives, aligned with the innovation strategy. A new product portfolio will accomplish the desired balance among project types to achieve these goals, just as an individual would balance his or her own financial portfolio to achieve a particular objective within a given timeframe. Project types for new product development are described above, while typically, balance is shown visually with a set of charts and graphs that clarify the portfolio decision trade-offs.

As described previously, portfolio management practices allow a firm to maximize value by selecting the best projects that will deliver the most value over the time period of interest. In the analogy of a personal financial portfolio, an individual balances the low-risk, short-term gains of a money market fund against the longer term growth potential and higher-risk, stock investments. To achieve the maximum value of the set of projects that are selected to be actively worked in the new product portfolio, the portfolio management team will balance the risk and return of those projects against the business strategy. This will include balancing the short-term profit from maintenance and support type of projects with the long-term return and higher uncertainty of projects requiring more technology and market development over a longer period of time.

New product portfolios may be distinguished by the business division or product line, especially if the corporate entity is very large or engaged in diverse industries. This segregation can assist in the decision-making process so that the most knowledgeable senior managers are directing the portfolio in alignment with the specific business unit strategy. In this case, each portfolio would be balanced for acceptable risk and reward trade-offs based upon the innovation objectives of each individual business division.

Recall the four common project types are breakthrough, platform, derivative, and support. Breakthrough projects typically require the most technical and market development and have high uncertainty, but can deliver windfall returns if the project is successful. Platform projects require slightly less technical and market development work, though these efforts still involve significant risk. The platform project is expected to deliver value over the medium- to long-term, since the platform yields a common architecture with follow-up derivative products that can profitably sustain the investment for a significant period of time. Derivative and support projects are normally lower risk and accompanied by lower returns produced in the near term. Derivative projects will offer product enhancements or feature additions within existing product families, while support projects may yield cost reductions or process improvements with very short term benefits.

Product Portfolio Management Software

There are many software tools available to assist with product portfolio management and many firms offer standalone software solutions. Other product portfolio management software is offered as a part of enterprise resource systems. For smaller new product portfolios (less than about 20 active projects), common spreadsheet and graphics software packages can be used to assist in the prioritization and visualization activities necessary to view the trade-offs in the portfolio for decision-making purposes.

Software designed specifically for project management and portfolio management is recommended for larger portfolios due to the difficulty of maintaining the dynamic and large databases with a high degree of accuracy. However, firms should be cautious in selecting portfolio management software to ensure it supports their innovation processes rather than driving system design.

Risk vs. Reward (Bubble Chart)

Balance in a new product portfolio will reflect the risk tolerance of the firm, as detailed by the strategic goals and expected rewards from innovation efforts. In Chapter 1, the product/market matrix (Figure 8) was introduced as a tool to assess the firm's growth strategy and position relative to competitors. The product/market matrix compares existing and new products within existing and new markets. Within the context of portfolio management, the product/market matrix can help the portfolio management team understand the risks and trade-offs of the specified growth strategy.

Similarly, risk vs. reward can be assessed from a technology perspective. In the following graph (see Figure 16) risk is determined by the probability of technical success shown on the y-axis while reward is shown as net present value on the x-axis. The size of the bubble represents the required investment to complete the new product development project. Projects with low-risk but correspondingly low-reward are identified in the lower left hand quadrant as "*dogs*". The quadrant showing high probability of success but only moderate rewards is identified as "*cash cows*" in the upper left hand section of Figure 16. Meanwhile low-risk and high potential reward projects are termed "*stars*" and are identified in the upper right hand quadrant of Figure 16. Finally, the highest risk new product projects with the potential for high reward are called "*wildcats*." Another frequent representation of the risk/reward chart uses an ocean analogy with corresponding terms of "white elephants", "bread and butter", "pearls", and "oysters".

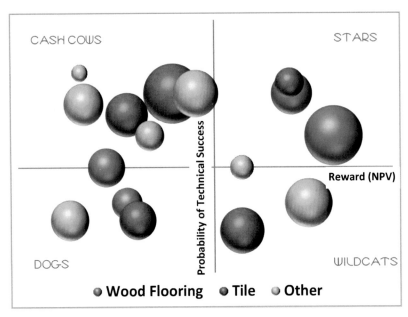

Figure 16 -Portfolio Management Risk vs. Reward

Graphs, such as the one shown in Figure 16, are used to stimulate conversation among the portfolio management team members. A portfolio discussion should evaluate the risk vs. reward of the entire portfolio relative to the dedicated innovation strategy, whether there are sufficient resources to work the active projects, and expected financial commitment to complete the projects in a timely fashion. For example, some items to note for the specific portfolio illustrated above may include the following.

- First, there is significant investment in the low reward, low probability of success projects - shown as "*dogs*" in the lower left-hand quadrant of the graph. Perhaps there is a very good reason for each of these projects to be included in the active portfolio; however, these projects should be investigated for fit with strategy since they appear to deliver low value. For example if the dog projects are part of a system or larger application, they should be pursued in concert with the organization's innovation strategy. The senior management team must understand how each of these projects enables the strategy and will help them achieve the goals of the business unit. Perhaps these projects are component parts of a new platform. Yet if there is not strategic justification to continue these projects as part of a system application or market entry effort, it may be a better decision to instead allocate scarce resources to projects that have higher probability of success or higher potential to add value.

Additionally, two of the four new products within the wood flooring division are in the "*dog*" category (see Figure 16). The portfolio management team should assess what actions should be taken to encourage innovation in the wood flooring division if it is an element of the firm's strategic growth. The firm must carefully consider growth objectives in each business arena in order to sustain long-term profitability.

- Next, because the flooring company has chosen to pursue a prospector type strategy, striving to be first-to-market with many new-to-the-world and new-to-the-company products, the portfolio team should question the high investment in "cash cow" projects. On the other hand, if the firm had aligned with an analyzer strategy, the distribution of project types shown in Figure 16 may be adequately aligned with the desired business and innovation goals.

- Finally, because there are relatively few business divisions for the firm, the color-coded bubbles give a visual indication of the portfolio balance. If the company had designed a strategic plan to grow the tile business and simply maintain the wood flooring and other flooring products, the balance of projects represented in the portfolio shown Figure 16 may be challenged as well. As illustrated, the new product portfolio is roughly balanced by the number of wood flooring and tile projects, with slightly more projects active in the other flooring category.

Bubble charts are used frequently in portfolio management to illustrate together projects from different divisions, varying risk, and dissimilar cost-to-benefit ratios. Candidates for the NPDP certification exam should be familiar with the basic structure and methodology used in a bubble chart to diagnose effectiveness and alignment of a product portfolio with a given innovation strategy.

R&D Spending (Pie Chart)

Another common chart utilized in portfolio management reviews is a simple pie chart, showing the investment split by project type (breakthrough, platform, derivative, and support). As indicated in Figure 17, the pie chart readily shows the R&D spending among project types, allowing senior management to quickly assess effectiveness in implementing a given strategy.

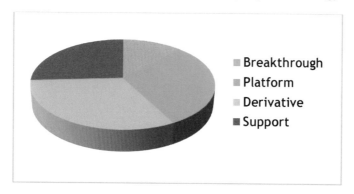

Figure 17 - Portfolio Project Pie Chart

The portfolio illustrated by the pie chart in Figure 17 indicates that the firm has invested nearly 60% of its R&D budget in derivative and support projects. Because there are a number of breakthrough and platform projects in the active portfolio as well, this particular firm is confident in the balance of projects to accomplish its assumed analyzer strategy.

NPDP CERTIFICATION EXAM: *a 24-hour study guide*

Other Charts

A multitude of additional charts and graphs are included with any portfolio management software package and can assist the senior management team in understanding the available project data. It is important for firms to optimize the charts and graphs used in a portfolio review for several reasons. First, the information should be consistent at each review so that decisions are made consistently. Second, the purpose of the portfolio review meeting is to allocate scarce resources to an active portfolio of new product projects. If there are too many graphs and charts provided, the discussion may fail to incorporate the advantages of each project in meeting strategic goals. A portfolio with too many, low-value projects executed by too few resources will hamper the firm in meeting its innovation goals. Finally, product portfolio software can be easily manipulated, often in real time, to give the portfolio management team additional views as necessary. Normally, a set of three to six charts and graphs can communicate the status of the active product portfolio, allowing the portfolio management team to make effective new product project decisions.

Other charts that the portfolio management team might include in a review are simple bar charts showing the number of active projects per stage, per business unit, or per expected release date. Bar graphs showing the number or type of projects to launch over the next three to five years are also useful to convey active portfolio information to the decision-making team.

Additionally, if the revenues from one or more new products are expected to fund next generation development efforts, graphs illustrating payback period, cash flow, or cost vs. timing are effective communication tools to evaluate project trade-offs within the NPD portfolio.

Remember that the most important role of the graphs and charts in a portfolio review is to provide a formal, consistent, and rigorous method to compare all active projects against one another. Discussions should utilize the data from the charts and graphs to assess strategic alignment of the new product portfolio, and not to validate the calculation methodologies. The outcome of the portfolio review meeting should yield an updated active portfolio of new product projects.

Product Portfolio Best Practices

Bob Cooper, Scott Edgett, and Elko Kleinschmidt have published the most comprehensive study of portfolio management best practices (2001). Approximately 200 businesses active in new product development were surveyed regarding their portfolio management practices. Many of the companies were members of the Industrial Research Institute (IRI) in the United States and represented industries including technology, advanced materials, industrial products, and healthcare among others. Like the PDMA studies described previously, the IRI study segregated "the best" performers from average performers and "the worst". Best performers were defined as the top 20 percent of businesses, measured by their success in using specific portfolio methods.

There are two important items to note from the IRI study (Cooper, et al., 2001). First, most firms (about 77% on average) use financial methods to make product portfolio decisions. The best, average, and worst performers all use financial methods to make portfolio decisions about equally. Second, and more importantly, businesses that use strategy as a portfolio method show the greatest difference between top and bottom performers - compare 73% of the best businesses in portfolio management using strategic alignment as a portfolio decision technique with just 26% of the worst performers (Cooper, et al., 2001).

Next the IRI study addressed which portfolio tool or method controlled in making portfolio decisions. Again, there are two distinct items to note from the IRI study. First, poor performers rely more heavily on financial methods as the dominant decision-making method in portfolio management as compared to the top performers. Cooper, et al. reported a significant difference between the 56% of the worst performers exclusively choosing financial methods to make portfolio decisions as compared to only 35% of best performers (2001).

Additionally, alignment with business strategy clearly distinguished top performers from poor performers. Whereas nearly 40% of the best performers relied primarily on the fit with strategy to make a portfolio decision, only 10% of poor performers evaluated strategic fit (Cooper, et al., 2001) as a key differentiator to include a project in the active new product portfolio. Lastly, it is also important to note that best performers utilized multiple portfolio tools in order to assign an active set of new product development projects. Most commonly, these techniques included an assessment of strategic fit, a financial evaluation (either using NPV or ROI), and a scoring model.

Ensure Strategic Alignment

After maximizing the value of the portfolio and achieving balance among the types of projects, the third objective of portfolio management is to ensure that the set of active new product projects is closely aligned with the business and innovation strategies. As indicated above, this is a fundamental responsibility of the senior management team. There are three common methods employed to align the product portfolio with strategic objectives of the firm: the strategic bucket approach, the bottom-up approach, and an iterative method.

Strategic Bucket Approach

A common approach to portfolio management is called the strategic bucket approach. This is a top-down method used to align new product projects with the innovation strategy. Using the top-down approach, senior management *first* clearly outlines the mission, vision, and values statements for the business to achieve innovation goals. Strategy is designed first, then R&D spending is allocated based on these pre-defined business segments or project types (called "buckets"). Lastly, individual projects are selected for inclusion in the active product portfolio using portfolio management tools and charts as described previously.

Thus, in the top-down or strategic bucket approach, management chooses up-front how to allocate new product spending, forcing alignment of the active portfolio with the strategy. Spending buckets may be allocated based on degree of innovation (such as breakthrough, platform, derivative, and support type projects), business unit (cars, trucks, vans, and hybrid vehicles), or geography (North America, Europe, Asia, and South America), for example.

To illustrate, assume that upper management has allocated $10M to new product development for the upcoming annual budget period. Based on an aggressive innovation strategy, senior management has also deemed that 20% of projects should be breakthrough, 50% should be new platforms, 20%

should be derivative projects to enhance existing product lines, and just 10% should be support projects. Thus, the R&D/new product spending for the year would be as follows:

- **Breakthrough projects:** $2M,
- **Platform projects:** $5M,
- **Derivative projects:** $2M, and
- **Support projects:** $1M.

By definition, then, the spending pattern assigned to specific buckets automatically reflects senior management's intention to focus on an aggressive innovation strategy.

To further illustrate, let's assume a different firm, working in the lighting industry, has chosen to aggressively pursue the landscape lighting business and to maintain their indoor lighting and specialty lighting businesses without significant growth in the following years. Thus, the company will assign new product research budgets as follows:

- **Landscape lighting:** 60% of R&D budget,
- **Indoor lighting:** 30% of R&D budget, and
- **Specialty lighting:** 10% of R&D budget.

In this way, the strategy is executed through new product development spending as the landscape lighting business is growing aggressively, while the small, low-growth specialty lighting business is supported to only a marginal degree.

Once new product development and/or R&D spending is allocated by senior management, division or product managers will then prioritize the individual projects within that "bucket". New product development projects within a bucket may include developing new technologies, new markets, and/or product improvements.

An advantage of the strategic bucket approach is that it forces senior management to make tough investment decisions up-front by allocating how and where money will be spent to produce the desired strategic outcomes. A disadvantage to the strategic bucket approach is that timing and risk of individual projects may not be fully considered due to the top-down nature of the approach.

Bottom-Up Approach

In contrast to the strategic bucket approach, strategic alignment of the product portfolio by the bottom-up approach requires less direct intervention by senior management. In fact, the bottom-up approach is often the default method used in portfolio management when no other definition is provided by upper management. In the bottom-up approach, independent project decisions are made during individual project reviews. This results in a single portfolio, across the corporation, of active new product development projects.

As discussed in Chapter 4, a structured NPD process will include individual project evaluations at gate reviews. Typically, the decision-making team that advances an individual project will be composed of mid-level managers rather than the senior management teams responsible for designing strategy and implementing portfolio management. Thus, projects are measured against internal standards for strategic alignment, risk, and expected return, and not necessarily compared to one another.

If the firm has very robust gate criteria, then the bottom-up approach may be successful in creating a product portfolio that is fully aligned with the strategic thrust of the business. However, in many cases, lower value, less risky projects are advanced at the expense of longer-term, higher-risk development efforts. Moreover, the portfolio of projects resulting from a bottom-up review is not necessarily designed to reach overall spending goals (buckets) as described above.

While it is advantageous to evaluate each individual project against a pre-determined checklist of strategic criteria, a disadvantage of the bottom-up method is that projects are evaluated on an individual basis alone. With a pure bottom-up approach, there is no consideration to weigh one new product project against another as in the top-down, strategic bucket approach.

Because many firms have very strong structured NPD processes in place, the bottom-up approach often becomes a default project selection technique. However, senior management must still conduct periodic portfolio reviews to assure that the active projects will achieve the overall innovation goals that they have established.

Best Practice: Align via an Iterative Approach

As implied by the name, the iterative approach to portfolio management combines the top-down/strategic bucket and bottom-up approaches. For firms just beginning to implement a portfolio management process, the iterative approach is fundamental to achieve the organization's strategic goals.

In the iterative approach to portfolio planning and decision-making, the senior management team will first lay out a clear strategy for innovation, using tools like the product and technology roadmap (see Chapter 1), to indicate when more innovative products will be commercialized and when product family enhancements will be implemented. Thus, the innovation strategy yields a first pass spending allocation among the strategic buckets, such as business unit or project type as indicated above. Projects within each bucket are then prioritized by the mid-management gate review teams by evaluating individual projects through the bottom-up approach.

One advantage of the iterative approach is that there is a single resulting portfolio, allowing comparison of breakthrough projects (with high risk and high potential for reward) in one business unit with derivative projects (lower risk and lower potential return) in another business unit. Projects are checked to ensure that they are strategically aligned with the firm's goals.

Moreover, senior management will review the entire portfolio on a regular basis, providing top-down feedback to the independent, bottom-up project decisions. Overall, decision-making for the entire organization will improve over time and project selection will be fine-tuned to implement the innovation strategy effectively.

Resource Allocation

Strategically aligning the new product portfolio with the mission and objectives of the firm goes beyond just selecting active projects to include in the portfolio. Recall that portfolio management is defined as a decision-making process to select the best new product development projects for the firm to actively work while *optimizing the use of scarce resources*. One role for senior managers in the portfolio management process is to allocate the firm's scarce resources, including time, money, people, and equipment, to the active projects.

To their dismay, as they first initiate the portfolio management process, most companies discover that they have too many low-value projects staffed by too few people. Starving the projects of appropriate resources results in poor quality implementation and can lead to significantly delayed commercial launches. Poor project execution has an immediate financial cost due to wasted efforts and loss of competitive advantage. In addition, team members may be demoralized as they are buried under a stack of low-value, uninspiring projects. Furthermore, when resources are overcommitted, a few names will typically appear repeatedly on project lists with concurrent work required. It is clear that such subject matter experts cannot produce quality product development efforts simultaneously on multiple projects.

Figure 18 - New Product Project Resources

Assigning adequate human resources to new product development projects within the portfolio management planning process can help to level resource commitments for each new product development effort. Chapter 6 discusses team and organizational best practices for new product success based on the complexity of the work; however, it is senior management's responsibility to assign adequate and appropriately skilled resources, *by name and function*, to each active project within the new product portfolio.

Resource Productivity

Steven Wheelwright and Kim Clark first documented the effects of project overload on resource productivity more than 20 years ago (1992, pp. 88-91). Other researchers have validated the effects of overcommitting resources to new product development projects with recommendations to enhance productivity (Carter & Bradford, 2012). Based on these studies, optimum productivity occurs when two projects (one large and one small) are assigned to each developer. Productivity is about 80% for each individual in this situation.

Note that 100% productivity is an unrealistic goal since most organizations require engineers, designers, and developers to participate in other tasks, such as completing payroll timesheets, attending staff meetings, and training for mandatory compliance. Additionally, project overhead can consume as much as five hours per week, accounting for time spent in meetings or conference calls, responding to phone calls or e-mails, and serendipitous "water cooler" conversations (Mascitelli, 2011, pp. 17-43). Unfortunately, many companies will assign greater than 100% of development time to individuals, especially high-demand subject matter experts.

In contrast, when a development resource is assigned only *one* project, s/he may experience excessive downtime while waiting for experimental data or customer test responses on the prototype new product. Working on just one project, as compared to two projects, can also lead to productivity losses. Thus, best practices dictate that under general conditions, two new product development projects result in optimum productivity for each development resource - whether that is an engineer, software developer, web designer, marketer, or process technician.

Resource allocation is most effective when team members are assigned to NPD projects by both name and function. A simple table can track the number of hours per project per week for each resource, allowing the project leader to ensure that productivity can be maximized for each new product development effort. Software, such as Microsoft Project™ or other applications specifically designed for product portfolio management, can assist in developing schedules with adequate human resource assignments.

Summary

Product portfolio management is an effective decision-making tool for new product development. Portfolio management is an interactive system that evaluates the entire suite of available new product projects in order to select the most valuable ones for future work based upon the strategic innovation goals of the organization.

Since portfolio management is directly tying the strategy to execution by defining an active set of projects, it must be implemented by senior management. Senior management holds several roles within portfolio management, including:

- Direction setter,
- Product line architect,
- Owning the portfolio, and
- Actively managing the portfolio.

Portfolio management addresses three primary goals within an innovation program. These are to maximize the value of the portfolio, achieve balance, and ensure strategic alignment. Portfolio value is assessed not only by financial consideration, but also scoring models. Non-financial scoring valuation methods are especially effective for early stage projects.

Balance of project types, such as breakthrough, platform, derivative, and support, is often visualized through a series of charts and graphs. These graphs will normally illustrate important trade-offs (risk vs. reward, market attractiveness vs. technical capability, etc.) so that senior management is better informed in the dynamic decision-making process.

Portfolio management can be accomplished from a top-down approach in which the R&D budget is allocated to ensure strategic direction, or can be approached bottom-up on a project-by-project basis. A best practice, especially for those firms just starting a portfolio management process, is to employ an iterative method in which investments in NPD are made through a top-down process, and then each project is evaluated for future work on an independent basis to inform the overall portfolio decision.

Projects that are selected to be included in the active portfolio should be assigned adequate resources, including time, money, people, and equipment. Special attention should be paid to assigning human resources to NPD projects in order to avoid overcommitting designers and developers.

Chapter 4 – NPD Processes

The new product development (NPD) process is a *structured* process designed to enhance the delivery of new products through innovation. Often the NPD process is called the Stage-Gate™ process based on the design of one specific innovation system.

Most people are familiar with the concept of a phased process for product development and many organizations have already implemented structured NPD processes to facilitate new product development. In this chapter, we will present a generic NPD process with various work stages and gate reviews. There will be many similarities between the generic process and ones used throughout industry.

In addition to describing a standardized NPD process, this chapter defines the fuzzy front end of innovation, details decision-making processes, and describes the roles and responsibilities of management within the structured NPD process.

As indicated in the Introduction and Overview, you will recall that NPD process accounts for 20% of the NPDP certification exam, fulfilling 40 of the 200 exam questions.

Learning Objectives

After studying this chapter you will be able to:

1. Understand the differentiating best practices for successful NPD processes.

2. Define the structured NPD process.

3. Explain the phases of innovation in the fuzzy front end.

4. Name and describe the purpose of stages and gates in the NPD process.

5. Outline the purpose of a post-launch review.

6. Describe the roles and responsibilities of the NPD process owner and facilitator.

Brief History of NPD Processes

New product development is generally a newer business process, with the first in-depth studies conducted in the 1980s. Compare this to lean manufacturing, for example, which Toyota pioneered as a business process in the 1970s. Industry-wide studies and university research by Bob Cooper, Merle Crawford, Steven Wheelwright, Kim Clark, and Clayton Christensen during the close of the 20th century have led to significant understanding of the processes yielding successful innovation. Many researchers continue expert studies through universities and trade associations today.

In a recent benchmark study by the Product Development and Management Association, over half of the companies surveyed reported using a formal, cross-functional process to develop new products. This number had been steadily trending upward, moving from 60% of firms reporting in 1995 to 69% of firms in 2003 (Barczak, et al., 2009). In addition, firms report increased utilization (20%) of formal, *sequential* processes (Markham & Lee, 2013). These trends indicate that structured NPD processes are becoming institutionalized as a standard way to conduct innovation projects and to translate novel ideas into commercially successful products and services.

Benchmarking studies also indicate that firms recognize the need for flexibility within an NPD process to capture both simple and complex NPD projects, as well as to balance short-term and long-term initiatives. Such efficiency steps may include using a "conditional gate pass", signaling that these firms have advanced to second and third generation NPD processes. In fact, most NPD processes should be renewed and revitalized to match the business strategy and cultural norms every two or three years. Firms with the best innovation performance constantly incorporate new learning into their NPD processes through continuous improvement efforts (Markham & Lee, 2013).

NPD processes are impacted by the maturity of innovation systems within the firm, organizational culture, pace of market changes (fast or steady), the degree of capital intensity required to compete in the industry, and complexity of technical hurdles. Not surprisingly, senior management's commitment to the NPD process is a critical role in the success of the process over the long run.

Structured NPD Process Definition

A structured new product development process is a *disciplined* and *defined* set of tasks and steps that describe the *normal means* by which a company *repetitively* converts *embryonic ideas* into *salable products or services*. Common to any structured NPD process is the grouping of product development activities into several phases, or *stages*, with review and decision points occurring between phases. Early stages of work are referred to as the fuzzy front end. Work phases include idea generation, information gathering, and prototype testing. Adhering to a structured NPD process can reduce the inherent risk of new product development at the same time as increasing the efficiency and time-to-market of innovation across a corporation.

> *A structured NPD process is a disciplined and defined set of tasks and steps that describe the normal means by which a company repetitively converts embryonic ideas into salable products or services.*

Disciplined and Defined

A *disciplined* process means that the system applies to everyone in the firm, whether they are scientists or software developers, as well as applying to senior management. A *defined* process means that the system includes a formally documented procedure, and all individuals working in new product development at the firm are familiar with the NPD process and practice it regularly.

Additionally, the defined set of tasks and steps have been agreed upon by upper management and the new product development practitioners in the firm. Procedures, checklists, and templates are aligned with the innovation strategy, business practices, and the culture of the organization. Steps required within the structured NPD process are understood by the users and are widely communicated throughout the company.

Normal and Repetitive

In the definition of the NPD process, *normal* means that the process is understood by all in the firm and the system is used consistently. Individual employees within the firm use the same terms and methodologies to describe the phase of development of a particular idea regardless of their function. *Normal* also means that the process is deployed unwaveringly day-in and day-out throughout all levels of the organization.

The definition of a structured NPD process indicates that the system can repetitively convert ideas to commercial products or services. Within this context, *repetitively* means that the NPD process is used *every time* a new idea emerges on the horizon. In other words, NPD phases and gates are not redesigned for every new idea. Additionally, new products are not commercialized if they have not been thoroughly evaluated within the systems defined by the firm's structured NPD process.

Embryonic Ideas and Salable Products

Within the definition of a structured NPD process, *embryonic ideas* include any new ideas, beginning with the first time the idea is considered at the company. Thus, the NPD process facilitates innovation management of new ideas as well as mature product development projects.

Finally, *salable* is an important part of the definition of an NPD process since innovations require a market to be successfully launched. Patent offices around the world are renowned for granting intellectual property to ideas that have no commercial use, yet innovation and new product development demand a significant market share in order for the company to remain profitable. Thus, even though inventions are interesting for new technologies, a product, service, or program must be sold into the marketplace as the final step in the NPD process.

Standard NPD Process

The NPDP certification exam covers a generic structured NPD process as indicated in Figure 19. Here, the light bulb represents a new product idea entering the process. As in a typical flowchart, the green rectangles represent stages of work in which the NPD team will conduct a series of tests and other data gathering activities in early stages while executing plans to manufacture and market the product in later stages. Decision points in the process are indicated by blue diamonds where new product projects are tested against pre-determined criteria in order to move forward to the next stage of work.

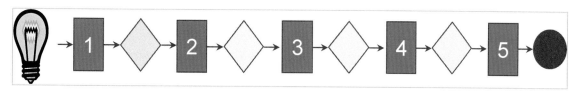

Figure 19 - Standard NPD Process

Normally, a gate approval will lead to the next stage of work. Typical NPD processes will include three to seven stages and gates; although, some companies may have as many as ten stages and gates. Firms that work in service industries or with very simple product improvement projects tend to have fewer stages and gates than those with more complicated or radical product developments, especially those that require significant technology work. The standard NPD process described for the NPDP certification exam will include five stages and four gates as indicated in Figure 19.

After the product is launched, best practices demonstrate that a review of the NPD process will lead to continuous improvements in the process itself. A later review of the product launch will also include financial metrics and whether the strategic goals of the project were met. This post-launch review is represented by the dark circle in Figure 19.

NPD Process Overview

New product development stages of work are distinguished by separate periods of time. Usually, an NPD team will complete all work in prior stages before moving to work in a subsequent stage. However, work does not automatically flow to the next stage. A gate review will ensure that the plan for future work is acceptable and that the new product project continues to meet the desired strategic criteria.

In each stage, specific work tasks are undertaken by the NPD project team. Each company will determine the particular actives to be completed in each stage, though commonalities exist across all successful NPD programs. Typically, earlier stages (Stages 1 through 3) will involve more discovery work, while the later stages include large-scale design, development, prototype testing, manufacturing, and commercialization of the product into the marketplace. Typical tasks required in each stage will be described below; nevertheless, it is important to understand that specific activities must be accomplished in order for a stage to be declared complete. For example, the product innovation charter (PIC, see Chapter 2), linking the strategy to the new product development team's work, must be completed in Stage 1.

Completion of the PIC document, for instance, is defined as a milestone or deliverable for Stage 1. Each NPD team will outline the key deliverables and milestones for an individual project that must be completed during each stage of work on the new product. Additional deliverables will be required to satisfy the firm's overall NPD process.

For example, a new chemical or materials product may require a milestone deliverable in Stage 3 to manufacture one gallon of the material in a laboratory setting. This deliverable would be agreed by the NPD team for the specific project at hand. Similarly, a milestone necessitating a full intellectual property search prior to commercial launch in Stage 5 may be a criteria required for all new product projects at a given organization.

NPD Process Gates

Again, gates are illustrated as diamonds in the standard NPD process shown in Figure 19. This generic process is built on five stages of work with four gate reviews, one after each development stage. Gates reflect the decision point after the new product development work has been completed in the prior stage and to approve the go-forward plan for the next phase of development work. Note that the final stage involves commercialization of the new product, thus, there is no decision point or gate review. However, the dark circle indicates that one or more post-launch reviews are conducted shortly after the new product is fully commercialized.

Gatekeepers

A cross-functional team of managers from different departments and functions are normally required to approve a project within the NPD process. These may be managers of the technology or R&D department, the sales and marketing division, operations and manufacturing, and finance or treasurer's department, for example. We often call this group of people the *gatekeepers*. Gatekeepers can either open a gate or leave it closed. Passing the project through a particular gate allows the new product development effort to move forward and indicates that the project continues to meet the strategic goals as outlined in the PIC. A "no-go" or "kill" decision by the gatekeepers, closes the gate and prevents the project from moving forward.

One distinction between successful innovation programs and those that are less successful is the type of gate review used within the NPD process. An *exit* gate is employed to approve the work in the prior stage and focuses primarily on the work that was already accomplished. On the other hand, an *entry* gate not only evaluates that previous work met the deliverable criteria, but also that the plan for the next stage of work is appropriate for the individual project to meet its strategic objectives.

It is important to recognize that the managers making the decision for a project to move forward must have the budgetary authority to approve the work scheduled for the next phase. Many firms fall into the trap of using exit gates by approving the work that was done in the prior stage without a thorough consideration of the upcoming planned development work. In order to approve future work via an *entry gate*, the gatekeepers must have full budgetary authority to approve for the next stage of work as well as the capability to assign adequate and appropriate resources to the project.

Gate Decisions

After the NPD project team presents the milestones and accomplishments of the previous stage, and presents a plan and set of deliverables for the next stage, the cross-functional team of gatekeepers issues a decision. There are three separate results of that decision:

- Go,
- No-Go, or
- Redirect.

Sometimes the go decision is called a gate "pass", the no-go decision is called a "kill", and the redirect decision is identified as "recycle" or "hold", depending on the particular situation.

Go Decision

A "go" or "pass" decision authorizes the NPD project team to invest given resources to advance the development of the new product project through the next stage. Gatekeepers authorize expenditures and agree to a set of deliverables designed by the NPD team.

No-Go or Kill Decision

In contrast, a "no-go" or "kill" decision means that the project will be halted. The NPD team will still be required to complete post-launch reviews of the project to transfer and build organizational knowledge; however, no additional testing or development should continue for the NPD project. Gatekeepers and senior management should ensure that the NPD team members are quickly reassigned to other challenging projects. Portfolio information will be updated to reflect the cancellation of the project as well.

Redirect

Finally, gatekeepers may occasionally issue a redirect decision. Because the NPD process is defined to continually recognize attractive new product development efforts to advance, the redirect decision should be used sparingly, if at all. In the most common form, a redirect decision requests that the project team "recycle" to an earlier stage to gather more detailed information for the new product. Gatekeepers may also choose to put a project on "hold" due to special circumstances, such as when market seeding for the new product is not complete or if there are not enough resources available for the NPD project to be staffed appropriately. Again, these decisions must be communicated to the portfolio management team to ensure that the overall product portfolio reflects current information.

Conditional Gate Pass

A *conditional gate pass* is one in which the gatekeepers recognize that not all of the deliverables and milestones have been met in the development work of the prior stage, but holding up a go decision would prevent the project from progressing at an acceptable pace. This can occur, for example, when capital equipment must be purchased with a long lead time or extended testing periods (such as a life test) are required for the new product.

Gate Criteria

In contrast to portfolio management (see Chapter 3), projects are reviewed *individually* at each gate. You'll recall that in portfolio management, the entire set of available new product development projects is reviewed to maximize the value of the portfolio bounded by the constraint of limited resources. At a gate review, the cross-functional management team will review a single new product development project against the criteria laid out in the product innovation charter and in the specific project deliverables.

In many cases, the gate criteria are similar to the portfolio management scoring criteria (see Table 3 in Chapter 3, for example). The senior management team that outlines the innovation strategy and is responsible for portfolio management will most likely assist in the development of a set of decision criteria that result in a gate pass for an individual project. Consistent decision criteria will enhance the quality of new product project ideas and will ensure that projects are aligned with the firm's innovation strategy.

Some typical gate criteria used within an NPD process are listed below.

- Does the project fit with the overall business strategy?
- Is there a clearly defined customer need?
- Is the market attractive?
- Is the project technically feasible?
- How can we leverage our core competencies?
- Can we manufacture a product that offers an advantage to customers over other competitors?
- Are there any special health, environmental, or safety considerations?
- What is the risk vs. return?

- Is there a complete cost/benefit analysis?
- Are they are showstoppers that could derail this project?

Gate criteria may be presented as a checklist for the gatekeepers to complete on an individual basis or as a group. If the gatekeepers all agree that the gate criteria are met, including deliverables and resource plans for the next stage of development work, then the project will advance to the next stage.

It is a best practice to train NPD project gatekeepers regarding the decision criteria as well as how to make decisions consistent with the firm's innovation strategy. It is not uncommon for firms to fail to kill NPD projects because of poor gatekeeping practices. Unfortunately, making no decision or delaying a decision until some future event occurs is the same as making a "no-go" decision but with continued spending. NPD projects will flounder without senior management gate approval and the product portfolio will swell with low-value, unattractive projects.

Project gate decisions must be made in a timely fashion. Commercial market windows are often limited for particular product offerings and technology developments must be initiated in time to meet specific product launch schedules. Thus, the timing of a gate decision is important and should be addressed in gatekeeper training, as well.

As discussed previously in Chapter 3, many firms will combine decision-making for individual new product development projects using a top-down or portfolio management process with a bottom-up, or gate decision process. This iterative approach will typically arrive at the best set of projects with the highest quality ensuring strategic alignment on a global basis.

NPD Process Stages

As shown in Figure 19, a standard NPD process is comprised of five stages and of four interceding gates or decision points. Typically, a staged and gated new product development process will consist of three to ten phases of work with corresponding gates. Activities and names of the stages can vary widely depending on the firm or industry. Many companies will link the names of the work phases to easily recalled acronyms tied to the overall NPD process. The NPDP certification exam uses generic terminology to identify the five stages. These work stages are also commonly utilized within the NPD processes of innovative firms around the world.

- **Stage 1** – Opportunity Identification
- **Stage 2** – Concept Generation
- **Stage 3** – Concept Evaluation
- **Stage 4** – Development
- **Stage 5** – Commercial Launch

Some older literature may identify Stage 3 as "Pre-Technical Evaluation" and Stage 4 as "Technical Development," however, both marketing and technology development activities should be conducted in parallel throughout all stages. As indicated in Figure 19, after the commercial launch phase is completed, the product is transitioned to the sales team and is no longer considered "new". If the firm utilizes product life cycle management, the product will also move into the standard brand and life cycle management processes after Stage 5 is complete.

NPDP CERTIFICATION EXAM: *a 24-hour study guide*

Fuzzy Front End

While some firms will have what is called a *pre-development process* or *technology phase-gate system* that precedes the formal NPD process, most consider the first three stages as the "*fuzzy front end*".

The fuzzy front end is aptly named because the product concept is usually not well-defined until Stage 3 (Concept Evaluation). Additionally, the work of the fuzzy front end precedes the more formal product development stages. The use of standard project management tools is described in Chapter 7, NPD Tools and Metrics; however, it should be noted that the formal project management tools covering scope, schedule, and budget are typically deployed in Stage 4 (Development), indicating the more structured nature of the work during the latter stages of the formal NPD process.

Early stage development work is crucial to laying the framework for a successful NPD project. The fuzzy front end encompasses the early "getting started" period of new product development work. During these early stages of the NPD process, where the firm is in the process of identifying customer needs and problems, the work can be very unpredictable and product concepts may be ill-defined. The fuzzy front end is comprised of new product development activities for Stage 1 through Stage 3.

Stage 1 - Opportunity Identification

Recall that *Stage 1, Opportunity Identification,* is closely tied to strategy development and involves a search for the available markets in which the firm should participate to achieve its strategic objectives. During Stage 1, the organization is proactively linking the market and business strategic plans with the technical opportunities for a new product. All levels of the organization are involved in this activity, as the senior management team has responsibility for the strategy, yet sales and marketing staff are often closest to the customers and can identify their needs and wants.

A particular activity completed during Stage 1 is to identify the market needs. Importantly, any opportunity that is identified for possible new product development should fit with the business strategy and innovation strategy of the firm. Attractive opportunities are those with open markets and not too many competitors, products that will be technically feasible to develop, and have few "killer variables".

Killer Variables

A *killer variable* is sometimes called a *showstopper*. Even in the idea stage, tests can be designed requiring a successful pass in order for a new product to go to market. For example, in the medical industry in the United States, new pharmaceuticals must undergo rigorous animal testing before a human trial can be conducted. If a new drug were to fail an animal test, that would be considered a "killer variable" since it would halt all further development on this project.

AG Lafley, the former CEO of Proctor and Gamble, has said that he asked one question at all project review meetings (Lafley & Charan, 2008). In essence that question was *"What are your killer variables?"* NPD teams need to demonstrate that these potential showstoppers can be overcome early in the process. It is very costly to pursue development of a new product and find out in a later stage, such as pilot manufacturing and consumer research, that there are technical or market hurdles which will halt the project. The NPD team will identify these killer variables as early as possible to eliminate them as quickly and inexpensively as possible. If killer variables cannot be overcome, then the project should not continue and resources should be assigned to more attractive NPD projects.

The key deliverable for Stage 1 is the product innovation charter. Recall that the PIC is a guiding document describing the market and technology opportunity, plans for the specific development effort, rules of the road for the project team, and any other special considerations (such as regulatory or legal requirements) for the new product.

Activities
- Strategic Fit
- Market Attractiveness
- Technical Feasibility
- "Killer Variables"

Deliverables
- Product Innovation Charter
- Market Opportunity Assessment Map

Figure 20 - Stage 1 Activities and Deliverables

Some firms will also include a market opportunity assessment map during this stage along with product roadmapping (see Chapter 1). A market opportunity assessment map examines the overall size of the market segment, potential growth rates, expected profit margins, strength of logistics (supply chain), and threats to the target market.

Stage 2 – Concept Generation

Stage 2 is called the *Concept Generation* stage. In this stage, the firm seeks to identify as many ideas as possible to solve the customer problems identified in Stage 1. The main question the NPD team should address during Stage 2 is "*How can we satisfy the market opportunity?*"

Brainstorming is a traditional tool used to create a large number of potential ideas that might solve a problem. For new product development, the brainstorming session should involve product experts as well as those who work in similar fields in order to generate the most ideas. Including individuals with only limited knowledge of existing product solutions can enhance the quality of ideas generated. Firms will pursue both internal and external sources for ideas at this stage and some companies will utilize customers in an open innovation or co-creation role during Stage 2 as well. Brainstorming and other ideation techniques are described in greater detail in Chapters 6 and 7.

Additionally, during Stage 2, the firm will conduct preliminary technical assessments. These may be so-called "paper studies" or literature reviews to determine what has been tried in the past, as well as preliminary market assessments to learn what products competitors are offering and how satisfied consumers are with current product offerings.

Idea generation as well as the preliminary technical and market assessments will lead to early approximations for the new product and rough estimates of both manufacturing costs and sales. The key deliverables for Stage 2 are the product concept statement and a preliminary business case.

Activities
• Brainstorming & Problem-Based Ideation
• Pursue Internal and External Sources
• Preliminary Technical Assessment
• Preliminary Market Assessment

Deliverables
• Product Concept Statement
• Preliminary Business Case

Figure 21 - Stage 2 Activities and Deliverables

Product Concept Statement

A *product concept statement* is a verbal or prototype expression that explains what is going to change in the product or service and how the customer stands to gain from the change. The product concept statement should clearly identify the benefits of the product (in the words of a potential customer), what form the product design will take, and the specific technologies required to fully develop and commercialize the new product.

For example, the great taste of a cola drink is considered a benefit, a cola drink with a dark color represents the form, and a cola made with a new sweetener identifies the technology. Thus, the form is the physical description of the new product, while the technology demonstrates the source by which the form will be attained. In this example, the sweetener and a color additive for the cola drink demonstrate the technology and form of the product concept, respectively. The product concept statement may read, in part, *"A new deep-colored, naturally sweetened cola that tasted fantastic, bringing pleasure to all."*

Perhaps the most important part of the product concept statement is describing the benefit to the potential customer. Benefits must be expressed in terms of what value the customer will gain from the product - the customer must have a need for the product in order to purchase it. Generally, there is an emotional linkage to the benefit (see Chapter 5 on market research), but the concept statement must also express the form and technology of the new product.

Preliminary Business Case

Also, in Stage 2, the NPD team will prepare a preliminary business case. This business case encompasses a wide range of cases, perhaps up to ±20 to 50% accuracy in sales forecasts and development expenses. Despite the wide range of probability of success at this point, it is important to understand if there is no profit potential, then the project should be halted at the gate review. If the probability of profit is high enough and the market is attractive enough, then the project should move forward. A preliminary business case can be developed for the leading concepts or for the new market, technology, and product in general.

Stage 3 - Concept Evaluation

Stage 3 is called the *Concept Evaluation* stage. After generating a high number of ideas in the Stage 2 ideation and brainstorming sessions, the NPD team works to narrow down the ideas to one or two concepts that will be further tested. Concepts that will advance to the next stage should be technically feasible, meet market needs, and deliver substantial benefits to customers. Some older literature refers to Stage 3 as the *Pre-Technical Evaluation Stage*, emphasizing the focus on customer need and early technical feasibility.

In this stage, the market requirements for the new product are finalized through concept testing. Concept testing is a particular market research technique that will be discussed in detail in Chapter 5. During Stage 3, the NPD team will investigate if the new product concepts identified will meet the customer needs and they will work to eliminate poor product models. Ideally, a single leading product concept will be identified that meets the needs of the intended customers.

At this point in the structured NPD process, the product development team will formally define the product attributes. *Product attributes* are a list of features and technical specifications required to deliver the specified product benefits to the customer. Attributes and product features can be described in technical terms for the product development teams, while the product benefits are designated with expressive words based on the customer's perspective and emotional linkage to the product.

Other considerations for the NPD and management teams during Stage 3 include the financial aspects of the new product development effort. Based on the leading concept of the product design, sales forecasts and manufacturing expenses can be estimated. In addition, capital investment requirements are determined if the new product necessitates building factories or improving production lines in order to manufacture the new product. The draft financial analysis is used to assess the project at gate reviews as well as through the portfolio management process.

The focus in Stage 3 is validating that the product concept meets consumer needs. One technique used in market research is called quality function deployment (QFD) and it is used to match the customer wants to the engineering specifications of the new product. Product attributes are further refined utilizing the QFD methodology. QFD originated as a technique to improve quality in the Japanese automotive industry and is a type of "voice of customer" market research. QFD is discussed in greater detail in Chapter 5.

Note that the formal QFD methodology is not commonly deployed in many industries. However, the basic theory that each identified customer benefit should be matched to a product feature or attribute is widely deployed at successful innovation firms. Again, the product should be evaluated through concept testing during Stage 3 to ensure that potential customers find that the new product will solve their problems and offer them a significant benefit over existing competitor products.

Product Protocol

Key deliverables from Stage 3 are the product protocol, the business case, and a project resourcing plan for the final development stages of work. The *product protocol* is a written agreement of exactly what needs to be done to complete the NPD effort and commercially launch the new product. It is fundamentally a go-forward plan for the remaining stages. A product protocol statement will communicate the essential activities required of all members of the NPD team as well as any ancillary functions. Used as a guideline for designers, developers, and marketers, the product protocol integrates all of the new product development actions and provides targets for outcomes of the effort. Importantly, the requirements are specified in *measurable* terms.

Activities

- Market Requirements Analysis
- Concept Testing
- Define Product Attributes
- Financial Analysis (including Capital Investment)
- Quality Function Deployment (QFD)

Deliverables

- Product Protocol
- Business Case
- Project Resourcing Plan

Figure 22 - Stage 3 Activities and Deliverables

As described above, the QFD tool matches the customer needs with product design attributes; QFD is a specific example of a product protocol. In some cases, firms will encourage the NPD team members to sign the product protocol and to incorporate the document as part of the overall project management plan.

Business Case

You will recall that Stage 3 concludes the fuzzy front end work of the NPD project. Small scale and technical feasibility testing is completed, while the concept tests validate that the envisioned product will meet customer needs. As the product development team verifies the product design and plans for upcoming Stage 4 efforts, significant investment occurs and trade-offs are made. Decisions to select one product concept over another will also include decisions to eliminate alternative product solutions. Additionally, product concept tests have gathered potential sales volume and pricing data directly from customers. Therefore, the business case is refined from Stage 2 and can be considered within a higher degree of accuracy.

For example, sales forecasts (including timing and volume) based upon the concept testing results will have a reasonable level of accuracy. During Stage 3, the NPD teams develop detailed project management plans for the final design and scale-up of the product, as well as preparing the market launch strategies for the new product. Information from similar projects is gathered from post-launch reviews to verify appropriate resourcing plans for the remaining project stages. Therefore, resources (time, money, people, and equipment) necessary to complete the development and commercialization work are predicted with a high degree of confidence so that the development costs are estimated with a high level of accuracy, perhaps ± 20%.

Project Resourcing Plan

Companies that routinely document NPD project post-launch reviews will have standard resourcing requirements available for each project type. Resourcing includes the time, money, people, and equipment necessary to convert the validated new product concept of Stage 3 into a commercially viable product. For example, company experience may demonstrate that a product derivative project will require 12 weeks of development time in Stage 4, with three full-time designers, six product engineers, and four marketing professionals assigned to the NPD team. Based on historical data, the cost to complete the stage is estimated using the direct labor costs of the NPD team with a multiplier (e.g. 50%) to cover investment in materials, supplies, and product use testing.

This exercise is completed for each individual project and presented at the Gate 3 review as part of the Stage 4 plan. If the product concept is radical or following a breakthrough innovation, traditional project management estimating tools (see Chapter 7) should be used to develop the go-forward project plan.

Stage 3 is a critical step in the structured NPD process. Concept evaluation involves trade-off decisions among many good product ideas as well as a significant amount of testing with potential customers. Poor concepts are eliminated from the pool of ideas while the few concepts that advance to the next stage will undergo substantial evaluation. Outcomes of Stage 3 include the product protocol to match customer needs with product attributes, a firm business case, and project resourcing plans for Stages 4 and 5.

Stage 4 - Development

Stage 4 is often referred to as the stage in which the "rubber hits the road", meaning that the development of the new product is finalized and the product is manufactured in this stage. While the previous stages may have involved small scale tests and literature searches, Stage 4 may involve numerous personnel across several divisions, supplier and distributor contracts, and potential capital investment to manufacture the new product. Depending on the quality of the work output from the previous stages, Stage 4 is normally a lengthier and more costly stage of work.

Because the purpose of Stage 4 is to develop and plan production for the final product in the marketplace, one of the most important activities is to develop prototypes of the product. These are working prototypes that have the look and feel of the final product so that they can be tested by real customers in the target market. The only difference between the prototype and the final product may be the origin or method of manufacture – for example, the firm may manufacture the prototypes for market testing on small scale equipment yet plan ultimate production in large factories. Alternatively, initial manufacturing may be limited to one factory while other facilities around the world will scale-up to full production later.

Having a full-functioning prototype is important for product use testing. Product use testing is a specific type of market research study (see Chapter 5). In short, the product use test allows the customer to use the prototype to see if the new product can really do the job for which it was designed and if it really addresses the problem customers identified in earlier stages of work. The product use test determines customer satisfaction with the product.

Activities
• Develop and Finalize Product Prototypes
• Product Use Testing
• Operations Planning
• Strategic Launch Plan
• Resolve Regulatory Issues and Intellectual Property

Deliverables
• Proven Product Prototype
• Updated, Comprehensive Business Case

Figure 23 - Stage 4 Activities and Deliverables

Additional activities to be completed during Stage 4 include developing a strategic launch plan and production planning. One of the many tasks in the strategic launch plan, for example, is sales account management. A cross-functional NPD sub-team will identify which existing customers should be converted to the new product or targeted for new sales. Other sales tasks that are initiated during Stage 4 include determining the acceptable sales cycle for the new product and managing existing customer communications regarding the new product or service. Marketing collateral will be prepared during this phase of development work, including a communications plan, sales literature and web sites, and advertising that demonstrates an emotional linkage with the new product's benefits.

Finally, any outstanding regulatory or legal issues need to be resolved during the development stage. It is important to ensure that patents, trademarks, copyrights, trade secrets, and other intellectual property are in place before the product is formally tested with potential customers. Without proper intellectual property protection, competitors may gain unrestricted exposure to the new product. Likewise, regulatory testing is often mandated by government institutions in order to legally sell a product under certain circumstances.

Proven Product Prototype

The key deliverables for Stage 4, Development, include a *proven product prototype* and a comprehensive business case. It may seem counterintuitive to consider the proven product prototype as a deliverable for Stage 4 instead of Stage 3. However, you will recall that Stage 3, Concept Evaluation, may yield two or three viable ideas needing further investigation regarding the market, technology, and product requirements for the innovation. Early in Stage 4, one of these concepts *must* be selected to move forward and into commercialization. Final selection of the one, best product concept pinpoints the proven product prototype.

An additional consideration for the proven product prototype is that it must be fully functional and meet the needs of the customers. During this phase of new product development work, the NPD team should validate that the proven product prototype will fully satisfy the potential customers and is a legitimate candidate for full-scale manufacturing.

Comprehensive Business Case

Finally, the comprehensive business case will have a high accuracy (± 5 to 10%) as compared to earlier financial estimates. This degree of accuracy is achieved as a result of completing the earlier testing and development phases of NPD work. During Stage 4, the NPD team will have obtained excellent estimates of the potential sales volume for the new product over a reasonable period of time, as well as both pricing and cost information for the new product.

Stage 5 - Commercialization

Commercialization is the last stage of the formal new product development process. The new product, service, or program is commercially launched and introduced to the market during *Stage 5*. Therefore, key activities in Stage 5 are oriented to the commercial launch of the new product and ensuring that appropriate inventory levels exist for the new product as it moves to full sale in the marketplace.

Activities

- Market Testing
- Strategic Launch Management
- Full-Scale Production
- Distribution Channels
- Transfer New Product to Mainstream Business

Deliverables

- New Product Introduction

Figure 24 - Stage 5 Activities and Deliverables

Market testing, which will be discussed in detail in Chapter 5, is the first time that the new product is verified with its marketing plan. There are several techniques that gauge the reactions of potential customers to the new product and to the marketing materials. If the reactions by customers are unfavorable or if sales are not reaching the anticipated levels, the strategic launch plan (designed in Stage 4) is implemented.

As described above, a critical activity conducted during Stage 4 is designing the strategic launch plan for the new product or service. In Stage 5 and beyond, the NPD team will monitor the effectiveness of the marketing plan. If certain trigger events occur, corrective elements of the strategic launch plan will be implemented. For example, if a particular marketing campaign is not achieving the expected sales response rates, the NPD team will implement the strategic launch plan by altering the advertising media, content of the marketing materials, and/or adjusting other elements involved in the sale of the new product. In essence, the strategic launch plan is a risk management tool that particularly assists with the marketing aspects of the new product innovation effort.

Note that the use of a cross-functional team throughout the development effort can significantly increase the speed of implementation of the strategic launch plan. The marketing plan will include items such as the customer value proposition, the emotional linkage to the product benefits, how the product can be positioned in the marketplace, and the impact of competitors on sales. For example, if the concept studies and market research showed that potential customers felt that the product was sophisticated and elegant, the emotional linkage and product positioning might address a luxury market or splurge purchase. Cross-functional team members will be familiar with study information obtained earlier in the development phases and can positively impact corrections necessitated in Stage 5 according to the strategic launch plan.

Market communications tie closely with the marketing plans. Once the product positioning and emotional linkages are determined for the new product or service, marketing communications will address how best to reach the target audience. Literature, brochures, and web sites are designed to connect with the potential customers in the best way. Today, social media sites, such as Facebook, Twitter, You Tube, and Pinterest are also important communication pathways for a new product or service and should not be neglected in the marketing communications plan. Advertising and sampling are also considered as a part of communications management within the strategic launch plan, as is branding the new product and platform. Many of these items will be described in greater detail in Chapter 5, Market Research.

Managing the commercial launch also involves managing the production capacity of the facilities manufacturing the new product. For international corporations, this may involve additional questions regarding supply chain, logistics, and distribution channels. In some circumstances, the new product is initially sold from a smaller production facility and as sales ramp up, manufacturing is expanded to other facilities. The NPD team and technical service teams must closely monitor the quality of the product as operations increase to full scale production and as manufacturing expands to multiple facilities across the globe.

Finally, production and distribution plans need to be developed for the new product. You'll recall that some of the concerns for the NPD team include where the product inventory is sourced, how fast production will be ramped up, quality of manufacturing, and the reliability of the distribution channels.

A key activity for the NPD team and for the management during Stage 5 is the transfer of the new product to the mainstream business. Notably, the team will be anxious to move on to work on the next project, yet the team members possesses a great deal of tacit knowledge about the design and function of the new product. Thus, some firms will hold the NPD team together for some time after the product launch to ensure a smooth transition to the mainstream sales and customer support functions.

New Product Introduction

The fundamental deliverable for Stage 5 is the *introduction of the new product* to the marketplace, sometimes called *commercialization*. The definition of commercialization is the process of taking a new product from development to market. It generally includes production launch and ramp-up, deploying marketing materials, training of customers and sales staff, as well as developing protocols for customer service and support

Post-Launch Reviews

Many studies demonstrate that learning organizations are more efficient and more productive in new product development. A learning organization is one that continuously evaluates the quality of work performance and undertakes improvement steps to reduce and eliminate waste. The product *post-launch review* is a critical step in the new product development process that encourages organizational learning to continually enhance and improve the innovation processes.

While is it recommended to always document the lessons learned during the implementation and execution of a new product project, it is especially important to do so once the product has been commercialized. The new product post-launch review is a critical feedback element for each new product development project. It is sometimes called the post-launch audit, a project post-mortem, the lessons learned review, post-implementation audit, retrospective, or post launch control study. Regardless of the terminology, it is crucial for continuous improvement that a review of the commercialized product and associated project work is conducted to enhance the knowledge of the organization and to offer feedback to inform the innovation process.

What is a Post-Launch Review?

At a post-launch review, there are three fundamental questions to be addressed. First, *what went well* in the project? This question encompasses the successes of the product development effort. Learning organizations will deliberately document the capabilities that enhanced the success by utilizing specific procedures, policies, and/or processes that led to a successful product launch. The list of things that went right may include items such as, using a structured NPD process, utilizing the skills of a cross-functional team, conducting market research studies with potential consumers early in the development cycle, following clear strategic objectives, and team cohesiveness.

Technical successes should also be documented in the post-launch review, such as having the proper testing equipment on hand, utilizing specially trained designers and developers, appropriate scheduling of technical tests and reviews, as well as the use of software and hardware tools to enhance the technical development of the new product.

It is a best practice to start any lessons learned review with the successful highlights of the product development effort. Describing successes first will help the team build trust with one another and ensure that the post-launch review is about the product and the development process instead of the people and personalities involved in the work.

The second fundamental question in a post-launch review is to ask *what went wrong* on a project. Understanding where there were roadblocks in the product development effort can greatly assist the next new product development program, especially for a similar project type (e.g. product improvement, derivative, or enhancement).

For firms that have not previously conducted post-launch reviews, findings of what went wrong will likely include compressed schedules, expanding objectives (known as *scope creep*), too few resources dedicated to the development effort, constrained budgets, and conflicting priorities. Additionally, many firms find that there are too many projects worked by too few people, and that market research studies were not conducted early enough in the process to stave off problems with customer satisfaction in the final product delivery.

Finally, the most important question to be addressed at the post-launch review is *what can be done to improve* next time? After all, documenting what went right and what went wrong on a project is a good practice, but providing recommendations on what to do differently next time is the best outcome of the post-launch review.

Benefits of Post-Launch Reviews

For example, if the first question (what went well) elicited responses from the NPD team regarding the great quality and timing of market research studies, these practices should be incorporated into the NPD structured process. In the future, then, a new product idea would not be allowed to pass an initial gate review without studying potential customer needs.

On the other hand, if the second question (what went poorly) revealed that the existing NPD process included too many duplicate checklists at each stage, the NPD process facilitator can improve the overall NPD process by streamlining phase and gate checklists.

It is especially important to incorporate the learnings from the post-launch review into process improvements. While the post-launch review is often overlooked in the NPD process, when it is actually completed, lessons learned are commonly filed or stored without any further communication to future NPD team leaders or the project management office. The role of the NPD process facilitator is discussed later in this chapter; however, it should be noted that s/he is responsible for communicating and implementing NPD process improvements from all product post-launch reviews to improve the efficiency and productivity of the NPD process throughout the firm.

Moreover, the importance of the feedback loop from the post-launch reviews cannot be overstated. If multiple product development teams working on a standard derivative project have learned that it takes an average twelve (12) weeks to complete Stage 3 work while the standard assumption for the new product development process only allots eight (8) weeks for Stage 3 work, nearly every project will fall behind the estimated schedule(s). It is critical for management and NPD team leaders to be honest and practical about the work required to develop a new product, rather than simply being optimistic and hopeful.

Not only will the post-launch review provide important feedback on the scheduling of new product development projects, the lessons learned reviews also yield information to improve future cost estimates for similar new product development projects. Cost of knowledge workers is best estimated by appropriate scheduling, while the post-launch review can also provide specific data regarding the costs of concept tests, product use tests, and other market research efforts.

When to Conduct a Post-Launch Review

Of course, it is a best practice to continually evaluate project standards and process execution steps. However, there are three critical times in which to conduct a post-launch review (PLR). As the new product or service is commercially launched in Stage 5 and before the NPD team disbands, the first post-launch review should be conducted, called PLR-1. Lessons learned at this team review are perhaps the most critical to improve the structured NPD process itself. The three fundamental questions of what went right, what went wrong, and what can be improved next time are focused on the execution of the structured NPD process. An outcome of the PLR-1 outlines systematic hurdles in the staged and gated development process, as well as any outstanding issues regarding market or customer research, timing, length, and cost estimates for each stage of the process, as well as communication or coordination constraints.

The output of the PLR-1 is crucial to continually improve the NPD process. As described above, best practices demonstrate that leading innovation firms *continually* revise and improve their NPD processes. In contrast, the poorest performing firms redesign the NPD process less than every five years (Markham & Lee, 2013). Feedback from the PLR-1 will allow the NPD process facilitator to continually revise and update the NPD process to optimize efficiency and productivity of new product development.

As an aside, lessons learned reviews, such as the PLR-1, should be also conducted for any project that is cancelled in a late stage of development. In such circumstances, management should identify why the product idea was allowed to pass gates when the strategic alignment, technical evaluation, or competitive environment were poor. Again, the lessons learned can improve the overall system and help to prevent such mistakes from occurring in the future.

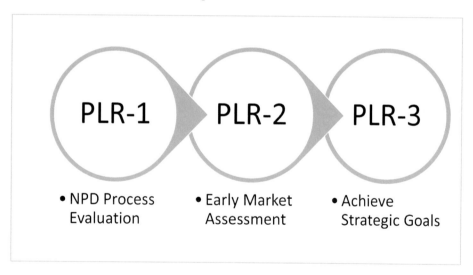

Figure 25 - Post-Launch Reviews

The second post-launch review (PLR-2) allows the NPD team time to implement and evaluate the strategic launch plan as necessary. The purpose of this second review is to determine if sales of the new product are at the expected level, if customers are satisfied with the new product, and if inventory is keeping pace with the required market needs. For example, if sales are lagging projections, then marketing plans should be altered according to the strategic launch plan. Alternatively, if the consumer product hotline is recording numerous quality or service complaints regarding the new product, then portions of the strategic launch plan and risk management plan should be executed to address these market needs immediately. Finally, in the happy case that the product is flying off the shelves, manufacturing plans may need to be adjusted to keep up with inventory demands.

Timing of the PLR-2 should be in accordance with the sales cycle of the product. For most products, the second post-launch review can be conducted just a few weeks or months after commercial launch. At this point in time, there is normally enough sales data and feedback from early adopting customers to evaluate and make any necessary changes to the marketing plans.

Some products, such as foods, beverages, and cellular telephones, have very short life cycles, perhaps on the order of 12 to 18 months before being replaced with a next generation product. In these cases, the PLR-2 should be conducted sooner rather than later after the commercial launch. Each company and industry will be able to identify the proper timing for this post-launch review based upon innovation and market experience.

Regardless of the timing for the PLR-2, the firm should evaluate data to ensure that the new product is gaining acceptance in the marketplace and that the profitability of the product is meeting expectations. In rare cases, adjusting the marketing plan may not improve sales significantly and the product may need to be abandoned. Again, this situation should be investigated further through the lessons learned process to ensure that poor product concepts are not passed automatically through the NPD system in the future.

Finally, the third product post-launch review should be conducted after the sales cycle is complete for most major customers. Again, the timing will vary depending on the product category and industry; however, yet about one year after product launch is sufficient for most products with medium- to long-life cycles. The PLR-3 review not only examines sales revenues and production cost information from a financial perspective, the review team should fully evaluate whether the project objectives were completely met.

Again, the feedback from the PLR-3 review provides critical information for future NPD teams, as well as feedback to improve the NPD process. In addition, information from the PLR-3 sends a strong signal to the management team regarding the health and strength of the innovation strategy by evaluating the subsequent success of the new product in meeting market, technology, and product category opportunities.

Management Roles in the NPD Process

Proactive involvement of senior management in the NPD process leads to greater innovation success. There are two management roles within the NPD process that are essential to an efficient and effective system for converting embryonic ideas to salable products or services: the NPD process owner and the NPD process facilitator.

NPD Process Owner

The *NPD process owner* is responsible for the strategic results of the NPD process, and therefore, works very closely with the operational manager of the NPD process (the NPD process facilitator, see below). Strategic results include elements of the innovation program, such as the throughput of the system, the quality of NPD ideas and projects, as well as cross-functional participation throughout the organization and firm.

For example, the NPD process owner will work with other senior managers to ensure that *all* new product and service innovation projects move through the staged and gated system. Ensuring that each and every new product project is carried out in accordance with the structured NPD process confirms the value of the project is consistently recorded and that the project is executed within the established quality standards. New ideas that enter the NPD process at the earliest stages are automatically evaluated via the portfolio management process as well. As such, any project bypassing the NPD process should not be included in the active project portfolio.

Often the NPD process owner is a senior manager who takes an active role to ensure all product ideas are introduced through the NPD process, but s/he is also active in helping to balance resource requirements as a result of portfolio management decisions. An NPD process owner may also serve as a member of the portfolio management team. As indicated, successful NPD projects require a cross-functional team for successful implementation and the NPD process owner is in a position to negotiate adequate staffing for the active new product projects.

Moreover, the NPD process owner helps to communicate the firm's strategic goals and objectives by working with the NPD process facilitator to ensure that innovation and business strategies are properly reflected in the phase and gate criteria as well as to provide training and implementation of the NPD process itself. Especially in the case of bottom-up portfolio decisions (see Chapter 3), in which active projects are included in the portfolio based upon gate passes, the NPD process owner must ensure that gate criteria clearly reflect strategic alignment.

Additional roles and responsibilities of the NPD process owner may include:

- Leading implementation of the NPD process throughout the company,
- Engaging new employees in NPD process training,
- Serving as a management focal point for all innovation efforts, and
- Ensuring strategic alignment of the firm's goals and objectives within the NPD process.

NPD Process Facilitator

While the NPD process owner may be a part-time role for an executive manager, the role of the *NPD process facilitator* is a full-time operational position. If the organization utilizes a project management office (PMO), the NPD process facilitator is assigned to the PMO to assist project leaders and to conduct training for innovation processes. In other firms, the NPD process facilitator may lead the new product division or may be assigned a senior role within the technology, marketing, or R&D groups.

Regardless, the NPD process facilitator possesses intimate knowledge of the firm's NPD process and is responsible for much of the implementation of the system. S/he is an expert in the detailed steps and tasks required for each stage of new product development, and provides both depth and breadth of understanding of the gate criteria required for any project to pass to the next stage. Normally, the NPD process facilitator will not be assigned as a gatekeeper to projects, however, s/he will be present at many gate meetings to ensure smooth transition of projects from phase to phase and to ensure that the process is functioning as it was designed and is documented.

Of course, attending gate meetings will provide the NPD process facilitator with feedback to continuously improve the NPD process. Continuous improvement and revision of the NPD process is necessary to ensure that the system is operating efficiently and is actively implementing the strategic objectives of the firm through new product development programs. Encouraging full participation across the organization is another fundamental responsibility of the NPD process facilitator.

Other important activities for the NPD process facilitator include training the NPD teams, gatekeepers, and other users of the NPD process. New employees coming into the product development group will be trained on the process utilized by the firm in order to ensure the common vocabulary and terminology are understood throughout the organization. Normally, the NPD process facilitator will schedule group or one-on-one training sessions for NPD team members, team leaders, and gatekeepers as necessary.

Because continuous improvement is a hallmark of successful innovation programs, the NPD process facilitator will play a key role in the post-launch review process. S/he will typically attend the post-launch reviews to ensure that lessons learned are proactively incorporated into system enhancements. A direct outcome of the post-launch review, coupled with continuous improvement of the system, is the increased quality of new product ideas input to the system.

Most firms find that as the gate pass criteria and steps required for each stage are communicated widely throughout the organization, the quality of ideas improves and they focus more on the strategic goals of the firm. The NPD process facilitator and the NPD process owner are directly responsible for the quality implementation of and continuous improvement of the structured new product development process within a company.

Designing and Implementing an NPD Process

While the overall design of the structured NPD process is normally initiated by senior management, the day-to-day implementation of innovation is led by the NPD process facilitator who reports directly to the NPD process owner. Continuous improvement to establish a repeatable, quality NPD program rests on the firm's long-term commitment to aligning innovation programs with the overall corporate business objectives.

At the outset, the structured NPD process must fit the organization's culture. For example, many large firms that work in traditional business arenas, like oil and gas, will tend to have somewhat formal NPD processes with a large number of stages and gates. Gate reviews will be official meetings and stage completions will only be accepted with checklists signed by the appropriate directors and administrators. Many of these firms will include a fuzzy front end process for technology development in advance of the more formal phased and gated process for technical and market development. Often a decentralized research division will be responsible for identifying new technology opportunities while integrated manufacturing and sales teams will explore markets and competition for new products.

Smaller firms, especially service companies and those in less traditional industries such as software development, generally tend to have fewer stages and gates. Gate reviews will require a management sign-off, but the presentation of work completed in prior stages is somewhat less formal and may follow a different format depending on the complexity of the innovation. In contrast to a traditional functional organization, these smaller firms often involve natural cross-functional teams to accomplish specific goals and objectives growing from an entrepreneurial culture.

Next, proactive and visible senior management helps to ensure success with the new product development programs especially during implementation of a new or revised staged and gated system. Senior management, with the assistance of the NPD process owner and the NPD process facilitator can help the NPD teams remove bureaucratic obstacles and streamline efforts to be more productive and efficient in developing new products and services. Senior management is responsible for allocating resources required for each NPD project according to the plans presented by the NPD teams at each gate review meeting.

Benchmarking studies show that the most successful new product development across industries focuses primarily on the market and the customer. It is crucial to enforce the early stage opportunity identification activities in the NPD process to gather potential market needs before going into the lab to develop the technology. Most new products fail because they have not addressed a customer's specific need while adding significant value. It is senior management's responsibility, and the joint authority of the NPD process owner and NPD process facilitator, to validate that customer input is gathered early in the process in order to lead to long-term innovation success.

Summary

Firms that execute innovation projects through a structured new product development process enjoy higher commercial success rates than those that do not implement formal systems. A *structured NPD process* is a disciplined and defined set of tasks and steps that describe the normal means by which a company repetitively converts embryonic ideas into salable products or services. NPD processes utilize stages to conduct development work and gates to review and approve the next phase of the effort.

The first three stages of the structured NPD process are called the *fuzzy front end,* where the work is more chaotic and less structured than later technical development stages. Sometimes, these early stages are called the technology development stages, encompassing Stages 1 through 3 of the standardized NPD process.

Foundational innovation activities are completed during Stage 1, Opportunity Identification, to identify the market, technology, and product category. Then, in Stage 2, Concept Generation, new ideas are generated, gathering a great number of diverse potential solutions to solve the customer's problems that were identified in the previous stage. An evaluation of the ideas leads to one or two being selected for further evaluation in Stage 3, Concept Evaluation. Potential customers are exposed to the new product concept to gauge their interest. The *product protocol* will translate product attributes into engineering specifications so that formal technical development can proceed.

Stages 4 and 5 are often considered more formal than the fuzzy front end. Project management tools are utilized in Stage 4 to ensure that the factories are built properly to manufacture the new product and that sufficient inventory will be available as the product goes to market. Early in Stage 4, a product prototype is proven so that the formal, comprehensive business case can be completed.

Stage 5 includes the *commercialization* of the new product as it is introduced into the market for sale. Market testing, in which the new product is first combined with the marketing plans, is also conducted in Stage 5.

After the product is launched, *post-launch reviews* are completed to ensure continuous improvement of the NPD process and to validate acceptable sales in the target market. An important measure of success that is evaluated during a lessons learned review involves customer satisfaction with the newly commercialized product. Feedback from the post-launch reviews provides data to improve resource estimates for future new product development programs and reinforces learning behaviors for the organization.

Finally, the roles of the *NPD process owner* and the *NPD process facilitator* ensure that the structured NPD process is implemented efficiently to achieve the strategic objectives of the firm. Both of these managers are key individuals to drive the successful implementation of the NPD process. When first designing an NPD process, it is important to maintain a focus on the customer and early stage investigations of the market potential. It is the responsibility of the NPD process owner and the NPD process facilitator to engage the organization and ensure that the focus on customer problems is maintained throughout the process.

Chapter 5 – Market Research

Like innovation strategy, there are many overlapping categories within market research that yield success with new product development. Additionally, marketing is a degree field unto itself, so the NPDP certification exam covers a broad range of topics describing how market research techniques are utilized within the NPD framework as well as specific marketing tools. For example, two common market research methods are the focus group and the customer site visit. A focus group employs both qualitative and primary market research techniques to gain in-depth knowledge of customers interacting with product concepts. A customer site visit might use causal observation and the voice of customer techniques from market research to identify potential consumer problems in the fuzzy front end of the structured NPD process.

While it is impossible to present an all-encompassing perspective of marketing to new product development, it is important for NPDP certification candidates to understand several classifications of market research and to identify market research techniques to deploy during the various stages of a standard NPD process to learn the most about customer behaviors regarding the new product, service, or program. Therefore, this chapter highlights definitions of foundational market research terms as well as simple applications of marketing tools to enhance and improve the innovation system for successful commercialization of new products.

Market research comprises 15% of the NPDP certification exam, or 30 of the 200 questions. Many of these questions focus on definitions of market research terms, require an understanding of the techniques, or validate the best techniques to apply during the various stages of work in the NPD process.

Learning Objectives

After studying this chapter, you will be able to:

1. Explain the importance and role of market research in new product development.

2. Differentiate between secondary and primary market research.

3. Understand the purpose of qualitative market research in contrast to quantitative market research.

4. Describe techniques of primary market research and when they should be deployed in the NPD process.

5. Define market research tools such as the concept test, three types of product use tests, and a test market.

Importance of Market Research in NPD

About eight or nine out of every ten new consumer packaged goods fail in the marketplace (Mattimore, 2012). Other studies show that less than 3% of new products achieve first year sales of $50 million or more in the US, considered the benchmark of a successful new product launch. In fact, American families purchase the *same 150 items weekly* to meet over 85% of their household needs (Scneider & Hall, 2011). Obviously, it is quite a challenge to successfully introduce a new product to the marketplace.

> *Market research is defined as information about a firm's customers and competitors.*

Leading causes of new product failure are lack of customer understanding and failed market execution. Best practices teach that if the firm has a solid innovation and business strategy, customer needs will be gathered *prior to* the initiation of technical product development efforts. However, because market research can be both time-consuming and expensive, the effort should be planned accordingly.

First, what is the burning question that the market research needs to answer? As you will discover in this chapter, there are different points in the structured NPD process at which consumers and potential customers should be queried for their interest in the product idea or concept. Activities within the NPD process will determine whether the product meets customer needs and if consumers are interested in purchasing the new product or service. Each of these tasks results in a different sets of questions for a target market and these details should be clarified prior to conducting a market research study.

Next, what is the objective of the market research? If the firm is testing a new concept idea, then the goal of the research effort should be to gather initial impressions from target customers to further refine the concept to meet customer needs. On the other hand, during the product use testing phase of the NPD process, the market research objective may be to ensure that a majority of target customers are satisfied with the product's features and functions.

Finally, what specific problem needs solving? The explicit problem that needs solving with market research should be clearly defined before contracting a market research firm. Most companies do not have the luxury of a fully staffed, experienced market research department. Thus, most new product development efforts require outsourcing some elements of market research. In order to maximize the budget for this portion of the new product development project, the goals of the market research study should be both concise and specific. It is important to remember in market research that if you don't ask the right question, you won't get the right answer!

Fundamental Market Research Definitions

One definition of market research is a **study of consumers' wants**: the gathering and analysis of information about what people want or like, and about the products and services they actually purchase. Other definitions explain market research as information about the firm's existing or potential customers, competitors, and markets in general. These are all crucial categories of information to gather and analyze within market research to yield successful innovation outcomes.

Failed NPD efforts are often attributed to a lack of understanding of the customer or the competitive landscape.

Market and customer information may be available from *secondary sources*, or those that are already published prior to the firm undertaking the NPD project. In contrast, *primary market research* is information that is collected to address a set of questions within a specific new product development project. Primary market research data is normally collected directly from potential consumers.

Finally, market research data can be either qualitative or quantitative. In the case of qualitative research, the firm gathers stories, opinions, and anecdotes in order to better understand customer needs to optimize the product development effort. Quantitative market research, on the other hand, can be analyzed with statistical methods, plotted on trend lines, and is used to generate sales forecast models for the upcoming product or service.

Keep in mind that secondary market research may be either qualitative or quantitative, as can be primary market research. Note that secondary market research is normally conducted *before* primary market research is undertaken.

Secondary Market Research

Secondary market research is often referred to as a "paper study" despite the fact that much secondary research is conducted using the internet today. The definition of secondary market research is *any* market research data or information that was collected by one entity for one purpose and is used again later by another party for a different purpose.

> *Secondary market research refers to any data gathered for one purpose by one party and used by a second party for another purpose.*

Some examples of secondary market research external to the firm include:

- Trade publications,
- Business journals,
- Newspapers,
- Books,
- Consultant reports,
- White papers,
- Case studies,
- Blogs,
- Library references,
- Professional trade association surveys, and/or
- Published government data.

Internal sources of secondary market research data may include customer service reports, sales call reports, and complaint records.

Advantages of Secondary Market Research

There are several advantages for a firm to use secondary market research data, especially in the early stages of a new product development effort. First, gathering and analyzing secondary market research data is comparatively inexpensive. In many cases, internet searches will reveal a substantial amount of market data that is readily available at no or very low cost. In other situations, access to large databases of customer or market information is available for low fees. Professionals, such as librarians, small business development centers, or market research reporting agencies, can also be helpful in accessing secondary market research data with little cost.

Next, secondary market research can be obtained quickly in order to help screen initial new product ideas and market segments. Especially in the case of an internet or library search, information can be often be found within hours, as compared to primary market research which may take weeks or months to gather. Such secondary data is valuable in circumstances in which a firm is trying to determine whether a particular new product idea has ever been tested, is already on the market for sale, or has intense competition within the marketplace.

Additionally, secondary market research can help the NPD team better clarify the customer problem that needs solving. Validating the needs of customers and the competitive landscape through secondary market research can identify gaps that need to be addressed later in the NPD project through primary market research. Secondary market research data provides the context and constraints for specific questions to be answered through the more time-consuming and expensive primary data collection techniques. In essence, a detailed understanding of potential customers, competitors, and the company can refine and streamline future efforts for the product development project.

Finally, some concepts are not well matched for development and commercialization. Secondary market research data can provide a supportive outside view, indicating whether an idea is truly great and worthy of full-fledged development. In some cases, secondary market research studies may expose prior testing of a like product in the marketplace, informing the NPD team of product requirements in order to successfully commercialize a new product in a given category.

Disadvantages of Secondary Market Research

Because secondary market research has been collected for one purpose by another entity, firms should exercise caution in evaluating the data for specific new product development projects. For example, in analyzing the data, a firm should question the accuracy and reliability of the source information. Data bias may have been introduced due to the nature or goals of the original study. This is of particular concern if the market research was sponsored with an end goal in mind, such as research funded by lobbying groups seeking data to support a given point of view.

In addition, assumptions made by the researchers in the original data set may not be well documented or detailed in the final report. Terminology and definitions used in the market study may be different than what your firm uses or may even be inconsistent with industry standards. It is important to completely understand how the market research data will apply to the market and customer opportunities for the specific new product development effort.

Next, when analyzing an external secondary data source, it is important to understand the purpose of the original market study. For instance, a long-term health study may be conducted to gather information on how smoking affects longevity. However, there may be data within the study that also captures the amount of coffee that the subjects drank per day. If you are investigating a new coffee product, this secondary data may be useful to you, but you do need to be cautious about extending the findings from a smoking study to coffee consumption.

Similarly, the use of secondary market research data may not be broad enough to match the market coverage needed for the current product development effort. The method of data collection for the secondary data is often not fully documented. In particular, the sample size of the secondary study may have been inadequate for the purposes of a current market research effort. Other concerns with secondary data are whether the sample was selected randomly or from pool of potential customers that equally represent the ultimate market for the new product or service.

Moreover, the age of the secondary data collection is relevant. For instance, if the data was collected during an economic downturn, it might not be representative of the current economic climate. Likewise, information collected in one geographic region cannot necessarily be transmitted directly to another country across the globe.

Finally, much of the available secondary market research data is open source, meaning that it can be used by anyone anywhere and is not specific to your firm. It is quite likely that your competitors also have access to this data. Conclusions from secondary market research data can lead to proprietary development activities, but competitive intelligence should be continually monitored as well.

Benefits of Secondary Market Research

As described in Chapter 4, Stage 1 of the NPD process involves identifying opportunities for a new product development effort by focusing on markets, technologies, and product categories. Activities within Stage 1 are closely linked with defining the innovation strategy for the business and product line. A key output of Stage 1 is the product innovation charter, a strategy document defining the work of the NPD effort that will achieve overall innovation goals and objectives.

Secondary market research supports the foundation of Stage 1 activities by identifying market, technology, and product opportunities. Because secondary research data is relatively quick and inexpensive to collect, the competitive landscape can be rapidly evaluated to pinpoint arenas of opportunity for new product development.

Finally, it is imperative to conduct secondary market research *before* initiating any primary market research studies. Secondary market research is completed first, and primary market research follows. Again, market research studies follow this order because the secondary market data provides a context for the later, more detailed and more expensive, primary market research studies.

Primary Market Research

One definition of *primary market research* is information that comes directly from the source--that is, potential customers. New product development teams will compile this information for use in the

innovation project. Alternatively, the firm may outsource primary market research to a specialty firm to gather specific information regarding the particular new product idea. The distinctive characteristic of primary market research is that the firm and NPD team control *all* elements of the primary research. Many of the questions addressed by primary research have been framed by and refined by earlier secondary market research studies.

Note that primary market research can be either qualitative or quantitative, meaning that it can be used to gather thoughts and opinions of potential customers as well as statistically significant analyses of information from direct respondents. Some of the techniques of primary market research include surveys and questionnaires, customer interviews, ethnographic research or customer observation, voice of customer, focus groups, and field tests.

In addition to gathering new market research data, internal company sources may also be used to collect primary market information. For example, technical service personnel often visit customers and can provide specific feedback on the use of products within the customer's environment. Other company records, such as customer complaint logs, warranty service information, and manufacturing databases, are all sources of primary market research data.

Primary market research techniques are used throughout the NPD process to ensure that the new product development effort is aligned with customer needs and to validate product designs. Again, in primary market research, potential consumers are directly tested for reactions and acceptance of new product designs.

Some market research techniques that are essential to understand for the NPDP certification exam include:

- Voice of customer,
- Focus groups,
- Customer site visits, and
- Surveys.

None of these techniques provides a full picture of the customer on its own or can be used in isolation to determine product features. Instead, primary market research tools should be used at different times throughout the NPD process and information from each technique compiled in light of the results of other market research.

Voice of Customer

From a marketing standpoint, the term *voice of customer* may encompass many different primary research techniques. The voice of customer is often associated with the quality function deployment (QFD) methodology to translate customer needs into engineering specifications. QFD, as a specific voice of customer tool, is discussed in Chapter 7.

Voice of customer is defined as a process for eliciting needs from consumers, often using structured, in-depth interviews to lead potential customers through a series of situations they have experienced and in which they have found solutions to the set of problems being investigated. In short, the voice of customer technique probes how customers have solved problems in the past in order to gather information on potential new solutions. Customer needs are identified through indirect questioning and by understanding how the consumers found ways to meet their needs previously. An important theme during voice of customer research is to clarify why a consumer chose a specific solution to fulfill their needs.

Voice of customer techniques often use anthropological or ethnographic research. Anthropological and ethnographic research are specific methodologies in which market researchers "live with" or shadow the potential customer while the customer conducts various activities. An expected outcome of ethnographic market research is to observe and learn about consumer behaviors and how potential customers interact with products.

As an example, a company that manufactures hand lotions might observe when a person applies the lotion, how they apply it, and what they do before and after applying the lotion. Ethnographic research might reveal that people apply hand lotion after washing their hands and that people avoid touching paper after applying the lotion. Voice of customer research will probe to identify the reason for this behavior when customers explain that greasy hand lotions can leave marks on office papers. It is only through this in-depth ethnographic market research that firms can identify a customer need and lead the new product development team to work on a less greasy formula for hand lotion.

Advantages of Voice of Customer

As described above, a common failure within innovation programs involves a lack of understanding of customer needs. Voice of customer research helps to uncover opinions and sentiments of potential customers to help the firm identify needs and opportunities to improve customer satisfaction. Additionally, ethnographic research methods help NPD teams to learn about customer concerns and emerging issues while capturing customer preferences. Proactively engaging consumers through voice of customer market studies helps to identify qualitative product benefits so that the NPD team can effectively design product features and attributes to meet consumer needs.

Disadvantages of Voice of Customer

Not surprisingly, voice of customer market research can be very expensive and time-consuming to gather. Most interviews last 30 to 60 minutes and will require participation from at least two team NPD members (interviewer and scribe). To fully understand market opportunities and customer needs, the NPD team may need to interview as many as 30 different customers.

An additional concern for voice of customer data is that conflicting results may be revealed among participants. This is valuable information that can lead to market segmentation and product positioning; however, the NPD team may need to invest significant effort in data analyses to sort through such conflicts and determine real customer needs. Some teams may also find it difficult to translate the customer stories into unique product features that will help the consumer solve his or her problems.

Benefits of Voice of Customer

Voice of customer market research is one of the best ways to interact directly with potential consumers to fully understand their needs. Since this is an exploratory and qualitative type of market research, designed to identify opportunities for the new product development project, voice of customer is typically conducted during Stages 1 and 2 of the NPD process.

Focus Groups

Focus groups are a popular way to collect information regarding customer needs. It is a form of qualitative market research because it is conducted with a small number of respondents to gain an *impression* of their beliefs, motivations, perceptions, and opinions. Firms use qualitative market research to gather initial consumer needs and to gauge the reactions of potential customers to an idea or concept. Note that due to the small sample size involved with qualitative market research, the results may not necessarily scale to the market in general. Indeed, the purpose of qualitative research is to understand **why** people might be interested in a product.

A focus group is a group interview technique held in a customized facility and is led by a trained moderator or a facilitator. The trained facilitator helps to guide the discussion, ensure that everyone participates, and will pursue new ideas within the context of the product development effort. Collaboration among participants in the focus group clarifies product features and benefits.

Normally, focus group participants are pre-screened to ensure broad and diverse representation from a desired customer base. Participants may include people that currently purchase the product as well as those who do not buy the product. Another selection criterion for focus group participation may indicate whether a person is happy with the level of service they are currently receiving. Participants may also be screened according to demographic information, such as age, gender, marital status, income level, education, etc. Selection of focus group participants that are representative of target customers is important in order to obtain the specific information that is sought through this type of primary research.

While the format of a focus group can take many forms, a typical focus group involves face-to-face interviews with the group participants. Once selected, the focus group participants are seated at a table in a conference room. Normally the table is in a U-shape in order to promote conversation and interaction among the participants and with the facilitator.

Generally, there are less than a dozen participants in a focus group. One of the advantages of a focus group is that it promotes collaboration and interaction among group members. If the focus group gets too large, interaction among participants will decline. On the other hand, if the focus group is too small, there are not enough opportunities for participants to build on other group members' ideas. A focus group of six to ten participants is common.

Focus groups are normally conducted in specialized facilities. The room is equipped with a one-way mirror so that the cross-functional team responsible for the product development effort can unobtrusively observe the proceedings. Additionally, focus groups are often recorded for later review. A separate audio transcript may be prepared so that the comments of the focus group participants can be shared broadly with the NPD team.

Advantages of Focus Groups

Whether captured through video or an audio transcript, the comments from potential consumers are completely unfiltered. This is especially important in primary market research since internal company resources and NPD team members can become overly enthusiastic about the product. Hearing direct words from customers and end-users can be difficult, but are revealing to the NPD team to learn what people think about the product. Firms will want to understand the reactions of potential consumers earlier in the process rather than later, while there is still time to incorporate their ideas into the final product design.

Again, the biggest advantage of a focus group is collaboration among the participants. Often, focus group participants will investigate using a product together, yielding potentially new uses and features for a product under development. Additionally, an experienced facilitator can add flexibility to the focus group in order to glean more information from the participants. For example, questions during the focus group might be varied in order to quickly explore new concepts or market opportunities.

Some participants may be reluctant to speak up and other participants might be dominating. Meanwhile, other participants might be joking or sarcastic such that the role of the moderator is critical to completion of a successful focus group event. A trained facilitator can redirect the group's discussion away from a dominant participant as well as draw out quieter ones. Moreover, a trained facilitator will have the flexibility to explore any new options for the product idea based upon the responses of the focus group participants. Many profitable new product ideas have been born through collaborative focus group discussions.

Disadvantages of Focus Group

With every market research technique there are both advantages and disadvantages. Focus groups add value to the NPD effort through the collaboration of participants and can lead to new insights regarding the product. On the other hand, group dynamics can sometimes suppress participation. People that are especially quiet or shy may not actively participate in the focus group discussion or may give yes/no answers rather than elaborating upon their thoughts and opinions regarding the new product concept.

Additionally, interpreting the participant's actual words and what s/he meant by the comment can add difficulty in perceptions of favorability of the product concepts presented in the focus group. It is also important for NPD teams to test concepts and prototypes that reflect the final product. A classic example demonstrating the complexity of interpreting focus group interactions involved the prototype testing of a new razor concept. The prototype was unrefined and did not reflect the final form of the product. Focus group participants spent most of the time joking about the ugly and rough appearance of the prototype and the firm prepared to abandon the project.

Only later, after carefully reviewing transcripts from the focus group, did the company choose to move forward with the new razor product. Buried within the focus group comments, the NPD team observed that each and every participant indicated he had experienced a very close, smooth shave with the prototype razor. The razor was successfully commercialized and permanently changed the market in North America.

Finally, focus groups are clearly qualitative, not quantitative, tools for primary market research. Focus groups are used to gather insights and opinions of potential customers in a collaborative setting. Therefore, it would be unwise to establish pricing information for a product based on the results of a few people in one geographical region. Multiple focus groups will offer support for the new product idea to the NPD team; however, focus groups can probe only a few of the millions of potential customers. Firms should also consider conducting different focus groups throughout the development cycle in order to ensure they are capturing the true customer needs and insights for the new product or service.

Benefits of Focus Groups

Focus group outcomes will include stories and anecdotes, descriptions of potential consumer behaviors, and ideas for market positioning of the final product. Results from focus group studies offer rich, contextual information on how and why a customer might be interested in the product. This information is valuable for product positioning and brand leverage as well as developing advertising media later in the NPD process.

Primarily used in Stage 3 of the NPD process, focus groups help to determine if the product concept meets consumer needs. Product use testing, conducted in Stage 4, may also utilize focus groups to ensure potential customers benefit from using the product and are left satisfied with the results. Focus group results should supplement other types of market research data for the new product development project, providing customer insights and generating interest in the concept.

Customer Site Visits

A *customer site visit* occurs when one or more associates from a vendor directly interact with one or more customers (or potential customers) of that vendor. Customer site visits are a form of primary market research since the data gathered is particular to the firm and the company is investigating customers for a specific reason to understand their needs for new products or improvements in existing products.

Customer site visits may be either exploratory or confirmatory in nature. *Exploratory market research* is a process that is used to discover needs or problems and is used in the early stages of the NPD process. A company will use exploratory market research to collect stories, anecdotes, feelings, and opinions of customers that lead toward product definition. *Confirmatory market research*, on the other hand, is used to support the decision-making process, specifically financial decisions, such as the go-to-market decision in Stage 5 of the NPD process. A confirmatory market research study is typically quantitative in nature.

In either case, the customer site visit will involve representatives from the new product development team and a customer or end-user that is a buyer or has the option of buying the new product. Customer site visits are frequently used in business-to-business situations, paralleling the ethnographic research techniques that are utilized in researching consumer packaged goods, for example.

While *customer site visits* may be planned and pre-programmed for the sole purpose of collecting market research information, many times an *ad-hoc* customer site visit provides information regarding customer and product needs. Technical service personnel, sales, and customer service representatives often visit end-users for a variety reasons and can be a source of new product information. In such cases, the visit is considered "*ad-hoc*" since the event was not purposefully scheduled to gather data for the innovation effort.

In the case of a planned or pre-programmed customer site visit, the vendor will often use a pair of researchers to improve the data collection process. One member of the NPD team will ask a series of pre-determined questions and make observations, while the other team member acts as a scribe, taking notes and documenting relevant data for the new product development effort.

There are three common elements for a successful customer visit. First, the end-user must be an "involved" customer, meaning that the customer has the need or problem which the company is trying to solve by designing and developing a new product. Customers that are fully satisfied with available product offerings are not as likely to yield actionable information for the NPD project.

The second characteristic of a successful customer site visit requires the NPD team to critically observe the customer who has the need or problem in the area of interest. As described previously, consumer research will use ethnographic or anthropologic studies to fully understand customer needs. This is an important characteristic of the customer site visit, as well, since the market research study should collect data on customer needs at the place in which the customer actually uses the product.

So, for example, if you are interested in a new faucet design for a kitchen sink, the market research should include observing people in their homes, specifically in their kitchens, while they cook and wash the dishes. In a business-to-business situation, customer site visits will include factory visits and tours of customer facilities to observe how the product is used in the customer's operation.

Finally, the third element of a successful customer site visit is talking with the customers who have the problem or need that the new product can address. This is sometimes called a voice of customer research technique because the market research is capturing the exact words of the customer. Speaking directly with potential customers is an important characteristic of both consumer and business-to-business customer site visits since a series of questions are asked and replies are recorded to better understand the customer needs. In other situations, the conversation can occur during the time in which the customer is conducting a task or activity that involves the product solution, providing feedback on the functionality and usability of the product.

For example, while considering a new kitchen faucet design, the researcher may ask the home cook to explain why s/he keeps a tea kettle on the stove all the time. When the consumer explains they like to have hot water available instantly, this can lead to insights for the faucet designer to provide an instant hot water dispenser as part of the new faucet design. Similarly, specially rigged tools or equipment in a business-to-business environment can signal opportunities to enhance product designs.

Advantages of Customer Site Visits

Like all of the market research techniques described herein, there are both pros and cons to the customer site visit. First, there is high impact on the NPD team from visiting customers and hearing their perspective on the product idea directly. Moreover, customers normally appreciate the extra attention from a vendor and value being asked to provide their opinion regarding new product design. Additionally, the NPD team can learn a lot about customer needs during a site visit that would be difficult to ascertain in any other manner. Customer site visits are especially relevant for team members, such as R&D or manufacturing functions, that do not normally have opportunities to engage directly with customers.

Next, face-to-face interaction offers rich communication through eye contact and observation of body language. Whenever the new product development team can increase the level of communication from asynchronous methods, such as e-mail, to synchronous, such as telephone conversations and live face-to-face discussions, the quality of information regarding the new product will be increased substantially.

Additionally, the first-hand experience can be quite compelling for the new product development effort. Many companies develop and sell products that are not used by the employees of the company, especially in the case of business-to-business products. Consider, for instance, a drilling equipment manufacturer. A customer visit to a deep-ocean drilling rig can help the new product development team better understand the problems faced with using the equipment when they directly observe it in service. The NPD team will better understand challenges faced by end-users after a customer site visit, leading to significant improvements in the engineering and design of a new product.

Disadvantages of Customer Site Visits

Of course, there are also some cautions in applying customer site visits to collect market research data. First, there is a potential for interviewer bias in the customer site visit technique. If the visit is an *ad-hoc* one, then the information may be incomplete or inconsistent. Even if the customer site visit was pre-planned, the questions asked and the way in which they are asked can bias the customer's response. It is important to try to take a neutral tone in the customer site visit so that the firm can learn as much as possible about the customer's problems and needs as possible.

Next, there is both instability and imprecision in the data gathered from a customer site visit. Suppose you interview the shop floor workers at one firm and learn about their needs. At another company, the NPD team may interview the purchasing agent during a site visit. It is unlikely that the same or even similar needs for the product will be revealed in these two customer interviews. Thus, it is important to plan customer site visits to consistently capture the desired market and customer information across a broad range of potential users.

Additionally, because products are typically used in conjunction with other products, a problem with one product element may be reported as a customer need. These conflicts must be resolved by the NPD team so that customer needs are fully understood for the product development effort and are not confused with ancillary problems encountered by some customers simultaneously using auxiliary products. For example, end-users may report a large number of 50-lb bags of raw materials are breaking open during routine handling. While the customer facility may be handling new product outside of expected normal parameters, the information can still be valuable to the NPD team. They may consider packaging in a different size or shape container as part of the innovation effort based on the observation.

Finally, customer site visits are both expensive and time-consuming for the new product development team. Therefore, only a few customers and potential customers can be interviewed, resulting in small data sets. As for most qualitative market research tools, it is important to not make extended sales forecasts or go-to-market decisions based upon a small number of exploratory customer site visits. On the other hand, a confirmatory market research study will indicate whether the new product is working as envisioned. This data can be used quantitatively to validate the product design (Stage 4).

Benefits of Customer Site Visits

Perhaps the biggest benefit of the customer site visit is the interaction between the NPD team and potential customers. Observing how customers solve problems currently can be revealing to the development effort so that customer needs are fully understood.

In addition to the NPD team, the sales staff plays a role in customer site visits. Sales personnel will interact frequently with customers and will retain tacit, in-depth information regarding customer needs, wants, and interests. The sales staff may be more aware of competitive threats than other functions within the firm, even with detailed market analyses. Additionally, the sales staff will be able to identify particular customers that have the characteristics described earlier for a successful customer site visit: being involved, open to critical observation, and access to decision-makers.

Moreover, since at least one of the customer representatives is a decision-maker, the customer site visit can enhance the relationship between the vendor firm and the customer's organization. Again, customers value being asked their opinions and are normally willing to provide data and information to improve product solutions. NPD teams should allow time during the site visit for customers to describe their own problems as well as identify suggested solutions.

Finally, if possible, during early stages of new product development, it is helpful to use visual aids or concept statements to help the customer understand proposed solutions. Customer site visits are often conducted during Stage 2 of the NPD process, and feedback regarding product concepts is essential to effective primary market research and subsequent new product development.

Surveys

Most of us are familiar with surveys. A *survey* is a fixed set of questions that are asked of a specific sample of respondents. Companies undertake surveys to learn about people's knowledge, beliefs, and satisfaction regarding products or services, as well as to measure the magnitude of these opinions in the general population.

Please rate the following statements, where 1 means strongly disagree and 5 means strongly agree.					
Product Characteristics	1	2	3	4	5
The product is easy to use.	☐	☐	☐	☐	☐
The product is attractive.	☐	☐	☐	☐	☐
The product functions as expected.	☐	☐	☐	☐	☐
The price of the product is reasonable.	☐	☐	☐	☐	☐

Figure 26 - Sample Survey

Unlike a focus group or an *ad hoc* customer site visit, the questions and answers for a survey are developed in advance. Often the responses are gauged on a Likert scale, where the respondent indicates his or her agreement with the statement on a scale of one to five for example, where a score of one indicates strong disagreement and a score of five indicates strong agreement with the survey statement.

The sample size in a survey is generally quite large; therefore, the data gathered from a survey can be considered quantitative market research in that it is statistically significant. Usually, surveys are distributed to groups of people based upon certain characteristics of the target market segment for the new product. For example, if you are developing a new toy truck, you may wish to distribute the survey to households that have male children between the ages of six and ten.

There are a multitude of ways in which to distribute a survey. Traditionally, surveys have been sent through postal mail. Other surveys are conducted over the telephone or in person. Finally, the internet has enabled quick polling and surveys through a variety of free and low-cost tools. Market research firms partner with industry organizations to collect general survey data and customer satisfaction surveys. Such organizations can also provide guidance to new product development teams based on analysis of survey and benchmarking data.

Advantages of Surveys

Surveys offer several advantages. Since the questions and responses are composed in advance, a survey can be both descriptive and precise. In addition, because surveys are normally quantitative in nature, the statistical analysis is robust, providing objective data that can be utilized by the NPD team in a variety of forms. Particularly useful information from surveys are data that show differences between groups (demographic, geographical, or market segments) and data showing trends over time when the survey is repeated.

For instance, many companies conduct customer satisfaction surveys on a routine basis. If there is a trend in one element that is declining over repeated surveys, the firm should take steps to address that problem with the customers. Perhaps, the wait time for check-out is increasing and the solution is as simple as adding additional check-out lanes at a retail store.

Surveys are generally considered a less expensive alternative to other forms of primary market research. However, to fully understand customer needs and motivation, follow-up market research may require interviews or other types of interactive engagement. In addition, to obtain statistically significant quantitative data, a large number of surveys need to be distributed. A common response rate to surveys is about 25% (Kaplowitz, et al., 2004).

Disadvantages of Surveys

As with all of the primary market research methods discussed in this chapter, there are some disadvantages to using surveys in gathering customer information regarding a new product development effort. First, because a survey will be comprised of pre-determined questions and responses, the data will reveal more answers regarding *what* than *why*. Statistical analysis of survey data can show, for example, the willingness of potential buyers to pay a given price for a new product or how many miles a customer will drive in order to find a retailer that sells the product. Unfortunately, because surveys are not good discovery tools, you will not be able to uncover the reasons *why* a potential customer is willing to drive ten miles but not fifteen miles to find a product available for sale.

Furthermore, surveys rely upon the motivation of the respondent. Typical return rates of surveys may account for only 20 to 30% of surveys distributed regardless of the method of distribution (web or mail) (Kaplowitz, et al., 2004). In order to obtain statistically significant data for a large market, a firm may need to distribute tens of thousands of surveys. Data analysis for this type of quantitative market research can also be extensive and require expertise in statistical analysis.

Surveys rely upon self-reported data and are not very rewarding for participants. Often, a small reward, such as a discount coupon or chance to win a drawing, is included as an incentive for survey participants to complete the information. Many on-line tools can probe potential participants for a match with the target customer segment so that a participant does not feel like s/he has wasted time and so that the firm obtains relevant market research data. Other capabilities of on-line survey tools allow the firm to track if and when participants may abandon a survey. Most surveys can improve the participants' experience by indicating the expected time needed to complete the survey in addition to offering a relevant incentive.

As described above, one of the advantages of primary market research techniques, such as focus groups, is collaboration among group members. Surveys, on the other hand, are individual market research tools and do not reflect any group thinking. This can be important in today's social-media connected world or with products that may be trendy, fashionable, or linked to short-lived fads.

Benefits of Surveys

Using surveys during the fuzzy front end of the NPD process can help the team understand customer needs and validate new product or service ideas. Surveys are beneficial in later stages of product development to verify product design and pricing models. In addition, surveys can be used to clarify trade-offs between features for a new product and can be used over time to gain insights regarding customer behaviors.

Since on-line surveys, in particular, are easy to build and administer, it is important to consider some additional factors when designing a survey. Market research firms can construct survey questions that verify an individual's consistency in responses. This is important since survey respondents sometimes are more interested in the incentive than they are willing to fully engage with the content of the survey.

One variant of a survey uses open-ended questions in a semi-structured interview. These open-ended questions allow the survey participant to elaborate on *why* they have ranked a given product feature at a particular score, what problems they encounter with the product, or what additional features or benefits they would find attractive for a particular product family. This type of survey offers the benefits of both quantitative and qualitative primary market research; however, it will require a larger investment to gather the relevant data.

Benefits of Primary Market Research

As a general rule, *secondary market research* is conducted *first*, in order to frame the context for the *primary market research* which is gathered *second*. Primary market research is information collected by the company for a specific reason, such as to learn about customers' buying habits or to understand consumers' need for a new product or service.

Primary market research can take the form of qualitative studies to learn about customers' wants, needs, and motivations. Common forms of qualitative primary market research are *voice of customer*, *customer site visits*, and *focus groups*. *Surveys* are a form of quantitative primary market research that can be used to predict customer satisfaction and potential purchase rates of the new product. Normally, primary market research is more expensive than secondary market research; however, the data is gathered for the specific new product development effort and is extremely valuable to refine product concepts and validate product designs.

The following table summarizes some of the market research techniques and recommended market tests for each stage of the NPD process.

Table 4 - Recommended Market Research per NPD Process Phase		
NPD Process Phase	**Research Method**	**Purpose**
1 - Opportunity Identification	Secondary Market Research Customer Site Visits	• Identify market opportunities • Market segmentation
2 - Concept Generation	Customer Site Visits Surveys	• Understand customer needs • Generate product concepts
3 - Concept Evaluation	Focus Groups Concept Testing	• Select projects for funding • Determine market application
4 - Development	Product Use Testing • Focus Groups • Customer Site Visits • Alpha, Beta Testing	• Test designs and prototypes • Validate new product designs
5 - Launch	Market Testing	• Test commercial launch plan • Measure new product success

Some of the market research techniques are utilized in more than one stage of the NPD process, such as customer site visits and focus groups. Other techniques, such as surveys, are useful in more than one stage of development work but may be deployed most frequently as indicated in the table. Data gathered from market research tools and tests should always be utilized in conjunction with other market research and customer information to fully evaluate the application of a new product and new technology in a new market.

Market Research Tests

Many of the market research tools discussed so far refer to the fuzzy front end of the NPD process. In the earliest stages of new product development, the goal is to identify markets, technologies, and product categories to solve customer problems. Both secondary and primary market research methodologies are used to brainstorm new product ideas and to test new product concepts. An important market research test, the concept test, is conducted during Stage 3 to ensure that the product idea will meet customers' needs.

After product concepts and market attractiveness are validated in the fuzzy front end of the NPD process, the new product project will move into Stage 4, Development. During this stage, different prototypes and designs are tested. As described in Chapter 4, an outcome of Stage 4 is a proven product prototype. *Product use testing*, discussed in this section, is used to verify that the new product design meets the needs of the customer. Normally, product use testing takes one of three forms: alpha, beta, or gamma. Furthermore, as indicated in Table 4, focus groups and customer site visits are utilized as confirmatory market research tools in Stage 4 to validate that the product works as expected in a live end-user environment.

Finally, as the new product is launched in Stage 5, market testing will probe customer responses to the new product with the proposed marketing campaign for the first time. Market testing may include preliminary roll-out of the new product. Thus, in the later stages of the NPD process, market testing techniques will emphasize concept tests, product use tests, and several distinctive market tests.

Concept Tests

A *concept test* involves rendering an embodiment or representation of the new product to current or potential customers to gauge their reactions. Thus, the concept test is a type of primary market research that is normally conducted during Stage 3, Concept Evaluation.

A product concept is simply an understood promise of the product, the customer value proposition, and the real reason why people should buy it. The purpose of the concept test is to compile the developer's perception of the product features and to check potential customers' reactions toward a particular feature set as well as their estimate of the benefits that those features will deliver. In short, a concept test will validate if the product idea, as envisioned by the NPD team will be a product that consumers are interested in purchasing.

Concept statements, as discussed previously in Chapter 4, may be written paragraphs describing the features and benefits of the new product, or may be visual depictions of the new product, including rough prototypes. For example, 3D computer imaging can be used to display a product so that potential customers can interact with the product and react to its design. For example, Disney is famous for using storyboards to test concepts of movies and character concepts internally.

Since concept testing is conducted relatively early in the formal development phases of the NPD process, the prime objective of this market test is to identify and eliminate poor product concepts. Such poor concepts should be eliminated from the active portfolio. An example is that even though the concept of a round-bottomed coffee cup would allow more efficient storage, customers will reject the concept since the round-bottomed cup cannot sit stably on a desk or table.

If the concept is not rejected out of hand, then the next objective of the concept test is to further develop the idea into a usable and salable product. An idea is typically modified significantly from the initial concept test until the final product is launched into the marketplace. In addition, the NPD team will need more information than a simple concept statement in order to fully design and develop the new product. Benefits of the new product concept will need to be transformed into engineering specifications describing the product attributes such that the product can be fully developed in Stage 4. You'll recall from Chapter 4 that the product protocol is a document that translates the customer needs into engineering design specifications for the development team.

Finally, most concept tests will include a question regarding a potential customer's intention to purchase the product as presented. Responses are often indicated on an interest scale, ranging from definitely would buy to definitely would not buy. Note that sales forecasting data collected during a concept test is generally not quantitative nor suitable for making a go-to-market decision. Instead, the estimates of likely purchase can be used as an early indicator of market success. In some instances, firms have past experience with concept testing, knowing that a 60% positive response at the concept testing level will translate to measurable sales increases. In these special circumstances, sales estimates from a concept test can be used with a greater degree of confidence to develop a formal business case.

Advantages of Concept Tests

Concept testing can be done quickly and easily, often before full prototypes are available. Testing a narrative statement or a visual image of the new product can help determine a buyer's need for the product or service. Potential customers will indicate the extent to which they find the concept interesting, practical or useful. Consumers will indicate if they like the concept and how likely they would be to purchase the new product as described in the concept statement.

There are several advantages to using a concept test in new product development. As described previously, the concept test helps to eliminate poor concepts early so that the development teams can work on the few, best ideas that solve customer problems. Furthermore, the concept test helps the NPD team align customer benefits with product features and attributes.

Thus, the product concept test can save time and money by eliminating poor concepts early in the process, minimizing investment. Some managers may question the reasons for concept testing due to the time or cost involved in gathering test data; however, the concept test allows the new product development team to get it right the first time, ultimately speeding up the project and saving the firm money in the long run.

Because the concept test is designed to gather perceptions and needs of potential customers, a company can learn much about buyer thinking to eliminate misunderstandings of the product's benefits, misperceptions of functionality, and other parameters that could potentially harm the successful commercialization of the new product. Information gathered from concept tests also allows the NPD team to improve the product design during the later stages of the NPD process. In particular, data collected from concept tests can lead to market segmentation information and future product positioning. Moreover, such information allows the marketing collateral to be developed in tandem with the product as a result of the concept test.

Disadvantages of Concept Tests

As with all research methodologies, there are a few disadvantages to concept tests that should be weighed against the positive outcomes. Potential customers may be exposed to the new concept for only a few seconds or a minute. Because the customer's exposure to the new product or service idea may be very short, it is sometimes difficult to obtain meaningful data for radical new concepts. New product designs that depart significantly from products currently available in the marketplace may also require additional definition or training that is beyond the scope of a concept test.

Since the customer's exposure to the concept is brief and cannot test personal preferences, a concept test may not be adequate to judge the reactions of potential customers when the technology is exceptionally novel or radical. Furthermore, customers may not yet know they have a need for the product and may need to be educated on how to use the product. For example, the first chewable antacid failed concept tests because people at the time assumed that all antacids needed to be taken with water. The product later went on to be successful in the marketplace, but consumers needed to be educated in a new way of administering the antacid.

Next, when the benefit of using a product or service is personal, such as with art or entertainment, a concept test may not accurately gauge potential customers' responses. Such personal preferences may not reflect general attitudes and opinions of a target market segment and are difficult to judge in advance. For example, concept tests may not be successful in measuring what the next fad will bring in the color of clothing for a season.

In some cases, the concept test cannot be conducted in an engaging environment where the product can actually be used. When people are asked to be a judge in these types of situations, human behavior may lead to over-endorsement of the concept, thus skewing the results of the test. Again, the concept is often only represented by a narrative, visual image, or computer model of the product. Potential customers may give positive feedback regarding the product concept in order to not appear negative or hurt the feelings of those conducting the test.

Finally, customer responses during a concept test are generally gathered through questioning and interviewing the potential consumer as s/he views the concept statement. As with all interviewing techniques, the NPD team should be aware of extending the data from a small sample set to the market at large. Depending on the number of consumers probed with the concept test and the quality of data collected, there can be a substantial investment in the concept test from both a budgetary and schedule perspective.

Benefits of Concept Tests

Concept tests provide extremely valuable market research information regarding customers' opinions about a new product idea. However, NPD teams should consider that the environment can change, sometimes drastically, during the time period in which the concept test is conducted and when the product is fully developed for commercial launch.

Most data gathered from a series of concept tests will provide conclusive information for the NPD team regarding customer impressions of the new product idea. However, data from concept tests can sometimes be mismanaged or researchers might not fully understand the analyses in a concept test report. For instance, if 35% of the respondents understood the main benefit of the product, while 10% of respondents find the benefit unbelievable, what does the data mean? Concept test data can be further complicated if the 10% who did not believe the benefit was achievable are also part of the 35% who fully understood the benefit.

Thus, the questions and interview techniques utilized for the concept test should be consistent and clear to fully evaluate the responses of potential customers. Data gathered from concept tests allows the NPD team to understand if the new product will bring value to customers and is used to eliminate poor product concepts. Stories and comments from potential customers regarding benefits and functionality of the new product can further refine the product design during subsequent development stages.

Product Use Testing

Product use testing is normally conducted during Stage 4, Development. Sometimes product use testing is called field testing, acceptance testing, or user testing. Product use testing validates the end-users' experience of the new product or service. Normally, this testing is done in a live or semi-live customer environment, meaning that the product is tested at the customer's location or at the place where the product is sold, consumed, or used. The essence of the product use test is that the customer actually *uses* the product.

For example, if you are testing automated check-out at a retail store, you would want to convert one check-out lane to the fully automated product. Similarly, if you are testing sport socks, you would have football players wear the socks during a real game. A key characteristic of the product use test is that the product is tested outside of a laboratory and under real usage conditions.

Product use testing involves varying degrees of complexity and integration with standard operations and product usage. Best practices demonstrate that the customer should be involved at all levels of testing and development for the new product; the product use test is an extension of earlier concept tests. Lead customer groups are effective for product use testing as well, since they will be familiar with the concept development and may have worked with the company in an open innovation or co-creation environment.

Note that the source of the product should be carefully considered when planning product use testing. NPD teams will need to decide whether pilot plant material is sufficient for product use testing or whether they require full-scale production. In any case, the product should be very close to its final form so that it can be used by the customer under normally expected conditions.

Alpha Test

An *alpha test* is a specific product use test that involves pre-production testing and is often associated related to quality control testing. The purpose of the alpha test is to find and eliminate the most obvious design deficiencies. Normally, the testing is conducted in-house with the company's own lab personnel or within the firm's normal operations.

In some cases, lead customers may participate in the alpha test. However, the environment is closely controlled and users are aware of the new product's functionality. When employees participate in the alpha test, they may be very familiar with the product, having worked on it throughout its design and development. Too much familiarity may skew the results of the test so internal participants for an alpha test should be identified with care.

For example, if the company is developing software for bookkeeping tasks, the software can be tested in-house with the company's own accounting department. However, since the testing is highly controlled, the product may not be placed under as rigorous and varied conditions as when it is externally tested by real customers. In such a case, the beta test helps the firm understand interaction with other products and customer behaviors.

Beta Test

The *beta test*, in contrast to the alpha test, is an external test of the pre-sales version of the product. Beta testing is used extensively in the software industry in order to expose the software package to various interactions with hardware, software, and end-user applications. The beta test checks whether the product will work as designed in the customer's environment.

In practice, the beta test places the product into a wide variety of situations to be validated under live conditions by real customers. For example, a software program may have been tested in-house on a Microsoft system, whereas the beta test will check whether the software works on Apple computers and on enterprise systems, like Oracle or SAP.

Because the beta test is investigating whether the product works for actual customers in live systems, the beta test is far less controlled than the alpha test. Of course, this is part of the objective of the beta test – to put the product through its paces and find out what situations may cause faults in the operation. Any defects that are discovered through beta testing can be corrected before the final product launch in Stage 5.

While alpha testing is common across many different industries, beta testing is traditionally associated with the software industry. Gamma testing, on the other hand, is often affiliated with the medical industry.

Gamma Testing

A gamma test is a specific product use test that not only examines whether the product works as designed, but also leaves customers satisfied. NPD team members will measure the extent to which the new product meets the needs of the target customers, solves the problem, and leaves the customer fully satisfied.

Gamma testing is most often affiliated with the medical industry, especially in development of prescription drugs and of medical devices. It is required testing in many countries to allow new applications to be certified by the appropriate governing body. For example, the United States Food and Drug Administration (FDA) requires extensive data on prescription drugs to be validated by gamma testing (called clinical trials) before approving the new medicine for public use.

Additionally, a gamma test measures whether the product actually meets the needs of the customer. This is unique to the gamma test, since the alpha test checks if the product functions as designed and the beta test validates whether the product works in a live environment. As a result of the gamma test, customer satisfaction is indicated to ensure that the product not only solves the customer's problems but also leave the customer fully satisfied with the solution.

With the example of a prescription medicine, then, the product must not only alleviate the symptoms of a disease or condition, but also leave the patient without further complaints. For instance, a headache medicine should relieve the person of pain, as well as leave the patient satisfied without side effects, such as nausea or upset stomach.

Advantages of Product Use Testing

There are many advantages to the product use test and many experts advise against any skimping on end-user validation of the product design. Product use testing is beneficial in order to understand the impressions customers have about the new product, if it is perceived as intended, and if the product is being used as expected. Occasionally, the product use test can also reveal new uses for a product that were previously unknown.

Of course the biggest benefit of a product use test is that it is conducted in a real environment with actual end-users. Apple is famous for designing products with new functionality that the company's own employees have requested, so the alpha test can discover whether the product functions as desired with a set of internal users. Internal testing of new products is typically less expensive than many other market research tests.

Beta testing has the advantage that the customer can provide significant insight into the actual use, functionality, and benefits of the new product. Customers who are chosen for beta testing are often early adopters when the product goes to market. Word-of-mouth from customers who have tested the product can lead to hype and excitement about the product in the general marketplace as well. This media exposure can aid in early seeding of the target market even before the product is formally launched and commercialized in Stage 5.

Finally, an advantage of conducting product use tests is that it constitutes a dry run for full-scale production. Internal readiness of the company's infrastructure to sell, deliver, install, and support the product are further outcomes of a product use test.

Disadvantages of Product Use Testing

While the benefits of product use testing generally outweigh any disadvantages, the NPD team should be aware of some trade-offs. If the planning and implementation of the product use test is not effective, the results can be disastrous to the new product development project. Customers testing a defective new product in a live environment might be soured on the idea altogether and will refrain from purchasing it even if deficiencies are corrected in the final version of the commercial product.

Product use testing is generally not confidential. Thus, competitors will typically be aware of the new product and may be able to quickly develop a highly competitive product in response. For example, while General Mills was conducting product use and market tests of "toaster pastries", Kellogg's was able to develop and market Pop-Tarts®. After more than 50 years on the market, Kellogg's Pop-Tarts dominate this breakfast food market segment with almost no large-scale competition.

Another difficulty with product use testing regards timing and scheduling of the test. Usually NPD teams are under pressure to complete market test studies to speed the formal product launch into the marketplace. However, customers may not feel the same time pressure as the development team to complete the tests or provide feedback to the NPD team. Customers may delay product testing for a number of reasons. Unfortunately, too many delays in gathering and analyzing product use test information can lead to a missed market opportunity, such as launching the product at a special trade show event.

Finally, as the product is tested with lead customers or early adopters, these individuals may accept the product only as it functions during the test. Later modifications of the product could change the functionality of the product, yet the firm is often still committed to providing the "original" product design to these lead customers. This situation can lead to one-off production that is expensive and time-consuming for the firm.

Benefits of Product Use Testing

Product use tests may take different forms (alpha, beta, or gamma) based on the type of information needed to verify product functionality and on common industry practices. Testing in the live environment can reveal unexpected deficiencies in the product design, especially in interactions with other products or services.

Like any aspect of market testing, the NPD team must clarify the objectives of the test before undertaking the research. For example, if the purpose of the test is to find out whether people can properly follow the assembly instructions provided with the product, the product use test will be structured differently than if the goal of the test is to find out if the size and shape of the product meets the customer's needs. Note that the goals of product use testing may be documented in the product protocol, an output of Stage 3 in the NPD process.

Determining how to conduct the test is a special consideration for product use testing and should be planned extensively to ensure that feedback from consumers is collected and analyzed effectively. The NPD team will need to carefully consider the characteristics of the customer test group. Elements of the product use test plan may include how the customers will be contacted, if the customers are existing or potential purchasers of the company's products or services, whether the test will blind or branded, and what instructions and/or company participants will assist with the testing.

Other items to include in the product use test plan are the number of end-users who will test the new product, the length of exposure the customer will have to the new product, and whether the product will be tested alone or with auxiliary products or services. In the latter case, most beta and gamma tests are designed to test the product in a live environment so that product interactions can be observed and understood.

An example of a product use test that failed to consider all these elements involved "new Coke" which was first marketed in the mid-1980s. While over 200,000 respondents preferred the taste of new Coke in a blind taste test, the brand loyalty to the traditional Coca-Cola soda resulted in a massive failure of the product in the marketplace (Smith, 2013).

As indicated, the time period for the product use test also needs to be carefully selected. For example, if the product launch is planned at a high profile media event, the testing will need to be conducted well in advance to allow time for gathering and analyzing product use test data. In addition, the time period for the test should indicate whether the customer can use the product for days, weeks, or months. These considerations depend, to a large degree, on the complexity of the product and how familiar customers might be with its functionality.

Again, the source of the product to be used in the field test also needs to be considered. Often pilot plant materials are different in minor ways than the final manufactured product. The NPD team needs to understand if the pre-production model will be sufficient to gauge customers' satisfaction and use of the product. Other sources of the product may be from multiple manufacturing facilities across the country or world. The NPD team conducting the product use test needs to understand if the product inventory is fully interchangeable or whether manufacturing variability could influence the results of the test.

As with all market research techniques, the interpretation of the test data should be made with care. Of particular interest is whether the data will be collected, analyzed, and interpreted by in-house experts or an external consulting agency with expertise in market research testing. Most importantly, the data should be interpreted in conjunction with the specific objectives that were incorporated in the product use test plan.

In summary, product use testing is conducted to ensure that the product functions as expected and as designed. Without specific reasons regarding confidentiality or competitive threat, product use tests should always be included as a market research task within Stage 4 of the NPD process.

Market Testing

As indicated in Chapter 4, the final stage of the NPD process involves launching the product commercially. During Stage 5, the marketing plan is first tested with the new product. This is called *market testing*.

The strategic launch plan developed in Stage 4 and implemented in Stage 5 goes hand-in-hand with market testing. Market testing occurs when the new product is tested with the new marketing plan. While it is presumed that much of the marketing plan will already be determined based upon product positioning, customer feedback, and learnings from earlier market research, the marketing plan should be verified as the product is formally launched. Solid business case numbers, such as sales volume and pricing, can also be determined from the market testing results.

One of the key outcomes of market testing is to simulate the marketing plan along with the new product. This is done in several ways including a full sale, controlled sale, mini-market, or pseudo sale. Additionally, though the terminology is confusing, another market testing technique is the *test market* which combines elements of the full sale and controlled sale marketing tests.

Full Sale

Full sale is a class of market testing techniques with no special restrictions on the sale of the product or the marketing campaign. In a full sale, the marketing plan is complete and advertisements for the new product will be placed in multiple media sources. Distribution and supply logistics for the product are formally in place as they would be for any other mainstream product sold by the firm to a general market. New product sales typically include normal transactions, including payment by the customer to the vendor and delivery of the product to the customer or end-user.

A full sale market test typically takes one of two forms. As indicated, one of the full sale methods is described by the confusing term of "test market". The other is called "rollout".

Test Market

A *test market* usually involves selling the new product in one or several cities while launching the proposed marketing campaign in only these selected cities. The marketing and distribution efforts are fully representative of the logistics processes that will occur in the national or international marketing scheme. A test market approach allows various elements of the marketing plan to be tested under fairly controlled conditions, such as utilizing different media or targeting alternate customer value propositions.

Consumers in the test market will independently choose whether to purchase the product based upon their exposure to advertising media. However, both the marketing campaign and product availability are restricted to limited geographical regions to fully test the new product with the marketing plan prior to formal product launch. A drawback of the test market approach is that the advertising media may extend beyond the geographical region in which the product is available for sale. Similarly, the product may not be available at all wholesale or retail outlets within the test market.

A benefit of the test market approach is that the firm can gather much information in a short time regarding the efficacy of the marketing campaign, in particular, through a test market. Data can then be used to fine tune marketing, distribution, and quality during the next phase in full commercialization of the new product.

Rollout

A *rollout* is the second category of full sale market testing, sometimes called "tiered marketing". The company has firmly committed to the full scale marketing plan, but it is "rolled out" in a staged or tentative fashion. For example, the product and marketing collateral may be first distributed to the East coast, then the West coast, and finally to the interior of the United States. Similarly, the marketing effort might be rolled out first to large cities, then medium cities, and finally smaller cities and towns. In other cases, a firm may choose to rollout the product to a mid-level market segment first, followed by a luxury segment, and then to a price-buyer segment.

Rollout has the advantage of continuous learning with the ability to adapt the marketing campaign based upon new data gathered during each phase of the rollout. In addition, the firm can better manage inventory and distribution in a rollout situation when the manufacturing operation or technology is new to the company.

Advantages of Full Sale Market Testing

There are many advantages to using a full sale market testing technique. First, the output of the studies offer an abundant wealth of information to validate the marketing plan with real customers in an actual purchasing environment. Whereas earlier sales estimates may have projected customer opinions or survey data, the full sale data confirms estimates as customers are actually purchasing the product, hopefully in direct response to the marketing plan.

Moreover, full sale market testing requires product manufacturing processes to be stable with factories operating at standard conditions. With full sale market testing, the distribution and supply chain systems are simultaneously tested to ensure that the product is distributed in a timely fashion from the factory to the retail point of sale. All of these elements can verify that the production and supply chain systems are working as required for the final push to full commercialization of the new product.

Disadvantages of Full Sale Market Testing

With any market testing technique, there are some disadvantages; for instance, a full sale market test can be very expensive. Additional concerns may arise regarding competitors that offer discounts in the same selected test market cities in response to the full scale market test. Such discounts could skew the market research results. Furthermore, some cities that are selected as test markets may not be truly representative of the national or international market, for the product and/or may respond differently to the advertising media than the broader market. Likewise, a product rolled out to one geographical region may yield different responses by customers than other regions due to local customs, trend, and fads.

Next, full sale market testing requires a significant effort on behalf of the NPD team to correctly administer the test and evaluate the resultant data. If the firm is launching a game-changing or blockbuster product, full sale market testing may take too long. Moreover, because the new product is widely available for sale during the market testing, a competitor with a fast follower strategy may work aggressively to capture sales in other regions. In some instances, competition may secure the majority share of a separate market while the original firm is still evaluating initial market tests.

Rollouts have the disadvantage that the trade media will not generally respond as aggressively as they would for a national launch. This can have a detrimental effect on word-of-mouth communication in promoting and improving sales rates of the new product. However, with increased utilization of social media, regional rollouts may generate buzz for a new product even before it is completely rolled out commercially in a broad market.

Controlled Sale

A *controlled sale* is another type of market testing that is frequently conducted to test marketing plans and the new product together. In comparison to full sale market testing, some element of the sale is limited, such as distribution of the new product.

By definition, a controlled sale market test, one or more dimensions of the sale is controlled. For instance, in the most common form of controlled sale, distribution is limited. The new product may first be presented to customers by giving away free samples of it. In other cases, the product will be shipped directly to the customer, bypassing the typical order fulfillment system. In essence, the NPD team will automatically assume distribution of the new product without fully investing in the required logistics and supply chain.

Distribution costs are reduced in the controlled sale market testing effort, while the marketing plan and new product are still tested under actual use conditions. For example, many supermarkets charge a slotting fee or shelf fee so that the highest profit/highest turnover items are placed in the most visible places at the store. By giving away free samples at a tasting station in the supermarket, a new food product can essentially achieve the same distribution as a well-known brand, without incurring high priced slotting fees. The marketing plan will be tested at the same time through in-store displays representative of the full commercial advertising campaign.

Informal Selling

There are three typical forms of the controlled sale. The first, *informal selling* situation is a typical market testing technique used at trade shows or in business-to-business situations for an industrial product. With informal controlled sales, the marketing plan for the product is highly refined - salespeople will show the product, approach potential customers, and pitch the product. Information is gathered on whether customers actually buy the product. In other cases, as described above, the product is offered as a free sample.

The objective of the controlled market test checks whether customers readily accept the free product, use it, and like it. A coupon for future product purchases may be distributed with the free sample to monitor future purchases. Informal selling is a very popular method of market testing and is often a predecessor to a full sale rollout or to full commercialization of the new product.

Direct Marketing

Direct marketing is another form of controlled sale. Normally, direct marketing is used for market testing of consumer products rather than for industrial products in business-to-business situations. As an example, a retail company may sell its products through the internet and via catalogs that are delivered to customers' homes. A direct market test would involve placing a new item in *some*, but not all, catalogs that are targeted to a specific customer segment.

Consider a firm that sells bedroom furniture through a catalog. For customers that had previously purchased a new bed frame, the direct market test might include new products for the company to sell, such as sheet sets and duvets. These customers would see the new products in the catalog, whereas customers who had not purchased bedroom furniture would receive a standard catalog without the bed linens advertised.

Social media is able to add a very personal dimension to the direct marketing technique as specific sales are offered based upon Facebook profiles, past searches on the internet, or browsing at an internet marketplace, such as Amazon® or eBay. Computer algorithms automatically make direct market recommendations on an individual basis.

Mini-Market

Finally, the third type of controlled sale is a mini-market. A *mini-market test* is a form of controlled sale where the sales outlet is small and may not be representative of the full market. The product is placed into these outlets while the marketing plan and advertising campaigns are significantly scaled back from schemes deployed for a full product launch. In this case, the primary objective is to validate whether customers are willing to purchase the product.

Black and Decker, a tool manufacturer, has used one or two Ace® Hardware stores as outlets for new products to test whether there is interest in the product. Note that sales may not be representative because many consumers will purchase these types of products at big box stores; however, the mini-market test gives the NPD team flexibility in the display, pricing, and other marketing variables to ensure that the full product launch is successful later. In this case, large scale advertising is significantly controlled, since only one or two stores in a region have the product available. Black and Decker will limit their advertising primarily to in-store displays and demonstrations, thus controlling the advertising reach.

Advantages of Controlled Sale

A key advantage of controlled sale market testing is that it is generally much less expensive than the full sale method, yet still represents independent purchases by real customers. Any challenges related to distribution or supply chain are easily overcome because the product is placed in only a few stores, as in the mini-market method, or are given away at a trade show, as in the informal selling method. Additionally, there is a high degree of flexibility built into the controlled sale because many different marketing elements can be tested quickly. For example, in the direct marketing method, Amazon might suggest a popular book on one topic to one person while simultaneously suggesting a new mystery author to other customers. Sales of the books, as well as search history, will then drive further marketing and product development efforts.

Disadvantages of Controlled Sale

As with any market testing technique there are some pitfalls in the controlled sale method. First, customers that are targeted with the controlled sale may not be representative of the market as a whole. For instance, if stores are selected for a mini-market test are primarily located in retirement communities, the purchase patterns and pricing options may not reflect a wider demographic range.

Furthermore, by definition, the controlled sale limits one or more elements of the commercial marketing plan. Many times, distribution is assumed, yet supply chain logistics can sometimes be a challenge for firms, especially if the product is perishable or fragile.

Overall, however, the controlled sale is an effective market test methodology to gain knowledge and information about customers' real responses in accepting and purchasing a new product. The information gleaned from the controlled sale is useful in later full sale rollouts or the full scale product launch.

Pseudo Sale

In comparison to the other types of market testing techniques, the *pseudo sale* is an artificial selling situation. A potential customer will perform various actions that demonstrate a reaction to the new product and its marketing plan, but the customer does not actually purchase or receive the product. In many cases, the product is not yet officially available for sale and the firm is simply trying to gauge reactions of potential customers to the marketing mix.

There are two types of pseudo-sale: faux purchases and speculative sales. The faux purchase is sometimes called *premarket testing* or *simulated market testing*. Again, these may be confusing terms. Premarket testing is perhaps the one term that you will encounter the most with sales personnel; however, the term *faux purchase* is somewhat more descriptive.

Faux Purchase

A *faux purchase* market test is typically utilized with consumer packaged goods when other market testing methodologies are not applicable. This technique may be an extension of concept tests or focus groups, in which a market research firm may intercept consumers during a shopping experience to gather new product sales forecast data. Potential customers will be asked to provide demographic information as well as provide feedback on the new product. The new product may be hypothetical if development efforts are not complete, yet advertising samples will likely be provided to customers. The faux purchase is designed to capture the likelihood of commercial success for a given product.

In practice, there are several steps to conducting a successful pseudo sale market test. First, participants are selected for the study. Often this is done through a mall intercept where people are approached in a shopping mall and pre-screened. If you are testing the marketing plan of a new toy, the mall intercept would screen people by asking if they had a child between the ages of six and ten, and if they are willing to participate in a short market research study.

Next, the participants are taken to a market research facility, often an empty storefront in the shopping mall. There, the participants are exposed to marketing materials for the item to be tested along with exposure to other media. For example, they may watch a television show with advertisements of the toy interspersed in it, or the toy may be a product placement within the television show itself. Magazines may have the advertisement under investigation included in the facility waiting room as well.

Participants are then given faux money or credits and are led into what looks like a convenience store. They are allowed to "purchase" whatever they want in the faux store with the fake money. Some participants may select no product, others may select the product of interest, and others may select a competitor's product. In some cases, participants may select a product that is not under study as a prime product or that is marketed by the competition. All of this data is important feedback for the NPD team to adjust the marketing mix and the pricing points of the new product as necessary. In addition, sales forecasts will be refined based upon the pseudo sale data.

In some cases, a few of the participants exiting the faux store will be selected for an additional focus group study. This follow-up focus group will probe the participants for reasons why they selected the products they did and to learn more about the customers' reasons for selecting different products in the faux store. Other participants may be asked to fill out a survey or questionnaire covering the same questions.

At the conclusion of the focus group, participants may be offered another chance to "purchase" products with the faux money. Again, the data gathered during the faux market testing exercise is valuable to the NPD team in verifying the business case for the new product as well as the proposed marketing mix.

Speculative Sale

A *speculative sale* is another pseudo sales market testing technique, primarily utilized in industrial situations. In a speculative sale, a salesperson will make a full pitch of the new product to a potential customer and conclude by asking the customers how likely they are to purchase the product. This type of market research is useful in situations where a business has a close relationship with key customers and if the new product is technically sophisticated, the company has tight intellectual property control of the new product, or the new product has little risk of failure.

Like the faux sale, the purpose of the speculative sale is to help forecast commercial success of the new product. In essence, potential customers are asked to speculate on their own likelihood of purchasing the product as described in the sales pitch. Note that older literature may refer to a speculative sale as a *bundle test*.

A typical inquiry during concept testing is whether the customer is likely to buy a product like the one represented. Thus, during concept testing, a firm may gather additional pseudo sales data if marketing media are also available. Concept tests will probe how likely a customer is to buy the new product if it is manufactured precisely as described. Because the product is not commercially available at this point in time, these methods may be considered pseudo sales market tests.

Advantages of Pseudo Sale

The biggest advantage to the pseudo sale method is that it offers little risk to the customer. In the speculative sale, there is no exchange of the product for cash. The firm, too, may have little investment in the new product as it may be testing a concept or prototype. In addition, the marketing mix is not highly refined and artist rendered sketches may be presented to customers rather than full-color, glossy advertisements. A pseudo sale is typically less expensive than many other market testing techniques.

Disadvantages of Pseudo Sale
Since the product "sale" is artificial in the pseudo sale market testing methodology, human behaviors can skew the results to potentially more favorable purchase rates than will occur in an actual sales situation. In particular, since the customer is not vested in the purchase (no cash or product is exchanged), consumers may provide overly optimistic feedback to the market testing team. On the other hand, with appropriate follow-up, the pseudo sale method can generate additional insights into purchasing behaviors for customers when they are exposed to different marketing media.

Pseudo sales market testing techniques are often used to screen product and marketing information to further design additional market testing techniques. For example, results of a pseudo sale market test may be used to influence the design of a future direct marketing campaign. Moreover, the NPD team will be able to glean much information regarding the reactions of customers to the early new product design and the marketing mix as an outcome of the pseudo sale.

Market testing techniques vary from the pseudo sale level (in which the product is not transferred to the customer) to more complex market testing techniques where the new product and the formal marketing plan are tested together in real customer environments. Oftentimes, firms will follow pseudo sale market tests with controlled sale or rollout market testing. It is not uncommon for firms to institute several staged market tests to fully understand customer needs and the impact of the marketing campaign on potential sales of the new product.

Summary

Market research is a vast field of study covering human behavior as well as financial considerations. New product development professionals should be familiar with basic marketing terms and tools that will lead to success with innovation. Some of the important terminology and market research techniques from this chapter are summarized below.

First, *secondary market research* was defined as a market research tool used in the early stages of the NPD process. Secondary market research is primarily a paper study that examines whether there is a favorable market opportunity available. Secondary market research is conducted *before* primary market research in order to frame the context for more expensive and time-consuming studies.

Primary market research is any research tailored to the firm's specific needs. It is often much more expensive than secondary market research, but reveals information that is precisely tuned to the questions that the NPD team poses. Primary market research is used to understand potential customer responses to the new product idea.

Second, primary market research takes one of two forms – qualitative or quantitative. In the case of *qualitative research*, the firm is seeking stories, anecdotes, and behaviors to understand *why* a customer might be interested in the new product. Equally important are the observations of problems that customers have with current product offerings. In studying customer problems, ethnographic or anthropological research is used to conduct "live-in" studies with consumers to fully understand their challenges. Another technique to learn about customers' problems is the *voice of customer* technique wherein the firm elicits responses from customers using a structured interview process, for example.

Three types of market research are used in the fuzzy front end of innovation in order to best match the market opportunities and customer needs with the product idea. These are (1) the *focus group*, (2) *customer site visit*, and (3) *surveys*. Many of these techniques are used as exploratory market research methods to gather customer problems early in the NPD process. Some of these tools are also deployed in later NPD phases in conjunction with market testing methods, for example, to act as confirmatory market research.

1. *Focus groups* use a small number of participants in a specialized facility with a trained moderator. Participants are led through a series of questions to learn more about their behaviors and reasons why they might be interested in a particular product idea or concept.
2. *Customer site visits* are often used in business-to-business situations where the vendor visits a lead customer at the customer's place of business. The purpose of the visit is to gain understanding of the customer's problems and how they are currently solving them. NPD teams will gather information on potentially novel solutions as well as their proposed new product idea.
3. Finally, *surveys* are a fundamental quantitative tool used in market research. Normally surveys are distributed to a large sample size yielding statistically significant data. Quantitative market research data is used to validate the business case for a new product and to advance the go-to-market decision. A disadvantage of surveys is that they rely upon self-reported data; however, as survey data is studied over time or among different demographic groups, it becomes even more valuable as a market research technique.

Next, new product development professionals must be able to define and explain the usage of basic market research tools. The *concept test* is usually conducted in Stage 3 of the NPD process to verify whether potential customers actually need the product. Concept tests will yield extensive data, providing customer insights to improve the design of the product and potential emotional linkages for future product positioning.

A *product use test*, on the other hand, tests the functionally of the product under real life conditions. The *alpha test* is done in-house and is closely related to a quality control test – the product is tested in the company's own labs to ensure it functions as designed. A *beta test*, commonly used within the software industry, tests the product in a real environment in order to ensure that it functions as designed under conditions that are not limited by any artificial performance conditions (e.g. laboratory conditions). Lastly, the *gamma test* is a product use test employed primarily in the pharmaceutical and medical device industries. The gamma test not only checks whether the product functions as specified, but that the customer is also satisfied with the product.

In Stage 5 of the NPD process, the new product is tested together with the marketing plan for the first time. This is called *market testing*. In the *full sale method*, the product is available for sale with no substantial constraints or restrictions. In a *test market*, the product and advertising media may be available only in restricted geographic area in order to complete final information analysis on the business case and customer responses to the marketing mix. *Rollout* is another full sale method in which the product distribution is limited at the beginning and then ramps up to cover the entire geographical market as desired. Full sale market testing can be expensive, especially if the earlier stage market testing has not been conducted to verify the best approach.

One type of market testing that is often conducted prior to a full sale test is the *controlled sale*. Normally, the distribution of the product is limited through the controlled sale so that the supply chain is not fully tested at commercial levels. However, the product and marketing plan are fully tested together. *Informal selling* is a controlled sale market testing technique that is often conducted at trade shows and may involve providing free product to the customer. *Direct marketing* selects target customers to be exposed to the advertising media and verifies whether they make a follow-up purchase. Finally, *mini-markets* will make a locally advertised product available for sale in select outlets but there is no widespread marketing plan in place. Mini-markets rely on store display advertising to validate pricing schemes and buyer interest. In all of these controlled sale market testing examples, the distribution is restricted or limited in some way.

Finally, *pseudo sale* is a market testing technique in which the product is not typically transferred to the potential customer. With consumer packaged goods, a *faux sale* will test whether consumers are interested in the new product as described with its proposed marketing plan. Potential consumers are exposed to prototypes of the marketing media and the new product. Participants are encouraged to make product selections from a variety of items, including the new product. This market testing technique can yield significant information to the product development team in understanding the marketing strategy.

In a business-to-business environment, the pseudo sale is referred to as a *speculative sale* wherein the marketing strategy is presented to a potential customer and the customer is asked whether they will buy the product. A financial exchange for the product does not take place and the customer may not receive any product at all. Pseudo sale is an important market testing technique to frame more extensive, and expensive, studies of the new product and the marketing plan.

Chapter 6 – Teams and Organization

Supporting the systems and processes of new product development are the people of the organization. In this chapter, you will learn preferred organizational structures that match the complexity of the project with the makeup of the team. Innovation requires a team of dedicated professionals in order to convert nascent ideas into commercially successful products and services. Furthermore, appropriate resources must be assigned to each project in order to lead to successful new product development.

As described in the Introduction and Overview section, teams and organization results in 20% of the questions on the NPDP certification exam. Since many work environments are designed around team functions, this section includes information that most people encounter on a daily basis. For example, team building is an activity in which many new product development practitioners have participated. NPDP candidates should be familiar with the best form of team structure for a given project type (see Chapter 3) utilized to implement a specific strategy (see Chapters 1 and 2).

> *"Talent wins games, but teamwork and intelligence win championships."*
>
> *Michael Jordan, NBA basketball player*

Learning Objectives

After studying this chapter, you will be able to:

1. Define teams as opposed to work groups,
2. Describe four common organizational structures utilized for NPD,
3. Explain how to build a team and select a team leader,
4. List the characteristics of a high-performing team, and
5. Name the roles of senior management on NPD teams.

Teams in New Product Development

A team is defined as a *small number of people* with *complementary skills* that are committed to a *common purpose*, a set of *performance goals*, and for which they hold themselves *mutually accountable*. Each of these terms in the definition of team is important.

A Small Number of People

First, a small number of people on the team translates, in practice, as six to ten core members. Often the core team members serve as leaders of sub-teams and represent a specific function, such as R&D, engineering, or marketing. By maintaining a small number of core team members, the decision-making process is more effective. If there are too many core team members, decisions can be difficult and time-consuming. Having too few team members does not allow for full cross-functional representation on the core team.

Famously, Jeff Bezos, the founder of Amazon, has a "two pizza" rule (Giang, 2013) – the size of the team should be small enough to be fed with just two pizzas. Realistically, the two pizza rule translates to about six to ten people who can come to a decision together.

Complementary Skills

The definition of a team includes people with complementary skills. Here, *complementary* means that the team is multi-functional and each technical, sales, marketing, and administrative function is represented in order to ensure that the project can move to completion.

A common failure within innovation programs is assigning phases of work within the NPD process (see Chapter 4) to a specific function. Successful innovation teams are structured throughout the life cycle of the project with cross-functional representation. Team members from relevant functions should serve on the core team throughout the NPD project, including idea generation, market research, and development phases.

A Common Purpose

Teams also require a common purpose. This is one reason that sports teams are good analogies for new product development and project teams. In sports, the common purpose is to win the game or match. With innovation, "winning" is delivering the project outcomes as requested, on time, and on budget. To this end, teams often use a set of specific performance metrics to measure their on-going success.

Performance Goals

In sports, the performance of the team is measured by the final score of a game, the number of games won or lost during a season, and participation in the championship series. Even individual performance metrics in sports demonstrate teamwork, such as assists, runs batted-in, or turnovers.

Similarly, the success of innovation teams should be determined through team performance metrics. Organizational behavior theory (Greenberg, 2010) indicates that teams will reach higher levels of collaboration when their performance is measured as a group rather than as individuals. In addition, teams are more likely to achieve stretch goals when they design the success metrics themselves.

Thus, NPD teams should help to define their performance measures for the given innovation project. Often these metrics will be designed during the kick-off meeting and should be incorporated in the PIC, or product innovation charter (see Chapter 2). The PIC will link the innovation strategy to the product protocol in which the team determines how they will achieve the work of the project.

In addition to the product protocol, the team will establish working norms during the kick-off meeting. The NPD team will agree upon processes for managing meetings, making decisions, and handling communications. Team norms are addressed in greater detail later in this chapter.

Team Members are Mutually Accountable

Finally, an important part of being a team member is holding yourself and other team members accountable for the work of the project. Extending the sports analogy to a football team, an offensive line that fails to block the opponent will share the blame with the quarterback and receiver for an incomplete pass. A successful touchdown relies upon every player completing his actions and working together to move the ball to the goal line. Likewise, team members in NPD are required to work together to complete all milestones and deliverables for the project.

NPD team members agree to honor team commitments, such as bringing data to meetings and sharing knowledge with other team members. The scope of work, schedules, and budgets should be realistic and deadlines should be respected by all team members. If a team member finds that his or her work cannot be completed as promised, the team will work together to find an alternate solution. Team accountability relies upon fair and open communication among team members who act to support their roles and responsibilities for achieving innovation success.

Functional Departments are Not Teams

In stark contrast, a *functional department* is *not* a team. For convenience, many firms will group professionals by skill set. For example, a firm may have departments of mechanical engineers, of sales staff, and of software designers. However, each individual within a department is likely working on a different project and does not share the goals and objectives of other people assigned within the same functional department. Performance metrics are individualized within functional departments, and the department is managed in order to achieve department goals.

New Product Development Teams

As defined above, teams require a set of complementary skills. In sports like baseball, the players may have special skills to play a specific position – the pitcher, the catcher, and the shortstop all have special skill sets that contribute to the success of the team. Similarly, in new product development, a *cross-functional team*, sometimes called a multi-functional team, includes representation of *all* functions necessary to convert the embryonic idea to a commercial product. Many of these project team members have special skill sets or capabilities required to complete the project.

Commonly, the cross-functional team will include representatives from engineering, research and development, marketing, and operations. While many of these individuals would not normally work together, it is necessary for the success of an NPD project that diverse functions are able to collaborate early in the process and throughout the innovation effort. Creating a successful new product is not solely the effort of technical or marketing departments.

Team Leader

The team leader is part coach, part orchestra conductor, and part technical team member. S/he is responsible for leading the new product development team and for accomplishing the project deliverables. Many organizations will refer to the team leader as a project manager, product manager, project leader, program manager, or team leader. Regardless of title, the team leader is responsible for shepherding the innovation project to completion.

In many cases, the team leader does *not* have any direct authority over the various project team members. As discussed below, some organizational structures rely on informal, part-time project leaders to guide the NPD effort, while others will include formal assignment of a full-time, dedicated project manager.

Organizational Structure for NPD Teams

In new product development, there are four types of teams typically utilized to convert the idea into a salable product or service. These organizational structures are (Wheelwright & Clark, 1992):

- Functional work teams (sometimes called a functional work group),
- Lightweight teams,
- Heavyweight teams, and
- Venture teams (sometimes called tiger teams or autonomous teams).

A project should match the organizational structure of the team to the complexity of the NPD effort (Jurgens-Kowal, 2012). While the simplest projects, such as incremental improvements, can be worked by a functional work team, the most risky and complex projects, such as developing a new-to-the-world product, will necessitate a venture team to be completed successfully.

Functional Work Teams

In Figure 27, the boxes represent various functional departments that might be involved in a typical new product development project. In this simplified case, R&D/engineering, manufacturing, and the sales and marketing departments are represented. The circles inside the boxes represent individual workers who are actively working on the NPD effort. Note that each person at the working level reports to his or her functional manager, identified by the letters "FM" in the circle at the top of each box in the figure.

Much of the development work in a *functional work team* is done sequentially. Frequently simple new product development projects will not require a full multi-functional team working concurrently. For example, in a technology push strategy, a scientist within the centralized R&D department at the corporation may independently conceive of a new product idea. This is illustrated in Figure 27 by the light bulb on the left hand side of the illustration. The idea is then transferred to the applied research and development or engineering departments. At this point the work is *handed off* and the originating function no longer participates in the new product development effort.

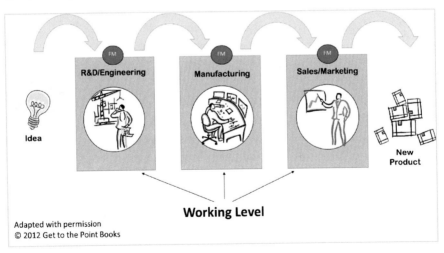

Adapted with permission
© 2012 Get to the Point Books

Figure 27 - Functional Work Team

Phrases like "tossed over the fence" and "handed off" are often used to describe sequential development when a project is transferred from one function to another, when each department completes their portion of work on the new product project. For instance, after the engineering department develops a scale-up plan to produce the new product, they will then transfer the work to the manufacturing department. When the product is manufactured and ready for sale, the operations department will alert the sales and marketing department so that the product can be introduced into the marketplace for sale.

Note that there is no formally identified project leader for a functional work team. The leader of the new product effort will either be a functional manager or will be a technical champion for the new idea. Responsibility for the work will shift over time from one function to another, such that the leadership of the project varies over the development life cycle. There is normally some degree of alignment regarding what jobs each function needs to complete for the project; however, there is no coordinated effort to encourage cross-functional interactions or coordinated project activities among the functions.

A functional work team structure is found most commonly in large, mature businesses that are organized by function rather than product line. Each function is thus responsible for the quality and quantity of work that is done. Priorities are set by the functional managers and there may be a noticeable lack of cross-functional collaboration in the work. Similarly, the individuals responsible for completing the work may suffer from a lack of coordination and communication, thus leading to lower levels of team commitment toward the NPD project.

One characteristic of functional work teams is that the new product project will compete with other departmental projects. Frequently, the time of staff members is fully allocated before the new product development project is initiated. In particular, subject matter experts will be forced to multitask and the company may struggle with the optimum use of such experts between functional and project work.

Project work is often accomplished through previously established, long-term personal relationships. For example, someone in engineering may phone a colleague in operations to alert her to the new product idea that is under development. However, new employees will find such an environment frustrating since they do not have the long-term relationships within the company in order to overcome these hidden communication barriers. This type of work is often described as being conducted in "silos," since collaboration and communication among functions is uncommon in many industry settings.

Very simple new product development projects, such as those that involve incremental improvements or cost reductions, are appropriate for the functional work team where the depth of expertise is more important than the breadth of experience. For instance, a cost reduction project may involve selecting a new vendor for a raw material. The customer should never be impacted by this change, yet the cost of manufacturing the product can be reduced leading to improved product profitability.

A new product idea may flow through the NPD process, having originated in the R&D department when employees attended a conference and learned of newer, less expensive raw materials. The R&D department would have worked closely with the engineering and manufacturing departments to ensure that quality control is maintained for the product. Sales and marketing may be notified of the change only when the new product is actually manufactured in the factory. Marketing may rapidly implement a "new and improved" tagline for the product to ensure customers continue to be satisfied with the product, since marketing was not involved early in the effort to ensure adequate emotional linkages to customer needs and wants.

Another arena in which functional work team structures are appropriate in new product development includes fundamental research, where the depth of expertise is more important than collaboration among functions. For example, many new technologies that are later utilized in platform products may be introduced through small scale, fundamental chemistry or biology studies. Such foundational studies can be successfully executed for new product projects with the functional work team structure.

Lightweight Teams

A *lightweight team* is tasked with somewhat more sophisticated new product development projects than a functional work team. Again, in the figure, various functions are represented by the boxes, indicating R&D/engineering, manufacturing, and sales and marketing are involved in converting the nascent idea to a commercial product. Individuals act as functional group liaisons on the project and are illustrated in Figure 28 by the circles. These individual team members report directly to, and only to, their *functional manager*, shown by the small circle with the abbreviation "FM" at the top of each functional box.

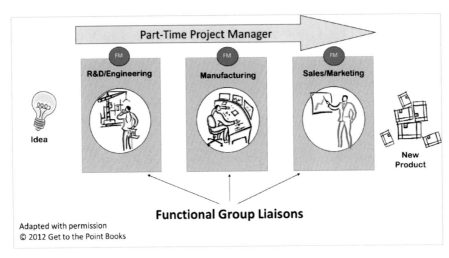

Figure 28 - Lightweight Team

In comparison to the functional work team, a lightweight team normally has a higher degree of coordination, indicated in Figure 28 by the arrow representing project management crossing all of the functions. While a new product is pushed to commercialization by a champion within a functional work team structure, a project manager will lead the work for a lightweight team. However, the project manager may be assigned only part-time, as s/he retains day-to-day functional duties or is responsible for a large part of the technical development effort for the project.

A lightweight project manager may be in his or her first supervisory assignment and does *not* have any direct reporting authority over the team members. Functional managers are responsible for task assignments, even if they may be in conflict with the project work. Thus, a great deal of time may be spent by the lightweight team leader in negotiating resources for the new product development effort.

Of course, the advantage of a lightweight team for new product development is that the team has improved communication and coordination of the project work. In this case, there is some degree of cross-functional coordination in the development of the product, which includes simple product improvements, enhancements, and limited addition of features. As compared to the functional work team in which work flows from department to department, the product development project is coordinated across all functions in the lightweight team. Communication is enhanced compared to the functional work team, as well, since the project leader will be actively engaged in designing and developing the new product.

A disadvantage of the lightweight team is that the project leader may be considered weak and of lower status within the overall organization. Such perceptions can increase the barriers to acquiring adequate project resources. Additionally, since department heads are independently responsible for the goals and work assignments of the lightweight team members, the project work may compete with other work priorities. Team members are often frustrated by their day-to-day burdens which conflict with their ability to advance the NPD project.

As a new product development project becomes more complex, a lightweight team is better suited than a functional work team is in completing the work with a degree of coordination and cross-functional communication. However, if the new product requires significant technical or market development, a heavyweight team may be more appropriate.

Heavyweight Teams

A *heavyweight team* is characterized by excellent communication and coordination among a group of core team members. Core team members continue to be retained within their home (functional) departments, represented by the boxes in Figure 29. Annual performance reviews, for example, are still conducted by the functional department heads, indicated by the label "FM" at the top of each box. However, the core team members and the project manager are assigned full-time to the project. Staff working on the new product development project may have a "dotted line" reporting authority to the project manager for the duration of the NPD effort.

Oftentimes, heavyweight teams are tackling new products that are complex, and the size of the team may number several dozen individuals with diverse responsibilities. Regardless of the overall team size, the core project team will remain small, between six to ten members, in order to maintain efficient decision-making. Core team members may also be responsible for a sub-team's work on the new product development project, especially within any specialized function. The core members of a heavyweight team are cross-functional by design and represent *all* functions necessary to convert the new product idea to a salable product.

In contrast to the lightweight team, the project leader is more experienced and will also maintain budget responsibility for the project. S/he is in a full-time management position and is not likely to be engaged in specific project tasks, technical design, or market development. Priorities and work assignments for the project are established by the heavyweight project team leader, and not the functional managers. Project managers of heavyweight teams bear primary responsibility for the successful outcome of the project and will report directly to a senior executive at the firm.

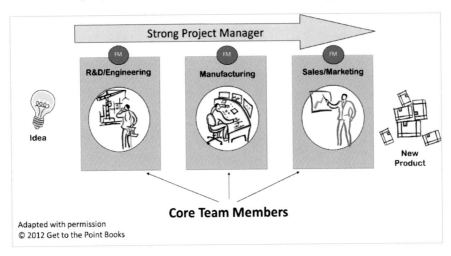

Figure 29 - Heavyweight Team

NPD projects that are undertaken by heavyweight teams generally have high visibility within the firm and are supported by the functional managers. A formal product innovation charter (PIC) documents the expected work of the team and may identify key functional roles for the project work. While they may be reluctant to release subject matter experts from departmental work, functional managers will indeed support the work of a heavyweight team with necessary resources. In fact, several staff from each department may play a role in the new product development effort over its life cycle. Additionally, support functions, like the legal department, IT, and customer service, may need to provide resources to the heavyweight team in order to ensure a full cross-functional perspective.

A heavyweight team incorporates excellent communication and coordination among the team members. As indicated, the project will be allocated a specific budget with clear accountability for the successful commercialization of the new product. Complex innovations with a higher degree of risk, such as next generation products and new platforms, are well-suited for work by a heavyweight team. For the most radical new product development projects, companies may instead utilize a venture team to complete the work.

Venture Teams

A venture team has great latitude in the decisions it makes to design, develop, and market a radical new product. Also known as *tiger teams* or *autonomous teams*, venture teams are staffed by highly experienced personnel with deep subject matter expertise and a strong project manager (likely a senior executive) tasked with the large, complex, and risky NPD effort.

The venture team project leader will have full accountability and responsibility for the project's scope, schedule, and budget, as well as direct reporting authority for the project team members. S/he will generally report directly to the CEO. In contrast to the lightweight team, for instance, the venture project manager will be highly influential within the firm and the breakthrough new product development project may be his or her last assignment before retiring from the firm. Venture team leaders are respected within their company and have established a long-standing record of success in management and product development.

As indicated in the Figure 30, the individual team members (represented by the circles), are pulled out of their home departments (illustrated by the small boxes). Team members include the core venture team leaders, representing high level managerial functions from the various departments, as well as subject matter experts and support team members. Due to the complexity of the NPD project undertaken by a venture team, there will multiple sub-teams reporting to each of the core venture team leaders and the project may involve numerous personnel and third-party contractors. To attain the highest levels of productivity and effectiveness, team members are co-located, typically in a location geographically separate from the home organization.

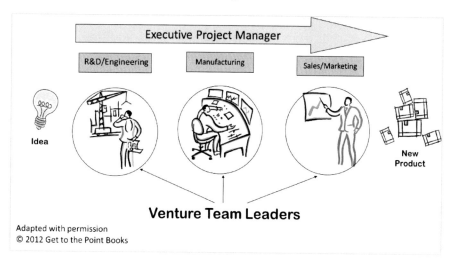

Figure 30 - Venture Team

Note that the venture team is used infrequently for very complex and radical NPD projects. There is a high focus on results. The development effort can be quite expensive due to the scale and higher levels of risk and uncertainty involved in the project. A new product developed by a venture team may lead to a spin-off or joint venture company for several reasons. First, due to the increased risk of developing a product that is largely new-to-the-world requiring significant technical and market development, the work may be segregated from the parent company. Next, the team members will view autonomy as a core value and will seek independence to tackle the new product challenges with unique solutions. Finally, when the new product is launched, the venture team members will remain as part of the organization to continue next generation product development and to provide initial customer service for the new product.

A classic example of a venture team was the Apple team that developed the Macintosh computer in response to IBM's recently released personal computer (Markides, 1999). A team of experts was convened, separate from the rest of the Apple organization and led by the CEO (Steve Jobs). The team was located in a different building and given freedom to work outside the normal hierarchy and bureaucracy of the company. Recognizing that the project was important from a strategic perspective, the team members performed at the highest levels - taking ownership in the project - in order to address the competitive threat. The team was highly focused on results and regarded autonomy as a core value.

Choosing an NPD Team Structure

No one type of organizational structure is perfect or promises 100% success in launching a new product. The organizational structures discussed above each have different strengths and weaknesses, as well as appropriateness for different levels of development complexity. Firms need to be flexible in choosing the type of team for each project based upon the needs of the product development effort and in light of the organizational culture.

Pros and Cons of a Functional Work Team

Functional teams are characterized by control and accountability, offering strength to developing a new product requiring depth of skill from the team members. In addition, resources are optimized offering expertise and depth of knowledge, especially for projects that take advantage of the firm's economies of scale. Individuals working on a functional team clearly understand how their work assignments align with their functional career path.

However, the disadvantage of a functional work team is that the project team may lack breadth of skills. Often organizations utilizing functional work teams for simple product development efforts, such as cost reduction projects, will employ formal, bureaucratic procedures and processes to ensure consistency with existing operations. NPD work is primarily cast as tasks needing completion rather than being viewed as project-oriented work with a multi-function collaborative effort. Complex product development projects will proceed slowly when assigned to functional work teams, due to the lack of cross-functional representation and strong leadership.

Functional teams are useful in rolling out minor changes to products, such as repositioning an existing product into a new market or improving simple product features. In the case of repositioning, for example, a new product can be introduced with support from the marketing function alone. Consider a firm that is marketing an existing whole grain cookie product as a convenient, on-the-go breakfast snack. This new product project requires little coordination among departments and can generally be advanced by the marketing function alone.

Cost reduction projects also fall within the expertise of a functional work team as well as fundamental research. Basic research is typically spearheaded by a single organization and requires little cross-functional collaboration to be successful in meeting technical goals.

Pros and Cons of a Lightweight Team

A lightweight team has the advantage of increased coordination and communication among the functions. With at least a part-time project manager guiding the new product development effort, tasks are likely to be designated to responsible parties; however, this weak project manager does not have reporting authority over team members. The project may or may not be initiated with a PIC.

The project leader and individual team members on a lightweight team may be frustrated since they will continue to work on day-to-day assignments but they will have little spare time for the creative project work. Especially challenging are decisions for work to progress in a lightweight team since the project leader has low status across functional boundaries and most decisions for team members' work assignments will be made by their department managers. Oftentimes, individuals prefer project work over routine tasks.

Lightweight teams are commonly used in many different new product development situations. Primarily, lightweight teams are deployed for derivative products, additions to a product line, and adding feature enhancements to an existing product. For example, a lightweight team may be responsible for designing and marketing different size packages of cookies when the primary product has been only as a 12-ounce package. Such a project requires coordination across manufacturing, sales, and marketing functions, yet is not a highly complex project from a technical or marketing viewpoint.

Pros and Cons of a Heavyweight Team

Heavyweight teams have a strong project focus and maintain accountability across multiple functions, including even the project's budget and schedule. The team has significant decision-making authority, yet it can be difficult to staff because the team members need to have both depth *and* breadth of skill. Team members are normally highly committed to the new product development project which may require a system solution with contributions from many different functions.

New products that are assigned to heavyweight teams are typically more complex and involve innovation in either markets, technologies, or both. Integration and synergies across functional boundaries can be a challenge for the project manager. However, the project leader is assigned full-time to the project, as are core team members, increasing the capability of the NPD team.

Projects executed by a heavyweight team will be guided by an approved product innovation charter and responsibility for project tasks will be laid out formally for the team members. Functional managers will be expected to support the NPD effort yet will maintain primary authority for the team members. For instance, performance reviews for heavyweight team members will be conducted by the department managers; however, the project leader will be providing much of the information since s/he is directing each individual team member's work on the NPD project.

Development of a new platform product is an example of a project in which a heavyweight team would be utilized. This type of new product involves significant technical development as well as market growth and penetration efforts. An example of a project for the heavyweight team would be to commercialize a new flavor of cookies (such as chocolate chip), supposing the company had previously only sold sandwich cookies.

Pros and Cons of a Venture Team

Recall that venture teams are also known as *autonomous teams*. This alternative name stresses the importance of independence and autonomy to the work of the venture team. These teams are highly focused on the results of the new product development project. Venture teams are motivated and usually personally vested in the success of the project which involves both new markets and new technologies.

Not only is the project manager assigned full-time to the NPD project, core team members will be responsible for various sub-teams in order to accomplish the work. The project is guided by a formal PIC and the project manager will have authority for the budget, schedule, and personnel involved in the project. A venture team's project manager is highly influential across the company and will report directly to the CEO for the groundbreaking work of the NPD effort. Again, a venture team may be co-located at a separate campus from the primary organization in order to allow the team to focus on the creative elements of the work and to have a degree of freedom from the company's mainline bureaucracy.

However, when team members are isolated from other R&D and product line work, the degree of coordination with the existing business could become a challenge. In addition, many individual team members may find it difficult to integrate back into their home organizations after completion of the project. Many of the team members will enjoy the independence of the project away from their day-to-day work and will have a vested interest in the long-term success of the new product from both a technical and market perspective.

Due to the higher risk nature of the product development effort, and the focus on independence as a core value for the team, venture teams are reserved for the most radical of innovations. NPD projects require significant technical development and extensive market development for new-to-the-world type of products. These projects involve breakthrough technical developments as well as entering brand new markets, sometimes which require building from scratch. For instance, the cookie company may wish to enter the ice cream market and will thus establish a separate organization to handle all of the technical and market development work.

Choosing an Organizational Structure

Choosing a particular type of project team requires flexibility on the part of team members, team leaders, and upper management. Figure 31 provides a quick reference to match the project type (based upon complexity of the technical and market development effort) with the recommended organizational structure.

Projects with greater complexity and novelty (breakthrough) will migrate toward venture teams or heavyweight teams while simpler projects may utilize a lightweight team. In some cases, a heavyweight team may be appropriate for breakthrough innovations. However, heavyweight teams are best utilized in developing platform and derivative projects. Heavyweight and venture teams are expensive to convene and can result in a waste of key resources for simple support projects.

Lightweight teams are appropriate for developing derivative or enhancement new products and may be used in designing and marketing well-defined platform products. Some incremental improvement projects may need the coordination, communication, and integration offered by a lightweight team in order to be successful, depending on the situation. Lightweight teams are not recommended for riskier breakthrough projects.

Functional work teams are used when the work effort is vertically integrated and requires depth of expertise, such as in support projects. In some cases, functional work teams are effective in developing derivative or platform products when the technical or marketing effort is limited.

Functional work teams are not recommended for breakthrough products due to the lack of collaboration across the various functions of the organization.

NPD Project Type				
	Breakthrough	Platform	Derivative	Support
Functional Work Team	N/A	Situational	Situational	Recommended
Light-weight Team	N/A	Recommended	Recommended	Situational
Heavy-weight Team	Situational	Recommended	Recommended	N/A
Venture Team	Recommended	N/A	N/A	N/A

Figure 31 - Recommended NPD Organizational Structure

In addition to considering the type and complexity of the new product development project, organizations should also consider the need for a part-time or full-time project manager as well as diversity, integration, and coordination among business functions.

Building an NPD Team

Building and managing a project team is common in every industry today. Effective project leaders will manage communications among team members and other stakeholders while striving to meet the objectives of the project, including schedule and budget goals. NPD project teams often involve cross-functional, dispersed teams, and the project leader must integrate tasks among team members who may have vastly different perspectives of the expected product.

In most situations, senior management will name the project leader and team members in advance of the project kick-off. Team members are selected based upon the project needs, skills sets of subject matter experts, and availability to work on the project. Senior and functional managers will consider career path and stretch assignments as well as other business needs in pre-assigning team members to an NPD project.

Senior management may, on the other hand, appoint the project manager for a new product development effort, relying upon his or her judgment to select the team members for the project. Some organizations post internal job announcements for project work while others actively solicit "volunteers" to assign themselves to the project. In the latter cases, project team members with the most interest in the product idea will likely volunteer to work on the project, ensuring a high degree of commitment over the life cycle of the project.

Team Structure

The basics of team structure are normally established at or during the project kick-off meeting. Teams should also develop their own processes for meetings and decision-making soon after the project kicks off. The team structure is made up of the type of team, the size of the team, and membership of the team. Recall that the type of team should be matched to the complexity of the NPD projects, taking into account the needs for technology and market development (see Figure 30).

When team members are self-assigned, all of the new product development projects are listed and the potential team members assign themselves to the project that is of most interest to them. This suggestion is validated by studies that show higher levels of output, enthusiasm, and motivation when people are working on the projects and technical problems for which they have the most passion. You have probably observed the phenomena of working on your favorite hobby and completely losing track of time due to an intense level of concentration and enjoyment of the task at hand. A similar phenomenon can be observed in the workplace as team members choose the NPD projects that enhance their highest levels of job satisfaction and commitment.

However, in most organizations, team members are typically pre-selected for the new product development effort by senior management. These assignments should be done in consultation with the project leader to ensure that all functions are adequately represented by the NPD team. Individual assignments of NPD team members by senior management will consider factors such as career development and growth, personalities, and training needs. Team members must act as part of the team, accepting accountability of the common purpose and deliverables of the project. Team members are assigned to NPD projects based upon their special skills and expertise to align with the cross-functional needs of the project.

NPD team members need to fully represent their function within the team. They need to provide functional expertise throughout the project and ensure that any functional issue that could affect the delivery of the new product on time, on budget, and on scope, are raised proactively within the team. Team members should participate in solution generation for any problems they identify, as well.

Team members also need to fully engage and participate in the activities of the project. This includes sharing responsibility for the project's results, and monitoring improvement actions so that the team can be more effective and productive. Recall that a part of the definition of team includes *shared performance goals*.

Note that for a heavyweight or venture team, the core team members often serve as leaders of functional or technical sub-teams. Thus, these individuals need to participate as functional representatives as well as team leaders. Keep in mind that the core team is a relatively small group, numbering six to ten, in order to maintain an environment conducive to efficient decision-making.

Purpose of the Team

Successful NPD teams clarify their purpose and own their project objectives. The product innovation charter, or PIC, defines the project work and aligns the deliverables with senior management expectations (see Chapter 2). Performance goals and measures of team success are documented in the PIC.

The most successful teams design the metrics of success themselves, usually during the project kick-off meeting, and these are aligned with the strategic goals of the innovation effort. Individual team members' performance should be measured against both individual goals and the agreed-upon team objectives.

Project Leadership

As indicated above, senior management will often pre-assign and name the project leader in advance of most major new product development efforts. Occasionally, for smaller projects of lower complexity, the leader will be self-selected or simply come forward as a result of the on-going work.

A project leader may be called the team leader, program manager, product manager, project director, or any of a variety of other titles. As indicated, the project leader is usually named by senior management in advance of the project kick-off. The vast majority of organizations pre-select the new product project leader to ensure the project will be guided by a person with specific skill sets and can advance the new product to successful commercialization.

Especially in the case of very small and simple projects, such as those implemented by a functional work team, the project leader may be self-selected. Alternatively, the project leader may simply be a person working on the project who voluntarily takes up some of the administrative tasks or who is a technical champion for the NPD effort.

Organizational Culture

One of the most important aspects of building a successful innovation team requires understanding the culture of the organization and of the project team. It is important for the project leader and senior management to fully understand the impact of the organization's culture on the productivity of the team. Many studies indicate that team culture is one of the key elements that leads to successful team outcomes. Groups with strong cultures typically perform more effectively as a team, as well.

For example, an organizational culture that is permission-based, requiring formal written requests for even minor tasks, may have difficulty integrating the work of an autonomous team designing a highly uncertain, radical new product. Instead, this type of project work requires a team needing freedom to pursue open innovation and co-creation work with a variety of end-users.

> *Organizational culture is defined as a set of customs and beliefs that are common among people in the organizational group.*

Culture is defined as *a set of customs and beliefs that are common among people in a group, division, or function.* Most corporations exhibit a certain culture, and project teams within the larger organization will also demonstrate a similar set of unifying traits and characteristics. Companies and teams that are most successful with new product development share a culture that focuses strongly on implementing the innovation strategy. All high performing NPD teams reflect a common culture.

Team cultures may reflect the overall organizational culture or the team may accept common behaviors that are independent of the parent organization. In addition, team cultures reflect the diversity of the individual team members, including their technical, business, and professional expertise, as well as the distinct personalities of team members. Some of the elements that determine an NPD team's culture include the basics of the team structure, the purpose of the team, and leadership.

New product development teams work the best when they have a high degree of autonomy, especially when the new product effort is complex and of higher risk. A productive team culture for an effective cross-functional new product development team will allow its members to bridge department boundaries to acquire knowledge and information needed for the project deliverables. Teams need to understand that it is acceptable to have an opinion that differs from senior management or the project leader, and team members should be encouraged to share differing points of view in order to gain the highest level of success in the innovation effort.

Team members also need to be free to make an honest mistake in the quest for a better way to do things. Often, it is only by making mistakes that we learn new information. Individual team members must feel comfortable in the work environment in order to fully participate in the tasks required to deliver the new product from idea to concept to sale in the marketplace.

Most human beings function best under an assumption of equality. In a new product development team, this means that the marketing representative has an equal vote to the R&D engineer and to the operations representative. Regardless of level or perceived status, the NPD team members should understand that no one is considered "above" or "below" the others. A team environment free of status can perform at high levels of effectiveness.

Formal management of and training of the team in a conventional perspective falls to the team leader with overall guidance provided by senior management. High performing teams will engage in continuous improvement and learning to enhance the effectiveness of the project team.

Span of Responsibilities

Many of the projects encountered in new product development will be suited to implementation of lightweight or heavyweight teams. Recall that venture teams will have a highly influential, senior manager leading the project with 100% dedication. Projects that lend themselves to a functional work team structure will have part-time leadership that reflects the department structure or the required technical expertise on an ad-hoc basis.

Leadership skills and characteristics are necessary for both lightweight and heavyweight NPD projects regardless of the common organizational culture elements. What will be different between the leadership characteristics of the teams is the span of responsibility (see Figure 32). These items should be considered when selecting the team leader.

A lightweight team, used for line extension projects, repositioning of products into new markets, and/or derivative and enhancement projects, will require at least a part-time project leader with a somewhat limited span of responsibilities. For example, the duration of the product development effort will be limited as will be the interaction between the team leader and potential customers or end-users.

In contrast, a heavyweight team leader will be responsible for new product development efforts with a greater degree of complexity, such as new product platforms, new-to-the-company, and/or radical breakthrough products. In such cases, the NPD project leader will have an extensive span of responsibility and will be assigned to the project full-time. A heavyweight team leader will be committed to coordination of project activities, multi-disciplinary skill development for team members, and can significantly influence various departmental functions, such as manufacturing, marketing, and engineering.

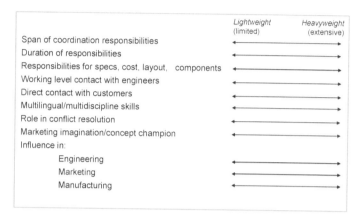

Figure 32 - NPD Project Leader Responsibilities

Heavyweight project team leaders will have demonstrated success in the organization and will understand the culture of the firm. Sensitivity to values, customs, and behaviors can improve the chances of success for a team tackling any higher-risk project activity.

Communications

New product development teams and team leaders need to manage a diverse network of communications regarding the project. Communications start with the project leader, while each core team member handles communications to and from his/her function.

Communications and status reports regarding the new product project are essential with the project sponsors and other senior managers. Recall from Chapter 3 (Portfolio Management) that the sponsor is the senior manager who provides funding and resources for the project. Thus, effective communications with the project sponsor are critical to the long-term success of the new product development effort.

Moreover, communications can take many forms – typically defined as *synchronous* or *asynchronous*. Direct, or synchronous, communications may include phone calls, meetings, or other face-to-face conversations. Asynchronous communications provide information one way, through e-mail, newsletters, or bulletin boards. Other asynchronous communications involve any communication between team members, leaders, and/or managers that is not conducted in real time.

For instance, a core team member may need to focus communications with sub-teams on their area of expertise, such as obtaining and refining customer requirements, product use testing, or executing the product launch plan. These communications are often synchronous and may require substantial commitment on the part of the sub-team leader to ensure the project is fully represented. On the other hand, weekly project status reports may be distributed asynchronously (via a newsletter or e-mail) to all of the project stakeholders.

Additionally, internal communications may require direct communication with the functional or department managers, and other organizational resources, such as the IT department, human resources, accounting, finance, or treasurers' departments. These types of communications are often well-suited to providing information to stakeholders in an asynchronous format.

Communications external to the core team will vary depending on the project type, the complexity of the development effort, and the needs of stakeholders. Project stakeholders, such as the legal department, will need to have a high level understanding of the NPD project in order to help draft patents and provide intellectual property protection for the new product. Government bodies and regulatory agencies may need to be informed of new product testing, construction of plant facilities, and to approve chemical formulations, raw materials, or ingredients used in the new products. Suppliers and vendors may need special communications to manufacture components with certain requirements and specifications necessary to further the new product development effort. As discussed in Chapter 5, Market Research, it is crucial to communicate with customers, potential consumers, and end-users of the new product to ensure their needs will be met and that they will be satisfied with the features and attributes of the new product.

As described herein, the project leader retains responsibility to ensure the NPD project is successful. Much of the success with new product development teams is rooted in effective communication. While the project leader's range of responsibilities varies depending on the complexity of the project (e.g. whether the project is executed by a lightweight or heavyweight team), s/he must dedicate a significant amount of time to managing both internal and external communications. One way to enhance the learning for a team leader is to evaluate post-launch reviews of recent and similar NPD projects. Lessons learned from effective internal and external communication procedures will have been documented as best practices.

High Performing Teams

Successful commercialization of a new product that meets scope, schedule, and budget goals are projects led by skilled managers and implemented by high performing teams. Groups develop through their shared organizational beliefs and by a pattern of personal interactions in which team members relate to one another to accomplish the tasks of the project. Team development stages were first proposed by Bruce Tuckman in 1965 based upon his empirical studies of small groups (2001). Today, we recognize the importance of team development in building a project team that will successfully deliver a new product under the constraints of scope, schedule, and budget.

High performing teams proceed through several steps; collectively these are known as the Tuckman model. As shown in Figure 33, steps in team development include: forming, storming, norming, performing, and adjourning. These stages effectively describe the transformation of an individual contributor to a productive team member and then back to an individual contributor as the project comes to a close. Individuals will adapt to the team environment with personal commitment while specific learning and growth elements for the team will be accomplished during each interaction.

Tuckman's original research (2001) builds upon small group studies in therapy, learning, and laboratory situations. However, over the years, Tuckman's model of team development has found widespread application. Individual behavioral elements as well as team tasks leading to successful product development projects are discussed below.

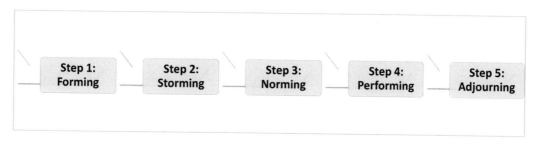

Figure 33 - Tuckman Model

Forming an NPD Team

As described previously in this chapter, team members for an innovation project are normally pre-assigned to ensure cross-functional representation and to align project assignments with individual career path goals. Normally, the team leader is also pre-selected for lightweight and heavyweight NPD teams.

During the kick-off meeting for the new product, senior management and the team members should progress through the forming phase of the Tuckman model. Step 1 includes individuals seeking behaviors to orient themselves to the work of the team. Individuals become attached to the group and will be breaking some functional ties in order to form the group bonds. Team members may be testing the leadership hierarchy of the team during the forming step while they are trying to establish their own role on the team.

From a task perspective, individuals become aware that the NPD team is a new group that may establish its own rules of conduct and its own culture. Team members may press to elucidate the boundaries of the project. Senior management and the team leader will need to define the work of the team and explain the overall business objectives of the project.

While no "work" is generally accomplished in Step 1, the team will begin establish protocols and approaches to solving the problem of working together. In particular, the team will address how the work will be accomplished. The kick-off meeting concludes with the issuing of the PIC (see Chapter 2), guiding the team's product development efforts so that they align with the firm's innovation strategy.

Storming on an NPD Team

Step 2 of the Tuckman model is described as storming. Individuals will be adjusting to their new project assignment and may even be suspicious or fearful of the new situation. This can be especially true if the new product is deemed high-risk in a conservative firm or if there are external economic factors influencing the potential for success.

Typically, the storming phase of the Tuckman model is associated with a high degree of emotional conflict as individuals compete to establish hierarchy in the new organization (the NPD team). Some team members may form factions within the larger group, advocating for a particular solution or approach to the customer problems. While every team must advance through each of the given Tuckman stages, a strong leader with excellent facilitation skills can help the team come to agreement quickly within step 2.

Tasks that are accomplished during the storming phase are usually not related to the project, but help to establish the team's working norms. Individuals will learn to cooperate and offer help to other team members. Additionally, learning about the scope of the project will help to reduce team members' anxiety. Individuals will begin to emphasize autonomy in the work over independent, self-directed goals. Two aspects of learning apply to NPD teams at this stage: building trust and project training.

Trust

Successful teams demonstrate intragroup trust. Robert Rosenfeld and colleagues (Rosenfeld, et al., 2011) have identified two types of trust that are necessary for effective team performance. *Intellectual trust* is an understanding that others are capable of conducting the project work. Team members will validate intellectual trust through educational achievement (e.g. a specific degree or certification), experience, and position or job title.

On the other hand, people need much more time and energy to build *emotional trust*. While this type of trust is specific to each individual's personality and life experience, emotional trust generally is exemplified by not causing another individual harm, offering support to others, and demonstrating selfless behaviors for the overall good of the team.

NPD projects with little risk can be accomplished by teams that have established only intellectual trust. However, most innovation projects involve some degree of risk, and therefore, team members must build emotional trust as well. Team-building activities, such as playing golf or dining together during the project kick-off meeting, will help individuals build personal relationships to strengthen emotional trust. Note that breakthrough projects are often implemented with a venture team. Autonomy of the venture team is a value reflected from a perspective with high levels of both intellectual and emotional trust.

Project Training

Training of the new product development team is another activity completed during project kick-off and is essential to moving a team beyond step 2 in the Tuckman model. To focus on shared objectives, team training will address building skills in support of the new product development effort. For example, any new software that will be utilized for project team communications should be described in detail when all of the team members are gathered together. Individuals should be given an opportunity to practice new skills and the team leader may choose to assign mentor-apprentice pairs within the team to ensure the product development effort can be delivered within the schedule constraints. Key stakeholders, such as the project sponsor and senior business managers, should participate in tool training as necessary to demonstrate commitment to the project.

However, training for the new product development team should not be rushed nor should it be delivered too early in the development cycle. For example, if the team has never before developed a strategic launch plan for a new product, management should recognize that specific training will be needed later in the project in preparation for Stage 4 activities. Prior work that is relevant to the product development effort should also be divulged at the kick-off meeting so that the team starts the project with a common knowledge base and does not need to engage in rework.

Leadership in Storming

Managing the team will rely heavily upon the team leader's personality, management skills, and the type of team – lightweight or heavyweight. However, in managing the team, the leader needs to keep the group enthusiastic and motivated toward the project goals. This is especially important as the team goes through the storming stage. As indicated, there may be a natural inclination for team members to become discouraged as they struggle with goals that seem too big or too far away for them to be successful. An effective team leader will help the team remain motivated through this natural slump in energy.

Motivation also includes securing appropriate incentives, recognition, and rewards for the team members. In particular, studies show that teams are more productive and effective when performance goals are tied to team activities. In fact, it is a common failure of leadership to encourage team collaboration, yet reward employees purely on individual performance goals. The team goals should be tightly aligned with the strategic goals of the project as outlined in the PIC. Team members should help design appropriate project goals during the kick-off meeting as well.

Norming for an NPD Team

As the team transitions from individual members (forming) and works through natural conflicts (storming), the group will become a cohesive unit and share a sense of being as a group. Group unification occurs in Tuckman's step 3, norming.

In step 3 of the Tuckman model, the group is unified around common goals, ideas, and purpose. Conflict of a personal nature is reduced and team values emerge as emotional trust grows. Individual team members recognize their interdependent roles and establish structural norms, such as meetings and discipline.

Tasks completed in the norming phase will include common ideation processes, practical logistics for team member inclusion and cohesion, and expression of opinions. Emphasis is placed on the evaluation of problems and categorization so that the new product development work will proceed efficiently.

The Team Contract Book

In establishing group norms, many teams will document their processes in a *team contract book*. The team contract book, sometimes known as the team charter, builds upon the information in the PIC, yet is specific to each NPD team. It will incorporate the guidelines, norms, and standards to which the team has agreed so that the group will function effectively. Establishing team guidelines within a team contract indicates the group is maturing in Step 3 of the Tuckman model.

Openness and exchange of ideas characterize the norming stage. As the team agrees upon standard working protocols, they will create the team contract book. Often, team members will sign their names to the team charter indicating agreement with and commitment to the project team guidelines. Adding a personal signature to a document solidifies an individual's commitment to completing the activities as well as a responsibility to adhere to the norms and standards of the group.

At a minimum, the team contract book should lay out the strategy, mission, goals, and purpose of the new product development effort to be undertaken by the team. The success criteria are brief and simple in the introductory executive summary of the team contract book. Providing guidance for team activities, the team charter will identify plans to achieve the project goals and objectives, the basic business plan (high-level benefits of the new product), team member roles and responsibilities, as well as preliminary budget and schedule information.

Much of the team contract book is specific to the given NPD project and the individuals assigned to work on the project. However, some general considerations for an NPD project should be included in all team charters. For example, the team contract book should discuss the general product development plan which includes items such as the commercialization schedule, expected gate review dates, materials and resources required to complete the work, and any work items specific to the new product development effort.

Additional sections of the team contract book may identify the product design plan capturing expected market research requirements, customer testing phases, and research and development efforts required. Quality assurance and quality control plans are also an important part of successfully completing a new product development project and should be fully documented in the team contract book. As the project is initiated, quality plans may be in outline format with detail added as the project progresses. Note that quality management for innovation is discussed in Chapter 7, Tools and Metrics.

Finally, in order to ensure a timely market launch of the new product, the team contract book should also include product testing and manufacturing plans, specific project milestones and deliverables, including gate review expectations and technical assessments, as well as the performance metrics that define success for the project, the product, and the overall program.

The team charter may take a significant amount of time to develop, and it can be designed as a living document to capture iterative plans while the process is implemented for developing the new product. However, it is important to ensure that the team members agree upon the contents of the team contract early in the NPD process to ensure there is commitment, responsibility, and authority to develop the new product. Again, the team contract book also allows the team to document their structural norms and practices so that the team can advance to the next stage in Tuckman's group development model.

Performing NPD Teams

In step 4 of the Tuckman model, teams are engaged in constructive work and attempting successful completion of previously identified tasks and activities. Individual team members' behaviors are characterized by understanding, analysis, and insight. Minimal emotional interferences are observed between group members as the team focuses its energy on supporting task completion through defined roles. In fact, team members often express positive emotions and enthusiasm during the performing stage.

In this advanced stage of team maturity, team members develop insights and accept change through collaborative processes. Team members utilize various methods of inquiry to further both individual and group development and to apply learnings to other situations. A high degree of interdependence exists among group members as they evaluate tasks in light of the global purpose of the team.

Once the team has moved into the performing stage, it functions at a high level to accomplish the goals of the new product development project. Because emotional responses are generally removed from the team's interactions, group members focus on idea generation and problem resolution. Most of the work of the NPD project is completed within the performing stage, including concept generation, concept evaluation, and technical development. Market research and product commercialization also rely on a high-performing NPD team for success.

Changes in Team Structure

Frequently, team membership will change over the life of an NPD project. At times new team members are added to absorb additional task activities, team members may transfer jobs within the firm, or individuals may leave the company altogether. Senior management and the project leader must deal with these changes in team membership in order to maintain focus on the new product development effort.

As new team members are added, the team is reforming with a new structure. The Tuckman model revisits the first stage – forming - as new individuals adapt to the group environment. Each stage of the Tuckman model must then proceed in order for the team to remain as a high-performing, cohesive unit. Typically, minimal changes in team membership will be met with very little emotional resistance from existing team members, and the group will rapidly progress through the forming, norming, and storming stages.

Adjourning an NPD Team

Tuckman's original model identified just four stages of group development: forming, storming, norming, and performing. A follow-up article (Tuckman & Jensen, 1977) recognized the importance of terminating the group and identified this stage as "adjourning".

By definition, NPD teams are temporary in nature. Teams are assigned a mission and will be organized around distinct starting and ending points. Temporary project teams may be in place for a few weeks, months, or years in order to accomplish the necessary work. At the conclusion of the work, these temporary project teams are disbanded. Tuckman's adjourning step describes the affective and task aspects of terminating the team.

As a new product project comes to a close, individual team members will become disengaged as they anticipate their next project assignment. Especially on highly interdependent venture teams, individuals may feel a sense of anxiety about separation and termination from the project. Team members will typically leave the group at different times even though the project termination includes a formal closing date.

Termination of the team in an NPD project introduces a key question associated with both the complexity of the project and cultural norms of the organization. In one instance, the team may be closed out early and the product transferred to the mainstream business as the product is launched in Stage 5 (see Chapter 4). In other circumstances, the team may not be discharged until some period after the product launch is finalized. For example, if the new product development effort involved a breakthrough project with high degrees of complexity and risk, the NPD venture team will know more about the product than any other function. The NPD team members can work side-by-side with customer service, technical service, and marketing and sales ensuring knowledge transfer of the product. Simultaneously, venture team members will address any concerns that arise and will gather additional information for subsequent next generation NPD projects and spin-off products.

In situations with simple product enhancements, the new product may be transferred to the mainstream business concurrently with the commercial product launch. Because the effort is less complex and lower risk than a radical innovation, the lightweight team can be disbanded in Stage 5, allowing individuals to return to their functional assignments with little disruption to the new product launch and market entry.

Note that as the NPD team is terminated, a post-launch review (see Chapter 4) must be completed to document project learnings. Lessons learned will include the life cycle of the team (forming, storming, norming, and performing) as well as specific project variables (sales, revenue, and customer satisfaction).

Team Values

Business strategies consist of the mission, vision, and values of the firm. Values are the guiding beliefs that designate the behaviors of employees. These are beliefs about what is important, or not, and what is considered good, or bad, thus guiding organizational behaviors.

Team values will reflect commitment and accountability for the new product development effort. NPD team members need to be committed to achieving project deliverables and milestones necessary to complete the project effectively and efficiently. By definition, teams are mutually accountable for the results of the NPD project.

Trust is often considered to be the key element of success within high performing teams. As discussed above, intellectual trust reflects that a person believes another team member is competent and capable to complete his or her assigned work tasks. Emotional trust, on the other hand, is essential for teams working on higher risk projects and reflects solidarity among the team members.

Team rituals reinforce team norms and standards, reflecting organizational values and commitment to the project objectives. For example, when new people join the team or others exit the team, a common ritual is to celebrate the occasion with a team gathering, such as an off-site luncheon. These rituals help to build the team's emotional trust as they become acquainted with the new team member and recognize the contributions of the departing team member. Other rituals include training to help the new team member become familiar with the product design, the project goals, and the team structure and processes.

Finally, learning is an important part of team growth and helps to make the new product project successful. Teams that value learning will improve the processes and information gathering tools necessary to ensure market acceptance and technical feasibility of the new product. Continuous learning will not only improve the capabilities of individual team members but can also enhance the overall performance of the team.

Dispersed Teams

Except for the unique situation of a venture team, most teams include members that are at different locations. Even as teams tackle breakthrough new products with autonomous teams, some team members may be situated at various business or customer locations. Some special considerations should be made for dispersed teams in order to achieve success with innovation projects.

Dispersed teams are defined as those that work from one or more locations. Some team members may work at different offices in the same city, others may have home-based offices, and still others may work in different geographical regions across the globe. Studies show that people working on different floors of the same building encounter dispersion because it is much easier to walk down the hall to speak to a colleague in comparison to taking the elevator to another floor. NPD project team leaders need to utilize additional skills to ensure that all team members are engaged in the product development effort, regardless of location.

Note that dispersed teams are also referred to as "virtual teams." In this case, "virtual" means that the majority of communication occurs through technology: e-mail, voice mail, and/or text messages. The term *"dispersed team"* is largely preferred over *"virtual team"* because the latter may imply that the team is not as important as co-located teams. However, the contrary is true today – we rely upon globally dispersed teams to identify market needs in different geographical regions and we rely upon the diversity of team members in various locations to guide development and commercialization of an idea.

Dispersed teams present unique challenges for an NPD project. Controlled studies demonstrate that the *quality of work* tends to decrease as the degree of dispersion increases (Hoegl, et al., 2007). For instance, dispersed team members face special difficulties in communication, decreased coordination of tasks, lack of mutual support, and a decline in team cohesiveness.

A recommended best practice for larger projects is to gather the team members in a face-to-face kick-off meeting. The kick-off meeting serves many purposes, including documenting the project goals and objectives in the PIC, laying out the team norms in the team contract book, and building trust among individuals who will be working together on the new product development project. A face-to-face kick-off meeting will ensure that the dispersed team members become acquainted with one another and can move rapidly through the forming, storming, and norming stages of the Tuckman model, yielding a high-performing, cohesive NPD team.

Communication Protocols

Next, following clearly established communication protocols can lead to a greater degree of success with dispersed teams. These communication protocols include agreements among team members regarding project conversations, discussions, and decisions. Communication protocols should address, for example, expected response times for e-mails and voice mails, as well as outlining times and schedules that various team members are and are not available. These agreements are especially important for team members working in different time zones and should be documented in the team contract book.

Some common communication protocols may include team member agreements to respond to all voice mails within one business day. Other protocols will include how and where project documents are stored, and what technology tools will be used for communication (e.g. e-mail, shared intranet, wikis, etc.). Dispersed teams should be trained at the kick-off meeting on the specific communication software and tools that will be utilized throughout the project, and these should not be changed unless all team members are trained on the upgraded system.

Meeting Protocols

Along the same lines as communication protocols, meeting protocols help a dispersed team work efficiently toward the new product project goals. Again, these meeting protocols should be established early in the process and may be documented in the team contract book. Formally established communication and meeting protocols are an expected outcome of a high-performing team (step 3 of the Tuckman model).

Dispersed teams often need to hold more *formal* meetings than a co-located team since distance will hamper routine conversations and sharing of information. Team meetings are best scheduled at the beginning of the week rather than the end of the week, so that team members can discuss the planned work together. Individuals tend to be more focused on the work to accomplish at the beginning of the week and reviewing go-forward work plans can improve overall project efficiency.

NPD team meetings should include periodic reviews of the overall project status, including scope, schedule, and cost. However, the project leader should generally limit the focus of meetings to decisions and information sharing among team members that cannot occur in any other asynchronous format. Especially for dispersed teams, project status updates may be more effectively communicated by e-mail, newsletters, or other bulletins.

The Dispersed Team Leader

Not surprisingly, a committed and engaged team leader can help make a dispersed team successful. The project leader is responsible for scheduling and facilitating the kick-off meeting, including developing the project success metrics to be incorporated into the PIC. Additionally, the team leader should help to decompose complex project objectives into smaller, achievable tasks and activities for the NPD project team members.

Also serving as the communications hub, the NPD team leader should plan to meet regularly with each individual team member on a one-on-one basis to fully understand the challenges that s/he faces on the project. This is especially important if there are any personality conflicts among team members and/or team members who fail to actively participate in team meetings. While working to maintain open communication pathways, the team leader will also be able to identify looming challenges to the project scope, schedule, or budget.

Because travel budgets are often limited for projects, the team leader will also serve as the liaison among the geographically dispersed team members. S/he should individually visit the team members at their primary location in order to demonstrate commitment to the project and to urge prioritization of the new product development effort for each employee.

The Team Contract Book

Also known as the *team charter*, the *team contract book* documents internal agreements among the NPD team members. As indicated above, the team contract book describes communication and meeting protocols. In addition, the team contract book may include the following items related to the execution of the NPD project:

- Executive summary,
- Business plan and purpose,
- Development plan,
- Work processes
- Communications and meeting protocols,
- Project schedule,
- Materials and testing,
- Resources (time, money, people, equipment),
- Product design plan,
- Quality plan,
- Manufacturing plan,
- Project deliverables, and
- Performance measurement and incentives.

Many of these items will be detailed from the product innovation charter and will be agreed on during the project kick-off meeting (e.g. performance measures). Work processes and communications protocols will be established as the team moves through the storming and norming stages of the Tuckman team development model. Other items, such as the quality and manufacturing plans will be outlined as the team progressively learns more about the scope, complexity, and requirements of the product development effort.

Work processes that are typically documented in the team contract book include the communications and meeting protocols. Meeting requirements, for example, will document team expectations and ground rules covering when and how meetings will be held. Many teams choose to have a regularly scheduled daily or weekly meeting to share information across the various functions involved in the NPD project. Work processes regarding meetings should include providing an agenda for the meeting in advance, electing a stand-in if participants are not available, respecting the meeting length and time commitments, and documenting the discussion and action item follow-ups. Often the meeting notes are maintained on a shared intranet site so that all team members can easily access group decisions and other project information.

RACI Chart
In addition, roles and responsibilities should be outlined as part of the team contract book. A common tool to help elucidate roles and responsibilities is known as the RACI chart:

- R – responsible,
- A – accountable,
- C – consult, and
- I – inform.

An example of a RACI chart is shown in Table 5. As indicated, a RACI chart may be developed for a single task or activity within a project phase, or the RACI chart may show overall roles and responsibilities for the core NPD project team throughout the life cycle of the development effort.

Table 5 illustrates an example of conducting a focus group on a new product prototype. As indicated, the NPD team's marketing representative will take the lead role in screening potential customers for participation in the focus group. The marketing team member may elicit the assistance of other NPD or functional team members; however, s/he is both responsible and accountable for ensuring that the focus group participants are screened to meet any criteria which the NPD team has agreed for this phase of work. Thus, the letters "R" and "A" are placed in the cell intersecting the row "Screen Participants" and the column showing "Marketing".

CONDUCT FOCUS GROUP	R&D	Engineering	Operations	Marketing	Legal
Table 5 - Example RACI Chart					
Screen Participants		I (Inform)		R (Responsible) / A (Accountable)	I
Select Venue		C (Consult)		R/A	I
Prepare Prototype	C	R	A	I	
Analyze Data	I	A	I	R	
Report Results	I	C	I	R/A	I

Note that the engineering and legal representatives will be informed by marketing as to the composition of the potential consumer group that is assembled for testing the prototype in the focus group. This is indicated by the letter "I" in the row "Screen Participants" and the columns labeled "Engineering" and "Legal" in Table 5. For various reasons, both of these core team representatives need to be aware of the actions and decisions made regarding participants for the focus group.

Similarly, the tasks of preparing the prototype is the responsibility of the engineering representative on the NPD team. However, operations is accountable for the actual production of the prototype, while the R&D group should be consulted (as indicated by the letter "C") to ensure that the prototype is manufactured to specification. The R&D group may provide feedback and other contributions regarding the prototype, though they are more involved in the work than simply needing to be informed. However, the R&D group is not responsible for performing the work nor in charge of (accountable) the prototype manufacture. Marketing is informed of the status and production plans for the prototype that is designed for the focus group test. Remaining tasks and roles are populated similarly.

While only one party is assigned responsibility for a given task, a RACI chart helps the NPD team to identify appropriate workloads for team members and to ensure a balance between functional and project responsibilities. In essence, the RACI chart clarifies the roles for team members while ensuring the new product project maintains a multi-functional perspective for all elements of work throughout the project phases.

In addition, a RACI chart can help to alleviate role confusion and it can assist in conflict resolution. In one example, the diverse backgrounds and experience of team members can lead to misunderstandings in discussions between the technical and marketing representatives. This is especially true if the NPD effort involves sophisticated technology development and there is extensive use of technical jargon. However, one of the primary goals of utilizing a cross-functional team in product development is to ensure that each individual on the team brings his or her expertise to the project and continually learns from others. The RACI chart builds on other team development activities to clearly lay out responsibilities for the specific work tasks. Carefully building the team and allowing the team to work through the Tuckman group development stages can further bond team members together with a set of common goals and objectives.

Concurrent Engineering

Utilizing a team contract book and a RACI chart will also streamline development efforts within a fully cross-functional team. Historically, many new product development project teams fail to include operations or manufacturing representatives in the early stages. While a new product may be easy to produce in a laboratory setting, full-scale manufacture may be difficult, expensive, and require significant adaptations in the factory. Further, operations departments are frequently assessed on their cost and quality performance which may introduce resistance to the processing of unknown new products.

The term *concurrent engineering* refers to developing a manufacturing process in parallel with the new product design. Integrating process design with the product development efforts from early stage development through full-scale production can save resources. For example, functionality, quality, and environmental concerns are addressed for the manufacturing process while the product is still in conceptual development. This leads to greater efficiency in converting the nascent idea to a commercial product.

Without full implementation of an integrated, cross-functional team, operations may become aware of a new product only as it is being introduced to the plant for production. This is called sequential development in contrast to concurrent engineering. A high-performing team will identify the roles and responsibilities of all core team members at the kick-off meeting. Manufacturing representatives on the NPD team can inform the team of any restrictions that limit the production of the new product. In addition, factory representatives will often provide realistic data to help the team improve cost performance of the product under development. Therefore, including manufacturing as part of the cross-functional NPD team can help to reduce the cycle time of new product development.

Decision-Making

Gate decisions were discussed in Chapter 4. In addition to the technical and marketing criteria that must be satisfied for a new product development project to progress toward commercialization, there are many other factors that can influence the decision. Some of these factors include the scope of the project; the schedule for delivery; and the cost to develop, manufacture, and market the new product. Furthermore, the NPD team is faced with a variety of decisions from managing team activities on a day-to-day basis as well as the longer term technology and marketing decisions.

Processes that will be implemented for team decisions throughout the execution of an NPD project should be documented in the team contract book. Project teams will agree upon decision-making methods while developing the team norms and standards. For example, the team will devise norms regarding whether subject matter experts are responsible for decisions for their function, at what impact level decisions should involve the entire team, which decisions will be made by the team leader, and importantly, when decisions should be escalated to senior management and the project sponsor. Because the product innovation charter directly links product deliverables and innovation strategy with how the team will work to achieve its goals, team decisions should reflect the organizational structure as indicated in the PIC.

Decisions range from autocratic to those made by consensus at a gate or portfolio management review meeting. An autocratic decision is one in which senior management or the team leader dictates a given solution. This type of decision-making authority is not generally recommended for NPD teams. However, situations involving safety standards or regulatory compliance may be fixed through an autocratic decision-making method. Decisions are more valuable when the entire team agrees and supports them.

Best practices, as described in Chapters 3 and 4, indicate that new product development decisions should be made during portfolio reviews and gate reviews. Recall that the portfolio review will compare the merits of a single project with all other innovation efforts at the firm. A positive gate review decision (pass) will indicate that the project has met its previous milestones and that the NPD team has presented an appropriate plan for future work on the new product.

Another common decision that an NPD team faces is how to manage problem-solving within the team. There are several group brainstorming techniques that are valuable to an NPD team, including nominal group technique, affinity diagrams, and the Delphi process.

Group Brainstorming Methods

Brainstorming is a general innovation technique used throughout the NPD process. More detailed information on brainstorming techniques is found in Chapter 7, Tools and Metrics. NPD teams may implement specific brainstorming tools at different points in a project in order to develop creative solutions for a customer's problem, to solve a vexing technical challenge, and/or to identify the emotional linkage for the new product's marketing campaign.

In general, brainstorming is defined as a group method of creative problem-solving. The fundamental basis for all brainstorming techniques is to generate as many ideas as possible *prior to* evaluating the merits of the ideas. Once a great number of ideas are documented, the team will combine and improve upon the ideas already discussed. Golden tenets of brainstorming are that "wild" ideas are acceptable and ideas should not be judged during the idea generation session.

The *nominal group technique* is a tool teams can use to clearly identify the problem, generate potential solutions, and reach a decision quickly. A key attribute of nominal group technique is that each individual's opinion is voiced and each team member's preference is recorded. Rather than a traditional vote which will lean toward a majority decision, team members rank the variety of ideas (e.g. first, second, third, and so on). Individual team members explain their logic for prioritizing the ideas, leading to better buy-in when the team reaches a final decision.

Next, *affinity diagrams,* sometimes called *affinity charts,* can be used to help NPD teams reach a decision based on group collaboration of idea themes. In creating an affinity diagram, teams will categorize the many potential solutions into a few categories or themes. Sorting ideas by similarities helps the stakeholders to review and evaluate a large number of ideas into selections with specific titles. This technique assists the project leader and the NPD team to visualize additional scope items that may not have been previously identified. The team will reach a decision and prioritize alternate solutions. An example of a completed affinity diagram is shown in Figure 34 for a project involving new software applications. Business solutions and coding solutions have been selected as the primary categories for problem-solving in this example. Ideas have been recorded on sticky notes for easy arrangement and rearrangement by team members into specific solution categories or themes.

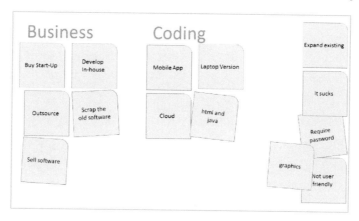

Figure 34 - Example of Affinity Diagram

Finally, the *Delphi method* is an interactive decision-making tool used to gather and refine the opinions of project team members to gain consensus. The Delphi method uses anonymous idea generation for gathering requirements, recognizing that not all participants are forthcoming in a group setting. Ideas are collected by the project leader and the submitter's identity is kept confidential. Responses are compiled and distributed to the participants. Several rounds of idea collection, compilation, and refinement lead to convergence on a group decision. In principle, the structured methodology in deploying the Delphi tool will lead to a better decision that is unencumbered by emotional responses that may be more prevalent in a face-to-face situation.

Group brainstorming is utilized frequently on NPD teams, regardless of the stage of the project. Collaboration among team members and knowledge sharing both offer extended benefits to support the group decision. Often the project leader will facilitate the brainstorming session; although, trained facilitators may increase the efficiency of decision-making if the team is large or the challenge is vast.

Senior Management Roles and Responsibilities

There are several important roles for senior management to serve the new product development team. Three specific stakeholders are identified to assist the NPD team in successfully reaching the goals and objectives of the new product initiative.

Champion

First, the *champion* is an individual who acts as a cheerleader for the project, constantly promoting the concept. A product champion is a party that is deeply involved with the overall goals of the project and will pull together people to ensure the NPD effort is a success. Innovation champions are passionate about the project, are persuasive, and are willing to take risks to move the project forward.

While the team members and the project leader also spend much time championing the new product or service idea, the project champion is normally not a member of the team. Instead, s/he may be a general manager in the marketing or R&D organization who is willing to sell the idea to meet business growth goals or to further develop technical capabilities.

Within an NPD effort, the product champion can help the team to gain resources and will assist in keeping the project alive even when faced with seemingly insurmountable challenges. Note that while the champion will assist the NPD team with appropriate resources, project resources are formally assigned by the NPD sponsor.

Sponsor

The project sponsor provides the resources to complete the innovation project. In particular, the sponsor will provide financial backing and human resources so that the NPD team can be successful in meeting the project goals. A senior management sponsor will guide and coach the project leader, while empowering the NPD team to act.

In addition, the NPD sponsor will act as an interface between the project team and other senior managers. Thus, the communication pathway is clarified for the NPD team, improving both project evaluation standards and performance measures.

As discussed previously, team norms and decision-making criteria will indicate escalation of problems to the senior management sponsor. Other decisions will be left to the project leader and the team as appropriate.

Other arenas in which the project sponsor will play a role in the specific NPD project may include (Wheelwright & Clark, 1992):

- Commitment of total resource requirements,
- Forecasting and recovery planning for schedule delays,
- Participation in gate and portfolio reviews,
- Planning for the transition of the new product to normal operations,
- Pricing for major customer accounts,
- Measuring team performance and providing incentive awards, and
- Optimizing resources among other projects and work assignments.

Facilitator

A third role for senior management in supporting the NPD teams is called the *facilitator*. The facilitator can help the team improve productivity by minimizing bureaucratic constraints or other organizational barriers.

For example, one NPD project facilitator is the NPD process manager, a role described in Chapter 4. While not a team member or decision-maker for gate and portfolio reviews, the NPD facilitator helps to remove roadblocks, assists with integrating multi-function activities, and works directly with the team on plans and decisions.

Because time-to-market is an essential variable for new product success, the NPD facilitator can improve the overall NPD process by expediting training for the project teams and by tracking the performance of the new product initiative. For example, the NPD process facilitator may oversee the IT systems utilized for innovation projects and can ensure adequate training, availability, and suitability for all NPD project team members.

Other Senior Management Roles

All three of the leadership roles – champion, sponsor, and facilitator - help to ensure the success of the NPD team. In addition to the three primary roles for executive leaders, senior management has additional roles to initiate and support the cross-functional team for a new product development project.

Senior management is responsible to ensure that a charter is established for the team's work. As detailed previously, the product innovation charter links management's strategic organizational goals directly to the NPD team objectives. Success criteria and performance metrics should be included in the PIC and in the team contract book for each innovation project.

In the twin roles of champion and sponsor, senior management provides energy and enthusiasm for the project. Management will ensure that the team has the resources, capabilities, services, and other support to get the work done. Project executives must ask what the project team needs to accomplish the new product deliverables and acquire these resources and skills on behalf of the team.

Senior management will manage project commitments by reinforcing the innovation strategy and coaching the team as they work through challenges and strive to meet stretch goals. All teams will have lulls in their energy level when new information is negative and teams will attempt to "gold-plate" the project when things are moving along efficiently. Senior management needs to remind the team of their commitments, as documented in the PIC, and hold the team to agreed-upon performance standards.

As coaches and mentors, senior management leaders can share their experiences with the team members and help deal with unforeseen challenges. Occasionally, the project boundaries and scope of work may need to be revisited. If so, senior management retains responsibility for making these significant decisions and communicating the new scope, budget, and schedule to the innovation team.

Finally, as described in Chapter 4, the NPD process manager and facilitator are responsible for ensuring that the innovation system is working effectively and efficiently. Continuous learning is maintained through project post-launch reviews in order for senior management to advocate on behalf of the NPD team members.

Senior Management Influence

Because most NPD teams involve crossing functional lines and integrating team members from various departments, senior management needs to influence the direction of the innovation work early in the process. In a typical project, senior management gives free rein to the team to brainstorm and test concepts with very little, if any, intervention. However, as indicated in Chapter 4, Stage 4 work can accrue significant expenses for the NPD project. As costs grow, senior management tends to become more involved in the project. Finally, as the product is ready to be commercialized in Stage 5, the brand may be viewed at risk and the firm's reputation is on the line. Therefore, senior management tends to micromanage the team's activities as the new product is closer to a commercial launch.

Unfortunately, at this point in the NPD cycle, factories have already been constructed, manufacturing has been initiated, and marketing campaigns have been launched. Management has little influence on the outcome without incurring drastic expenses to change the product design. Changes to the new product are easiest when the idea is in the concept stage rather than ready to go to market.

A preferred response involves management interaction with the NPD team early in the process. At this juncture, senior executives can voice their opinion on the markets, technologies, and product categories to strategically influence the new product development effort. Questions such as brand management and reputation of the firm can be built into the development effort and verified through the structured NPD process.

In addition to offering early strategic direction to the project, senior management's early involvement in an NPD project provides motivation for the team. Senior management commitment to a new product project as early as the opportunity identification and concept generation stages lends credibility to the project. Team members increase their commitment to the project because their work is seen as valued by senior management.

Summary

Cross-functional teams are a necessity for success in new product development. The definition of an NPD team is a small number of people with complementary skills that are committed to a common purpose, a set of performance goals, and for which they hold themselves mutually accountable.

There are four types of organizational structures for new product development projects. First, the *functional work team* is well suited for vertically integrated projects that require depth of expertise and/or are very simple in nature with little impact on the end customer.

Next, the *lightweight team* has improved coordination and communication relative to the functional work team. It is used for incremental product improvements, derivatives, and enhancements. The team may be managed by an inexperienced project leader who does not have authority over the team members. Individual team members balance day-to-day work with the NPD project but continue to receive specific work direction from their functional managers.

A *heavyweight team* has excellent communication and coordination of all work activities for the new product development effort. It is often used when the firm is developing a new platform. The project has a significant amount of complexity involved in either technical or market development and is staffed by cross-functional core team members and associated sub-teams. Heavyweight team leaders are experienced and will manage relationships with functional managers to negotiate subject matter expertise for the NPD effort. Functional managers, however, retain authority over most of the project team members.

Lastly, the *venture team*, also known as an autonomous team, values independence and is often comprised of highly skilled experts who are co-located to complete a radical development. The venture team's project may lead to a spin-off for the company and is encountered infrequently due to the higher risk, expense, and complexity of the new product development effort. Venture teams may be co-located at a location separate from the company's base operations and will be led by a highly respected and accomplished senior executive.

Both the structure of the team and the team leader are selected based upon the complexity of the project. The span of responsibilities of an NPD project leader varies between a fairly limited job scope to extensive innovation experiences for the most common types of NPD project teams (lightweight and heavyweight).

Team structure, culture, and processes can help the project team become more successful with new product development. All teams will progress through Tuckman's five phase model for developing a high performing team. Team norms are established and documented in a team contract book, supplementing the team's objectives from the product innovation charter.

Dispersed teams face special challenges due to distance. Standards for communication and meeting protocols help dispersed NPD teams function more effectively. Various brainstorming techniques assist project team with decision-making by identifying different alternatives.

Senior management supports the NPD team via three primary roles. These include the *champion* who serves as a cheerleader for the project, the *sponsor* who offers financial and other resources to support the project, and the *facilitator* who helps to streamline processes and remove roadblocks so the team can work productively.

Chapter 7 – Tools and Metrics

As you'll recall from the Introduction and Overview, tools and metrics account for 20% of the NPDP certification exam, or 40 questions. The exam is split with 60% of the questions (24 questions) identified with tools and the remaining 40% (16 questions) on metrics. Tools are useful methodologies to assist management and NPD teams throughout the innovation process to more effectively and efficiently deliver new products to the market. Metrics, on the other hand, indicate how the company or project is performing relative to specific goals and objectives.

Some common NPD tools have already been introduced in earlier chapters. For example, portfolio management (Chapter 3) is a tool that is utilized within NPD to manage the selection of value-added innovation projects. Moreover, market research (Chapter 5) also includes a set of tools used throughout the NPD process to better understand customer needs and to validate new product ideas with potential customers.

Many of the tools described in this chapter will be familiar; however, others (such as quality function deployment) are peculiar to new product development. Additionally, many of the topics in this section are substantially condensed, such as project management, risk management, and engineering design which can comprise entire fields of study on their own merit.

After studying this chapter, you will be able to:

1. Describe three methods of idea generation used in new product development.

2. Define and explain the use of quality function deployment.

3. Be able to name several engineering design and analysis tools.

4. Understand basic project management tools and the triple constraint.

5. Explain different financial analyses employed in NPD.

6. Describe a set of commonly used innovation metrics.

Idea Generation

Idea generation is sometimes referred to as *ideation* or *brainstorming*. During the divergent processes used in idea generation, a large number of ideas or solutions are generated to analyze new market opportunities, solve customer's problems, or satisfy functional product requirements. *Divergent thinking* is the ability to spawn multiple solutions to address an open-ended question. In contrast, *convergent thinking* attempts to derive a single solution or set of potential solutions that address a clearly defined problem or question. Idea generation will normally focus on divergent thinking methodologies early in the fuzzy front end of the NPD process (see Chapter 4) while convergent thinking narrows the new product ideas. The idea generation process is illustrated in Figure 35.

Divergent Thinking Methods

Many of the techniques utilized in idea generation are familiar. For example, *brainstorming* was briefly introduced in Chapter 6, Teams and Organization. Brainstorming is a technique used extensively in Stage 2 of the NPD process in order to identify as many solutions as possible to take advantage of the market, technology, and product category opportunities identified in Stage 1. Brainstorming is one of many divergent thinking tools.

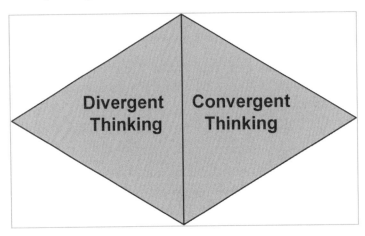

Figure 35 - Idea Generation Model

The definition of divergent thinking is a technique performed in the initial phase of idea generation which expands thinking processes to record and recall a high volume of new or interesting ideas. Divergent thinking seeks new perspectives and encourages creativity. Expected outcomes from divergent thinking are novel ideas, unique combinations of ideas, and new solution pathways to solve problems.

Brainstorming

As defined in Chapter 6, brainstorming is perhaps the most widely used group creativity tool for innovation and problem-solving. Typically, a brainstorming session will involve gathering subject matter experts and others with related experiences to generate as many ideas as possible in a short amount of time. A problem statement is provided and the group attempts to generate creative solutions to the problem. Ideas are shared verbally and a facilitator records the ideas so the entire group can view them all at once.

Normally, the problem statement will be posed at the start of the session and group members are charged to come up with new ideas to solve the problem. A facilitator will jot the ideas on large flip chart paper so that all participants can view the current set of ideas. Ideas at this stage are encouraged to be wild and even impractical. Therefore, even if an idea sounds crazy or breaks the laws of science, the idea should still be recorded. It is said that innovation is largely a numbers game, so that the more ideas that originate from a brainstorming session, the more likely one will be ultimately successful as a new commercial product or service.

Fundamentally, the concept of brainstorming is to record hundreds of ideas of which just a few will be selected as game changers in the next phase of idea generation (convergent thinking). As the innovation team continues to evaluate concepts, each idea generated in the brainstorming session may have a nugget of information that will be a component of a larger idea later.

It is important to build upon the ideas that have already been articulated. Often the idea will be described as just a word or phrase on the flip chart paper. As the participants in the brainstorming session contemplate these ideas, they may propagate new ideas or new combinations of ideas that build upon those already recorded.

In order to create a high number of unique and novel ideas, brainstorming sessions usually follow four primary rules (Thota & Zunaira, 2011).

1. **Generate as many ideas as possible.** Wild ideas, even those that violate scientific principles, are encouraged. Divergent thinking should focus on a large number of ideas rather than validity of the concepts.
2. **Reserve judgment of ideas.** A key feature of brainstorming is to generate ideas even if the team does not currently have a plan for implementation. During the later convergent phase of idea generation, ideas and concepts will be grouped together for further evaluation. To encourage participation by all group members and to maintain a rapid flow of ideas, analysis should be withheld until later.
3. **Improve on ideas and offer combinations of ideas.** It is not unusual for group members to build on ideas that have already been stated to improve the concept. Combining elements of previously documented ideas can offer new and unique solutions to a given problem as well.
4. **Encourage wild ideas.** Ideas that may have a basis in science fiction or break the "holy grail" of knowledge often include a nugget of information that can be relevant to addressing a real-life problem. Brainstorming can encourage wild ideas as seeds for new combinations of ideas and to stimulate creative thought among the group members.

Composition of the group gathered for a brainstorming session should include the NPD team as well as subject matter experts. Including customers or individuals who have tangential knowledge of the problem can enhance the creative outcome of the brainstorming session as well. For example, in a brainstorming session to address school bus designs, the team may wish to include subject matter experts from high speed rail since these individuals are familiar with transporting large numbers of people and may offer a unique viewpoint to solving the problem.

Nominal Group Technique

A divergent thinking method that is often used hand-in-hand with brainstorming is *nominal group technique*. Nominal group technique allows for face-to-face contact among group members and encourages direct communication. A growing number of studies indicate that techniques, such as nominal group, lead to a greater number of creative ideas (Thota & Zunaira, 2011). The prominent characteristic of nominal group technique is the output of ideas that are ranked or prioritized.

The steps involved in nominal group technique are (Kerzner, 2013):

1. Convene a panel of subject matter experts and knowledgeable others.
2. Individuals record ideas in writing.
3. Ideas are listed on a flip chart for discussion among the panel.

4. Each group member prioritizes the ideas.
5. Steps 3 and 4 are repeated until the group gains consensus on final rank ordering of the ideas.

In addition to generating a large list of ideas, the nominal group technique encourages participation by all group members. Furthermore, a resulting outcome of the nominal group technique produces a catalog of ideas that are rank-ordered and prioritized. This process has the added benefit of a high level of buy-in and support for the final selected ideas among the group members.

Brainwriting

Closely related to the nominal group technique, *brainwriting* involves recording and sharing written ideas (Mattimore, 2012). Prior to the ideation session, participants will be provided the problem statement and asked to generate a written list of ideas in isolation. The list of ideas may be shared as in the nominal group technique or through a shared brainwriting exercise.

In other instances of brainwriting (Mattimore, 2012), each individual in the group will write his or her idea on a sheet of paper. The paper is then passed to another person who either records an additional new idea or builds upon the idea already listed. After a few minutes, papers are passed again, and new ideas or combinations of ideas are recorded. The process repeats for a few rounds, passing the sheets with collective ideas. At the conclusion of the final round, the paper is passed to the originator (the person who recorded the first idea) who then selects one or two of his or her favorite ideas. These top choices are then shared with the group in a traditional brainstorming or nominal group session.

Brainwriting has the advantage that people are able to share their ideas when they enter the room, rather than waiting for an opportunity to speak as in traditional brainstorming. The technique also offers the advantage that an idea can be fleshed out during the session and allows equal participation by all group members. Finally, traditional, verbal brainstorming tends to favor extroverted individuals while brainwriting may be viewed as a more democratic process disengaged from personality types.

Electronic Brainstorming

Another divergent thinking technique that addresses group collaboration and attempts to address the primary drawbacks of traditional brainstorming is *electronic brainstorming*. Electronic brainstorming (EBS) is a divergent thinking tool that combines the advantages of brainwriting with the group collaboration of traditional brainstorming. Research suggests that EBS is more effective and productive than traditional brainstorming or nominal group techniques (Gallupe & Cooper, 1993).

Simplistically, EBS uses computers to gather ideas from group participants. Ideas can be solicited in real-time or asynchronously. Group members are gathered in a specialized computer facility or may be dispersed in multiple locations with a network connection. Software can be used to assist in the idea collection process in which individuals submit their ideas anonymously. Lists of ideas will be displayed for each participant, including their own and a random list of ideas from other participants. This allows opportunities for group members to build upon other ideas and collaborate as in a traditional brainstorming session; however, EBS eliminates bias toward specific experts or managers who may be participating in the ideation session.

Electronic brainstorming is also capable of handling much larger groups than traditional brainstorming sessions. While traditional brainstorming sessions are most effective with about a dozen participants, EBS can handle fifty or more individuals submitting ideas simultaneously. A drawback of the increased participation, however, is that evaluating and selecting ideas for further concept development becomes a larger task. IBM has successfully utilized EBS with very large groups and offers a public platform to collect ideas (ideajam.net).

Productive *divergent thinking* may involve several different tools prior to or during an idea generation session. In proliferating a high number of creative ideas, teams may use one or more methods of brainstorming, nominal group technique, brainwriting, and/or electronic brainstorming in combination and over a period of time. Divergent thinking is deployed extensively during Stage 2 of the NPD process but may be utilized whenever the NPD team faces a particularly vexing problem requiring group collaboration.

Problem-Based Ideation

Problem based ideation is another idea generation tool used extensively in new product development. It is different than conventional divergent thinking methods in that the problem needing a solution is not identified in advance. Traditional brainstorming methods, including nominal group technique, brainwriting, and EBS, all assume the problem is defined in advance of gathering the group to generate ideas. Problem-based ideation, on the other hand, searches for the problem *prior to* moving into divergent thinking.

> *Problem-based ideation is a technique used during idea/concept generation which is a problem-based approach to finding and solving customer problems.*

Deployed during the idea generation or concept generations stages of the new product development process, problem-based ideation is a technique that uses a problem-based approach to finding and solving customer problems. In comparison to traditional divergent thinking tools, the problem is not pre-determined. Problem-based ideation is an ideal tool to apply when searching for unknown or unmet customer needs in the earliest stages of the NPD process. At its foundation, problem-based ideation assumes that if we can study the problems with a product, then we will be able to come up with solutions for these problems.

The process used in problem-based ideation is comprised of just three steps. First, the innovation team will study the situation to identify problems. This can be accomplished using anthropological or ethnographic observation as described previously in Chapter 5, Market Research. Next, the list of resulting problems is screened for ones that offer opportunities for the firm. Many teams find that a SWOT analysis (strengths, weaknesses, opportunities, and threats - see below) or other categorization technique is helpful to highlight and select problems regarding which active innovation projects should be initiated. Finally, the team will develop concept statements addressing the specific problems for further evaluation. This last step is similar to generating concept statements in Stage 3 of the structured NPD process (see Chapter 4).

One of the challenges that most firms recognize is gathering the problems in the first instance. As indicated, using ethnographic or anthropological market research techniques can help to identify customer problems. Problems can be observed during customer site visits as well as through lead user analysis. Other ways in which problems are collected include tapping into existing marketing and technical staff experience. Consumer products can be introduced to the NPD team for their own use to help discover problems, while role playing can also be useful for teams to better identify customer problems. Furthermore, open innovation sources and customer communications (such social media, complaint hotlines, etc.) can further help to identify customer problems.

For example, many product problems may be documented in the customer service records, sales call reports, and other internal or external product reports. These documents can readily identify circumstances that are ideal for problem-based ideation and product innovation. Additionally, NPD project stakeholders may offer various problems through interviews, focus groups, and observation. Finally, scenario analysis is a technique that can be used to gather different end-user problems by examining various situations in which customers might use the product and how they might use the product. Scenario analysis can also be used to consider a picture of the future and how new products might be used to solve customer problems at that time.

Once the team has gathered potential customer problems, the innovation team must find ways to select and solve given problems through a focused innovation effort. Various methods to solve the problems include group creativity, such as brainstorming, nominal group technique, Delphi method, or affinity diagrams. At this stage of divergent thinking, judgment of ideas should be deferred until a later time when the primary categories or themes for solutions are developed in a convergent thinking session.

SWOT Analysis
SWOT analysis is a commonly used technique during strategy development and problem-based ideation. Strengths, weaknesses, opportunities, and threats are keywords that assist an innovation team in assessing the firm's competitiveness. Strengths and opportunities are exploited when the firm has a technical or marketing advantage over the competition. Weaknesses and threats should be addressed through new products or business model development. Note that strengths and weaknesses focus primarily on the firm's internal capabilities, while opportunities and threats involve external factors, such as competitors, technologies, or market trends.

Scenario Analysis
Scenario analysis is a tool that helps NPD teams envision different future states in order to create alternate strategies and solutions to future opportunities and challenges. Scenarios are speculative stories crafted to paint a picture of the future. These scenarios may be narrative descriptions of generic personas conducting actions under presumed circumstances of researching products, selecting products, and purchasing products.

Using scenario analysis, NPD teams can expand customer problems and gain insights in a variety of ways to solve issues that consumers may face in the future. Scenario analysis will identify how customers might use a product and will identify opportunities to improve features and attributes of existing products. Typically, scenario analysis will be used in conjunction with other divergent thinking techniques to build new product concepts.

Convergent Thinking

Convergent thinking is defined as a technique generally performed in the initial phases of *idea generation* to help funnel the high volume of ideas created through divergent thinking into a small group of ideas or a single idea on which more effort will be focused.

Often two or three strong candidate ideas or concepts will be revealed through the categorization efforts of convergent thinking. Different companies handle these ideas in various fashions. Let's presume that three idea categories are determined to be worthy of further innovation efforts. One option is to pursue small scale experimentation concurrently with all three ideas and later cull the poor concepts. Another option is to conduct further "paper studies" on the ideas to better understand the needs of the market, the customers, and the technology development. Lastly, another alternative may be to choose the "best" idea to move forward and mark the remaining two ideas as "next-up" in case the first idea fails to deliver a successful outcome in the development process.

Firms will handle approaches to generating the final concept differently depending on their acceptable risk profile and innovation strategy. In addition, the firm's competitiveness and existing product portfolio will influence decisions on narrowing the many new product ideas to one or two that will be advanced in the later stages of the NPD process. Convergent thinking provides a framework to narrow the hundreds of ideas generated during divergent thinking or problem-based ideation. A key feature of convergent thinking is to build upon the documented ideas and combine them into actionable innovation concepts.

Guidelines for Convergent Thinking

A primary guideline during a collaborative convergent thinking session is to not negatively criticize the idea generator. The purpose of the convergent thinking session is to capitalize on the positive aspects of the various ideas presented in the divergent thinking session in order to capture novel concepts to move forward in the NPD process. Thus, it is important to always note the positive features of an idea before building on the concept to maintain an open, collaborative environment in the convergent thinking session.

For example, you might say, "A perpetual motion machine would certainly help our customers save time and money; however, our firm does not yet have the technology to develop this type of product. Instead, we could add a battery to the product to extend its shelf life." Such a statement is preferable to one that indicates the idea is unworthy without providing additional information to categorize the many ideas from the brainstorming session. Undue criticism of ideas could hinder idea generation in a future divergent thinking session if people feel their suggestions are not valued by the group.

Another guideline to categorize ideas in the convergent thinking session is to follow a systematic approach. Categories for the various ideas might include different business units of the firm, various existing product families, or opportunities for growing or sustaining the business, and radical technologies. Again, a SWOT analysis can be useful to categorize ideas or themes at this point in the ideation process.

Tools for Convergent Thinking

Affinity diagrams, described in Chapter 6, are an ideal way to categorize (converge) the many ideas resulting from a brainstorming session. Because of the sheer number of ideas that are identified during a divergent thinking session, there is often a degree of overlap in the listed new product concepts. The affinity diagram method allows a team to consider high-level themes that are common among the ideas, and then prioritize these for further evaluation. An NPD team can expect to identify as many as a dozen themes from the output of a typical brainstorming session yielding 200 to 300 ideas.

Democratic voting on the raw ideas or the categories of ideas is another method to categorize, prioritize, and select concepts for further development work. Voting can be accomplished by a show of hands, secret ballot, or multiple selection. In the multiple selection method, each individual is assigned a proxy of three or four votes to assign to his or her top new product ideas. The proxy may be a colored sticker or some other visual indicator. Ideas with the highest concentration of votes are then selected for further development.

Like any voting process, there are advantages and disadvantages for open voting system as compared to a secret ballot. As discussed in Chapter 6, anonymity in idea selection may quickly lead to consensus without political influence. However, open voting allows the NPD team to discuss the merits and drawbacks of each theme to a greater extent. Voting selection methods will depend upon the culture of the firm and the data available to quickly evaluate the probability of success of each category of ideas.

Convergent thinking is not meant to be complicated. Idea selection should emphasize the positive aspects of the ideas or categories of ideas from a customer's perspective as well as the fundamental considerations for innovation: the market, technology, and product category. Teams will generally move quickly through the convergent thinking process to begin rapid trial and experimentation to verify the concepts selected for further development. Additional engineering and design tools will be deployed during the next stage of the NPD process, building on idea generation tools and techniques.

Quality Function Deployment (QFD)

Quality function deployment, QFD, was briefly introduced in earlier chapters. QFD is a voice of customer technique used to link the customer needs and wants to an engineering design specification. A structured method, QFD uses matrix analysis to link what the market requires to how it will be achieved within the NPD effort. Primarily used during Stage 3 of the NPD process, QFD will engage a cross-functional team to frame the product concept in terms of product features and specifications that meet consumer needs. Key advantages to using QFD include the multi-functional viewpoint for the development effort and the mechanism to minimize the omission of design characteristics most desired by the target market.

Benefits of QFD

Some key features of QFD are:

- Understanding customer needs from the customer's perspective,

- Learning what value means to the customer,
- Deciding what features to include with a new product or service,
- Determining a level of performance,
- Helping the team stay focused,
- Allowing easy management and peer review of design activities,
- Presenting customer and technical information graphically, and
- Linking customer needs with design and development work.

While traditional quality management tends to focus on reducing negative variables (e.g. defects, repairs, rework, and scrap), QFD identifies the customer requirements to maximize the positive quality that creates value. The principle objective of a QFD is to enable the new product development team to organize and analyze relevant product and service information. Benefits of QFD lead to reduced engineering changes during the product design and development phase. Additionally, QFD can help to reduce production issues when the product is manufactured, ultimately improving customer satisfaction.

Conducting a QFD

There are five steps in conducting a quality function deployment:

1. Determine the voice of the customer,
2. Survey customer needs,
3. Develop the QFD matrix rows with product needs information,
4. Design the QFD matrix columns with technical information, and
5. Analyze the matrix for actionable product development requirements.

An example QFD matrix is shown below in Figure 36. Any number of market research techniques can be used to gather the voice of customer, as described in Chapter 5. Customer information is translated into product and service needs as necessary in order to construct the horizontal rows of the matrix. For example, a consumer may say, "I can never find a parking place." This statement translates into a customer need of "convenient parking close to the entrance."

Conjoint Analysis

Once the customer information and needs are determined, customers may be surveyed in order to rank and prioritize their identified needs. Again, any number of market research techniques can be useful in helping customers prioritize a list of needs and can be utilized for QFD. For example, *conjoint analysis* is a market research technique that allows a company to gain insights regarding customer viewpoints of product features and attributes. The tool allows the NPD team to collect user trade-offs among a set of variables, estimate the value system of buyers, and make predictions of customer choices.

In *conjoint analysis*, customers are presented with two attributes from the many possible combinations of new product features. The end-user selects the one feature from the pair that is most important to him or her. After a series of rounds of ranking just two needs, the researcher is able to construct a prioritized list from the entire list of needs that were previously identified.

Repeating the exercise with multiple customers will lead to a consensus list of ranked customer needs. Software tools are available to assist in the data collection step of the QFD analysis.

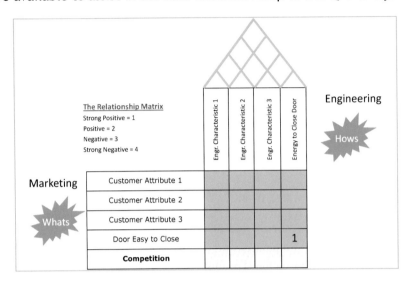

Figure 36 - Example QFD

Other ranking activities to prioritize customer needs for the rows in a QFD analysis may assign a potential customer a number of points. The customer is then asked to allocate the points among the needs that s/he views as the most important in the new product. For instance, in a new product development study for a new drink cup, a customer may allocate 50 of 100 points to "doesn't leak," 35 points to "easy to hold," 10 points to "interchangeable lids," and just 5 points to "fits in cooler." Analyzing the prioritization of a large number of customers will result in a set of features necessary for the new product design.

Essentially, the voice of customer is tracked with the prioritized product attributes shown in the rows of the QFD matrix. Thus, the rows of the QFD matrix are populated with the desired customer attributes. Figure 36 illustrates a sample QFD matrix with the fourth element of a vehicle design being "door easy to close".

Technical Requirements

Next, the vertical portion of the QFD matrix is populated. The NPD team must determine how they can meet the customer needs through technical solutions. As shown in Figure 36, the marketing "whats" are translated into engineering design "hows". Technical requirements must be measurable and specific. In order for an automotive engineer to design the car door, s/he will need to design a spring with a specific tension. A column is added to the QFD matrix indicating "energy required to close door."

Finally, the relationship between the marketing needs (rows) and the technical specifications (columns) is evaluated by the NPD team. In the example shown above, there is a strong positive correlation between the car door being easy to close and the required energy to close the door. This example of QFD also uses a number system (the relationship matrix) to indicate strongly positive, positive, negative, or strongly negative correlations. Thus, the cell intersecting the customer need (door easy to close) and the technical specification (energy to close the door) is populated with a "1". Other forms of QFD may use symbols or letters to indicate the relationships between customer needs and technical product requirements.

Once the group has evaluated each prioritized customer need and the corresponding technical requirements, the matrix is analyzed to determine the most important features for the product development effort. Note that not every cell in the matrix will be populated, so a visual assessment is often adequate for the NPD team to agree on priorities of the feature set design and development needed to meet the most pressing customer needs.

Additional Considerations for QFD

The QFD matrix is sometimes referred to as the *House of Quality* (Hauser & Clausing, 1988). Linking the customer needs to engineering specifications in the matrix will reveal the most important features for the development team. In addition to surveying customers regarding needs and attributes, the firm may ask customers to rank their existing products against competitors. Competitor information may be added by constructing additional rows at the bottom of the table (i.e. a basement in the house of quality).

Furthermore, co-dependent technical specifications will be indicated in the "roof" of the house of quality to further refine the required engineering design for the new product. Analysis of the technical requirements allows the team to determine the importance of these variables and informs the NPD process. Additional information may be added to the matrix (as additional rows or columns) to indicate the state of competition from a technical standpoint as well as to document any specific regulatory requirements.

How to Use QFD in New Product Development

Originally developed for the automotive industry and strongly linked to lean manufacturing and Six Sigma quality management, quality function deployment is a structured method using matrix analysis to link what the market requires to how it will be accomplished in the product development effort. In essence, the NPD team is asking what do the customers want and how will we give it to them? The QFD method is most valuable during the stages of development when the cross-functional team agrees on how customer needs translate into product specifications and features that will address those specific needs.

Many teams find it challenging to compose a full house of quality, including the competitive analysis, regulatory requirements, and basic customer needs data. While most firms do not use a formal QFD structure, the technique is widely utilized to limit the chance of omitting important design characteristics or interactions among the various design features and attributes of the new product. Many companies, in practice, will use a simple checklist that documents the most important features required in the product ranked by customer inputs and then ensure that those design elements are incorporated into the final product.

Because QFD provides detailed matching of the marketing "whats" with the engineering and design "hows," it is a crucial part of promoting cross-functional communication within the NPD team. Marketing and engineering team member relationships often encounter a natural degree of friction because the jargon used in the two fields is significantly different. QFD offers an opportunity for the marketing and engineering team members to work collaboratively in designing a product that meets the customer needs based upon quality design specifications.

Engineering Design and Analysis Tools

Like market research, engineering tools are used throughout the new product development process and often require specially trained subject matter experts. Product design engineers may encompass mechanical, chemical, biological, and many other specialty fields of study. During the prototype design and manufacturing phases of the NPD process, electrical, industrial, and/or civil engineers may conduct necessary work to ensure that production will meet demand for the new product.

Engineering design tools can be as simple as a pencil and calculator, or as sophisticated as a time-of-flight secondary ion mass spectrometer. Every project should identify the research and engineering staff required for the NPD project during the early stages. The engineering function is crucial for the success of a cross-functional development team, and will provide significant input to the technical concept for the new product during brainstorming and development stages.

Moreover, many candidates for NPDP certification have an engineering background and are highly qualified within a specific field of expertise. Engineering is a complex field of study on its own and technical experts serve the NPD teams to help identify the best solutions for customer problems. However, since other candidates for the NPDP certification have specialized in marketing, business, or project management, the NPDP certification exam includes only a high-level overview of engineering tools. Many of these tools are advancing at a rapid pace, such that foundational engineering concepts, rather than cutting edge tools, are presented on the NPDP certification exam.

Engineering design tools are focused in two arenas: design and analysis.

Table 6 - Engineering Tools Commonly Used in NPD	
Design Tools	**Analysis Tools**
Computer-Aided Design (CAD)	Computer-Aided Engineering (CAE)
Concurrent Engineering (CE)	Simulation
Design for Excellence (DFX)	Rapid Prototyping
Failure Mode and Effects Analysis (FMEA)	

Engineering Design Tools

While engineers use many different tools, models, and practices to design new products, a few of these may be featured on the NPDP certification exam.

Computer-Aided Design

CAD, or *computer aided design,* is one engineering tool that has experienced significant advancement in recent years due to increased computing capabilities. CAD and CAM (computer-aided manufacturing) software represent technologies that allow designers and engineers to use computers to complete design work. For the purposes of the NPDP exam, please keep in mind that CAD is assumed to be a static design tool.

Computer-aided manufacturing (CAM) has also seen widespread growth and adoption in recent years with the evolution of 3D printing. The technique of 3D printing not only allows rapid prototypes to be developed for concept tests, it can assist engineers in formalizing designs of new products. In addition, many manufacturing processes are fully automated and make extensive use of robotics. Taken together, 3D printing and robotics are enabling radical new uses and applications for innovation design.

Concurrent Engineering

Concurrent engineering (CE) was already introduced in Chapter 6 (Teams and Organization). You'll recall that concurrent engineering brings together the manufacturing and operations staff at the front end of the product development process to ensure that the new product design envisioned by the engineers can be manufactured in the plant. A more formal definition of concurrent engineering is when product design and manufacturing process development occurs concurrently or simultaneously instead of in series.

Benefits of concurrent engineering include gathering the inputs of the cross-functional team early in the process, ensuring that product concepts can be manufactured as envisioned, and improving cost and schedule estimates for development and commercialization. Participation from the operations and manufacturing departments can yield valuable information regarding the feasibility of producing the new product as well as providing data regarding the capability of existing factory equipment.

DFX Tools

Design for excellence incorporates a vast number of engineering tools. Abbreviated as DFX, these tools are widely used by manufacturing organizations to clarify customer service and technical support needs in the new product development effort. Designing for excellence includes methods to improve design performance by proactively taking into account the manufacturing, assembly, and servicing capabilities during the initial design process. As an example, consider *design for service excellence* where the product may be manufactured with basic components that allows upgrades or repair by simply plugging in a new part.

Occasionally, design for excellence may be indicated by alternate acronyms, describing the specific feature of the process. For instance, DFS may mean design for service, while DFM represents design for manufacture. In any case, design for excellence involves a cross-functional team to examine the product concept early in the NPD process in order to focus on the engineering design. DFX encompasses a systematic consideration of all life cycle issues for the product (manufacturability, reliability, and maintainability) in the design and development of the new product.

Failure Mode and Effects Analysis

Failure mode and effects analysis (FMEA) is a technique deployed during the product development process to uncover ways in which a product may fail (cause) and then to evaluate the outcomes (effects) of each type of failure. FMEA is an engineering design tool that helps the NPD team to identify risks and quality issues early in the development of the new product.

As a result of the analysis of potential failure modes, design characteristics of the new product can be altered to eliminate or reduce the risk of each failure mode so that the customer will ultimately be satisfied with the reliability and functionality of the product over its lifetime. In the design and development stages, hardware, functions, and interfaces are all examined for potential failure risks. Information and data gathered from the analysis is then incorporated into the product design to ensure a better product for the end-user.

Engineering Analysis Tools

Most of the engineering design tools are used to help engineers plan and design functionality of the new product. Engineering analysis tools, on the other hand, help engineers and NPD team members to understand if the product will work as designed.

Computer-Aided Engineering

Computer-aided engineering (CAE) is closely related to computer-aided design (CAD). CAE is defined as a technology that allows engineers to use computers for analysis work. For example, some computer-aided engineering software programs will help engineers understand finite element stress analysis, thermal analyses, and circuit timing. The primary difference between computer-aided engineering (CAE) and CAD is that computer-aided analysis involves a dynamic simulation, and as discussed above, CAD is considered a static engineering design tool.

In the example image shown in Figure 37, output from the CAD program is shown in the upper half of the image while a CAE image is illustrated in the lower half. Note that the CAD image indicates the highlighted gear may be studied for spacing and alignment with the other gears, and whether the number of teeth on the gear is appropriate. The CAD image is static and examines *physical* engineering characteristics of the new product design.

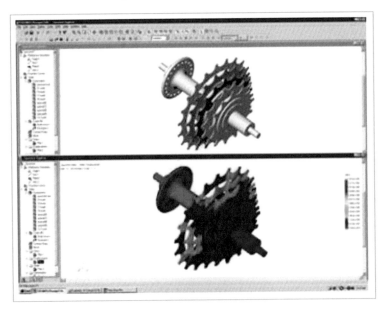

Figure 37 - Comparison of CAD and CAE

A snapshot from a simulation is shown in the lower half of Figure 37. Here, a computer aided engineering analysis is illustrated in which the computer was used to model compression stress while the gear is in motion. The color codes indicate compression stress on the axle when the particular gear is selected. CAE is normally a dynamic model used to assist engineers in designing the functionality of a new product.

Please keep in mind that these definitions and descriptions of computer tools used in engineering design and analysis are significantly simplified. Engineering design is rapidly advancing due to the expansive growth in computational power; however, candidates for NPDP certification should understand that engineering tools are divided into categories of design and analysis. Both CAD and CAE may utilize two-dimensional (2D) and three-dimensional (3D) modelling. For the NPDP certification exam, you will want to be familiar with simplified examples of each engineering tool such as those presented herein.

Simulation

Simulation is often considered a specialized engineering tool by itself. Simulation for new product development is defined as using computers to simulate design performance before building expensive prototypes for manual testing. For example, modern 3D CAD programs allow engineers and operators to simulate "walking through" a plant to ensure that equipment clearances are adequate and that future maintenance work can be performed effectively. Be careful, however, not to confuse simulation utilizing CAD software with CAD itself as an engineering design tool.

Other examples of simulation include electrical loading of transformers when new motors are added to a facility, layout of robots in a lean manufacturing plant, and virtual reality testing of dashboard designs for airplane cockpits. Simulation allows engineers, designers, and even potential customers to inexpensively examine the functionality of a new product. With computer modelling and simulation, product design can be tested and improved before more costly manufacturing steps proceeds in later phases of the project.

Rapid Prototyping

Rapid prototyping is yet another engineering analysis tool. In particular, rapid prototyping encompasses a variety of processes that avoid tooling time to produce a prototype of a product or its components such that the prototype can be produced within days or weeks instead of months or years. Often the prototype is non-functioning but it can be used to quickly test whether the product is feasible or not and whether customers are interested in a specific design.

The recent advent of 3D printing is greatly assisting the ability of firms to rapidly prototype products that will later be manufactured from metal, wood, or other dense materials. For example, producing a 3D printed model of a new coffee cup is far less expensive than creating a mold for a ceramic cup. In addition, 3D printing allows very rapid simulation of new product concepts, whereas traditional prototypes may require additional investment in time and money to build.

In summary, engineers will use a variety of tools and analyses to assist in the new product development process. Technical personnel should be involved throughout the NPD project in order to aid in ideation and brainstorming as well as to construct a new product with the desired functionality and quality to satisfy customer needs.

Project Management Tools

Another set of tools that supplement new product development overlap with those of project management. Many of the project management tools are deployed during Stage 4 of the NPD process; however, an NPD program may involve multiple projects in each stage of work in order to accomplish the overall, multi-functional objectives required of an innovation.

The definition of a project includes a specific start and stop date for the work as well as achieving specific goals with a temporary team (Project Management Institute, 2013). Therefore, there may be many different projects executed within the framework of one new product development program. For example, in Stage 3, several new product concepts may be tested as individual projects; while in Stage 5, different marketing collateral may be designed via separate projects. Taken together, these individual projects support the overall goal of developing and commercializing the new product.

Following the framework of the Project Management Institute, steps in a project include the following (2013):

1. Initiating,

2. Planning,

3. Executing,

4. Monitoring and Controlling, and

5. Closing.

You will note that the steps in project management are somewhat similar to the stages defined for the structured NPD process; however, the primary difference is that the project management steps are iterative and may be implemented multiple times within a single NPD program. For example, testing the new product concept with potential customers may constitute a stand-alone project in which the testing will be initiated, planned, executed, monitored for success, and closed. A separate project for the same new product may include designing a new packaging facility for the product, which again will require initiation, planning, execution, monitoring and control, and closing of the stand-alone project.

One of the most common challenges with any project is managing the *triple constraint*. The triple constraint consists of balancing the project scope, schedule and budget as shown in Figure 38.

Illustrated as an equilateral triangle, if one of the core elements of a project is changed, the project becomes unbalanced. Normally, project plans will outline an appropriate schedule and budget to accomplish the scope of work. When the scope of work is enlarged, both the schedule and budget must be adjusted in order to accommodate additional product requirements. Likewise, if the budget is cut, the project can only provide a reduced scope of work. If the schedule is tightened, the budget and scope will adjust to the new timeframe with a likely increase in costs and a reduction in scope.

Figure 38 - Project Management Triple Constraint

The triple constraint indicates that the scope, schedule, and budget of a well-planned project are highly intertwined and changes in one characteristic of the project plan will impact the other elements. A structured NPD process is utilized to help define the scope of work with clarity; however, changes in scope, schedule, and budget may be anticipated for large or complex innovation projects.

Scope of Work

As discussed in detail in Chapter 1, the innovation strategy is perhaps the most important variable in defining a successful innovation program. Similarly, the scope of work parallels the strategy in the realm of project management tools. Just as it is critical to get the firm's strategy right to be successful in the long run, it is crucial to get the scope right for a project. There are many techniques for gathering customer requirements and building a scope of work for the project. A common tool to visualize and capture all of the necessary tasks to complete the project is the *work breakdown structure* (WBS) for the project.

The WBS is a decomposition of the overall scope of the project into the smallest tasks that can be completed for the project. A common rule of thumb is to break down the work into tasks that can be completed by one person or during one work shift. Regardless of the breakdown used, each item comprising the scope of work must be included in the WBS as it is used in later project management processes to build the project plan and execute the work.

As an example, let's consider a project in which a company is designing a solar power system for residential installation – such as solar panels on the roof of a house that provides power to the homeowner and will also send power back to the grid when there is excess production capacity. A solar power system, then, can be broken down into categories such as the photovoltaic cells that are installed on the roof of the house, the storage or battery system, and a mounting system so that the solar panels can be physically attached to the roof of the home. The WBS for this project is shown below in Figure 39.

Note that each of the primary tasks can be further broken down into sub-tasks. For example, the storage system would need to include a battery that is charged when the sun is shining and then provides power at night (discharging the battery) or when the sun is not shining. The project would also need a sub-system called a limit circuit to control whether the solar panels are providing power to the home, using the batteries for power, or if the solar panels are generating excess power that is sold back to the grid.

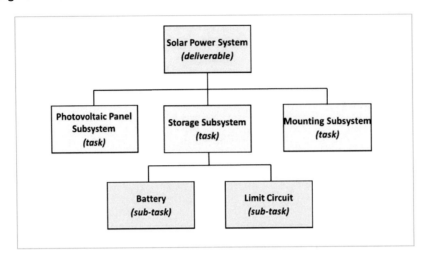

Figure 39 - Sample Work Breakdown Structure (WBS)

Note that each of the tasks and sub-tasks need to be completed so that the overall project (solar power system) can be finished. Each sub-task in Figure 39 also represents the smallest set of activities and work that can be done to complete all of the items in the scope of work.

Frequently, the WBS is then utilized to construct a project timeline, or schedule, since the duration of each activity (task or sub-task) can be estimated with a high degree of accuracy. For instance, we can easily estimate how long it will take to design, construct, and install the batteries and the limit circuit for the solar power system. It is also possible to estimate the project budget from the WBS, as a project team can readily estimate the costs for each sub-task and then sum these to generate a comprehensive project budget.

Project and product managers will often use Microsoft Project™ or other software tools to input and track the triple constraint items. The WBS allows the project leader to track the scope, schedule, and budget of the project throughout the execution and monitoring and controlling phases. Project management software is often integrated with portfolio management tools to ensure successful implementation of new product development efforts.

Schedule

Project schedules are often illustrated visually using a bar chart or Gantt chart. Named for Henry Gantt, an industrial engineer first utilizing this procedure in the twentieth century, this bar chart displays activities or tasks plotted against time on the x-axis. The length of the bar represents the amount of effort required to move from one point to another in the project. Each bar typically represents a task or sub-task from the WBS.

Gantt charts may also include project milestones, such as initiating and completing the project, as activities with zero length of time. Milestones are shown as diamonds on a typical bar chart as shown in Figure 40, illustrating the sample schedule for the solar panel project. The amount of time elapsed between the start of the project (first milestone) and the end of the project (final milestone) is the length of time required to complete the entire project. For example, the solar power system project is expected to take 25 workdays to complete, starting on 1 May and finishing on 4 June.

In any project, the initiation of some work activities are dependent upon the completion of other activities. For instance, Task #6 (Current Transmission) cannot be started until Task #5 (Voltage Design) has been completed. These activities are identified as *critical path* items in which the critical path is defined as the longest path through a project determining the shortest possible project duration. Critical path items are highlighted in red in Figure 40.

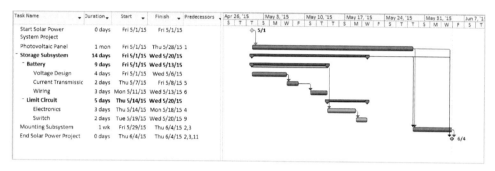

Figure 40 - Sample Project Schedule

In new product development, task dependencies will often reflect the necessity of completing market research before finalizing product designs and completing prototype testing prior to manufacturing the new product. Task or sub-task dependencies may be mandatory, as dictated by the laws of physics or by regulation. Other dependencies may be discretionary, reflecting specific company practices or preferences in new product development.

Note that some tasks in Figure 40 are *not* considered on the critical path. For example, Task #10 (Switch) includes *slack time*. Slack time, sometimes called *float*, indicates that there is leeway in the scheduling of the task that will not impact the overall project completion date. Thus, Task #10 has six days of slack, meaning that the activity can start as late as 27 May without causing any delay to the project. On the other hand, if a critical path task, such as Task #5 (Voltage Design) is delayed, the entire project schedule will slip, forcing the completion date to be later than planned.

Schedule Compression

Often, the new product launch date is fixed due to imposed dates and external commitments of the company or the product development team. If the project falls behind schedule due to the late start or delayed completion of a critical path activity, the entire project's schedule is impacted. *Schedule compression* encompasses methods to shorten the duration of the project schedule without significant reductions in the scope of work. However, recalling the trade-offs of the triple constraint (Figure 38), schedule compression will normally add some cost to the new product development project in order to speed up the work to meet accelerated schedule deadlines.

Schedule compression techniques include *fast tracking* and *crashing*. Both of these methods involve some risk to completing the scope of work as planned. Fast tracking is a schedule compression model in which tasks are conducted in parallel that were originally planned to be conducted in sequence.

For example, detailed product design drawings should be issued prior to completing product prototype testing. If the product concept is well-defined, there may be little risk in conducing prototype tests while design drawings are still being finalized. However, there is some uncertainty to the successful completion of the example project if a major change is identified during prototype testing that requires rework of the design drawings.

Crashing, the second most common method of schedule compression, involves adding additional resources to the project in an attempt to shorten the duration of the overall project schedule. Examples of crashing include approving overtime, hiring additional team members, and/or paying additional fees to expedite delivery of critical path items. A primary risk in deploying crashing as a schedule compression technique involves increased cost for the additional resources while the method may not produce a viable project alternative.

Budget

Budget, or cost, is the final element of the triple constraint in project management. An accurate and complete budget will allow the project to deliver the scope of work on time. There are several ways to prepare a cost estimate, or budget, for a project, including:

- Bottom-up,
- Parametric models.
- Historical data, and
- Company-specific methods.

Bottom-Up Budgeting

First, the WBS elements can be used to build a budget as described previously. Because much of the cost in new product development is related to labor performed by knowledge workers, the WBS can be used to provide a first pass, rough estimate of the budget.

Individuals responsible for the tasks and sub-tasks can estimate the workforce hours required to complete activities assigned to them. Additionally, responsible parties can also estimate any non-labor expenses necessary to complete tasks, such as capital equipment purchases, travel, and testing. An overall project budget is then determined by summing all of the cost elements from the WBS. Furthermore, since cost estimates start with the lowest level in the WBS (work packages), the technique is called *"bottom-up" budgeting*.

Parametric Models

Next, *parametric models* are often used for estimating the cost of a new product development project. These models assume the cost of one unit and then multiply that cost by the number of units in order to determine the overall budget for the project. Suppose, for example, that the project was constructing a new housing division. It is known that the cost of one house is $100 per square foot. Thus, a 2,000-square foot house will cost $200,000 and a 3,500-square foot house will cost $350,000.

Parametric models are most accurate when the scaling variable has a linear relationship with the overall project. Labor hours is one such variable since the overall project cost will scale linearly with the number of workforce hours conducted to develop the new product. Other parameters that can be used to estimate parametric budgets for new product development projects may include expected factory throughput (e.g. 100 units per hour) or number of components (e.g. 50 chips per circuit board).

Historical Data

Estimating the budget for a new product development project may take advantage of multiple forecasting techniques. *Historical data* is often used in conjunction with parametric models, for instance, to provide an accurate basis for the "per unit" cost. Data collected from complete NPD projects during the post-launch reviews is also used to estimate the cost of future innovation efforts.

Many firms will find that the majority of innovation projects fall within a few classes or categorizations, such as derivative, enhancement, incremental improvement, and/or support projects. Because the type of work performed for these NPD efforts will often be similar in nature, the historical data can provide a budgetary estimate with a significant degree of accuracy.

Recall from Chapter 4 that the post-launch review will capture not only product specific data, but also project-oriented information that is used for continuous improvement of the structured NPD process. Data, such as the duration of each stage of work and the number of required staff to complete the phase, can be extrapolated to estimate the cost of a future innovation program with similar characteristics. The NPD process manager should take an active role in collecting and disseminating this data to build consistency among budget forecasts for future NPD programs. An example of historical project cost data is illustrated in Table 7 below.

Table 7 - Historical Project Cost Data					
Company: ABC					
Product Type: Derivative					
Historical Database: 15 completed projects					
Additional Information: Last completed project in XYZ division, 31 Dec 2014					
Stage	Probability of Completion	Average Workforce Hours	Average Cost per Workforce Hour	Estimated Cost	Probability Adjusted Cost
1	25%	80	$100	$8,000	$2,000
2	40%	240	$100	$24,000	$9,600
3	50%	240	$100	$24,000	$12,000
4	60%	5,200	$150	$780,000	$468,000
5	80%	600	$110	$66,000	$52,800
Totals	N/A	6,360	N/A	$902,000	$544,400

In this example, the firm has compiled information from 15 completed projects and determined the average workforce necessary to finish each stage. They have also calculated the average cost of stage deliverables for each stage of work, including labor, equipment, travel, testing, and other expenses. Thus, an average cost of conducting a derivative product development project will be approximately $902,000 at this sample company.

Additionally, Table 7 shows the probability of an NPD idea moving from one stage to the next. This data can be applied to the expected stage cost to generate a "probability adjusted cost" for the project by stage. Using the historical data for similar projects, senior management and NPD team leaders will be able to build a project budget based on factual evidence tailored to their own organizational processes and experiences.

Company Specific Methods

There are many other alternate methods to estimate the cost of an NPD project. Firms that utilize a project management office (PMO), will have specific procedures and guidance to calculate the budget for a new product development project. Often, PMO staff will provide governance, coaching, and mentoring to NPD teams to ensure that project budgets are prepared according to consistent standards and baselines. In other cases, the finance or treasurer's department may be involved as cross-functional team members or affiliates to assist with preparing the project budget for an NPD program.

Project budgets will account for estimated costs including the workforce labor costs and capital expenses. Other components of a cost estimate may be less apparent and involve purchases, office supplies, and administrative staff. Travel expenses, especially for dispersed NPD teams, should be included in the overall project budget as well.

For longer term projects, the budget may need to include taxes, inflation, and predicted currency exchange rate impacts. These items are generally handled by the team liaison in the finance or treasurer's department; however, NPD project leaders will generally be held responsible for meeting a project budget regardless of the degree of detail included in the forecast.

Risk Management

Like project management, engineering, and marketing, *risk management* is a career field unto itself. For NPD, risk and uncertainty are inherent in developing new technologies, new markets, and new product categories. Tools described elsewhere in this book include best practice techniques to reduce the risk of failure when a new product or service is commercialized. In particular, the structured NPD process (Chapter 4) helps to reduce risk by gradually scaling the size of the effort and the financial commitment to a specific project as more information about the potential new product idea is gathered. Moreover, the portfolio management (Chapter 3) process helps to reduce innovation risk by selecting active projects which offer the greatest overall value to the firm.

Risk management is the process of identifying, measuring, and mitigating the business risk in a product development project.

Risk management is defined as a process to identify, measure, and mitigate business uncertainties in the NPD project. Project uncertainties may result in either a negative or a positive outcome for the product (Project Management Institute, 2013); however, as discussed herein, risks are presumed to negatively influence the success of an innovation effort. Risk may also be categorized as explicit or implicit, and finite or persistent (Walker, 2013).

NPD teams will need to use risk management tools to properly identify project uncertainties. More importantly, assumptions about the markets, technologies, and product categories are essential for the NPD team to fully understand so that the execution of the innovation project is smooth and efficient. Senior management, along with the NPD project leader, will also need to clarify the business assumptions and external risks that could influence the successful commercial launch of a new product or service. While many NPD project risks are of a technical nature, business risks may include unanticipated competition, inadequate project funding, and restrictive government regulation, for instance.

Project management tools include processes and procedures to evaluate risks and uncertainties from both a qualitative *and* quantitative basis (Project Management Institute, 2013). Many qualitative uncertainties in new product development are addressed through the structured NPD process and via portfolio management reviews linking the innovation effort to the comprehensive business and innovation strategies. Risk tolerance relates to the acceptance of uncertainty by the senior management team and is reflected in the degree of innovation (radical vs. incremental improvement) sought through the new product development strategies (see Chapter 1).

The Risk Management Process

Independent, specific risks to a new product development effort should be quantified to the greatest degree possible. As indicated, evaluation of individual risk responses will rely upon the risk tolerance of senior management and of the NPD team which is reflected in the firm's innovation strategy. For example, a prospector strategy may imply a firm is *risk-seeking*, demonstrating increased satisfaction when higher levels of project payoff are at stake. A defender strategy may arise from a firm that is *risk-averse* and gains less satisfaction with higher investment in new product projects. Finally, a balanced, or *risk-neutral*, approach may be reflected by an analyzer strategy in which risk of new product development is offset by attention to stable operations serving existing markets.

Once a set of project risks and assumptions have been identified by an experienced cross-functional team, the NPD team will plan mitigation and contingency steps should the future risk event occur. These mitigation steps include how the project team will respond to the uncertainty by changing elements of the technology, project scope, schedule, or budget in order to counteract the expected negative outcome of the risk event.

Finally, risk reports should be completed to document the assumptions, both qualitative and quantitative, and to list the trigger events, mitigation plans, and responsible party for monitoring the uncertainty throughout the project execution. An issues log or risk register may be used to track uncertainties throughout the NPD project life cycle.

Quantifying Risk

NPD project leaders can chart the probability and impact of uncertainties on a *probability impact matrix*. As shown in Figure 41, the x-axis shows the probability, or likelihood, that a particular risk event will occur. The y-axis plots the impact of the event should it occur. Figure 41 shows axis labels of high, medium, and low; however, some firms will use standard numerical systems instead of the general consequences of NPD risk. In these situations, the probability of the risk event occurring will range from zero (0) to one-hundred (100%) percent, while the impact may range from one-in-a-million (1:1,000,000) to one-in-ten (1:10), for example.

Many firms will use a risk probability impact matrix to quantify individual risks and to determine which uncertainties will require further assessment for mitigation and contingency planning. The shaded areas in Figure 41 guide the team to the degree of response necessary for each risk. Risks in the upper right hand corner (shaded red) are of relatively high probability with correspondingly high impact. Project teams will introduce risk mitigation plans to completely eliminate these uncertainties due to the high potential and severe negative impact to the project. For example, technical aspects of the new product may be entirely redesigned to avoid the occurrence of Risk A or Risk D.

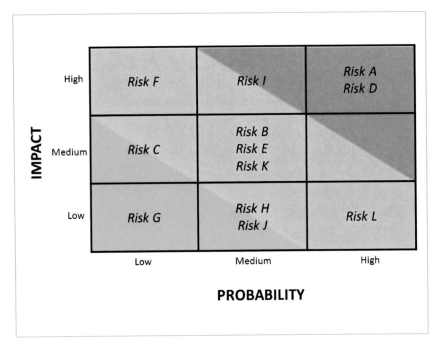

Figure 41 - Sample Risk Probability/Impact Matrix

At the other end of the spectrum, uncertainties plotted in the lower left hand corner, shaded green in Figure 41, may fall below a response threshold for the firm. These risks are not likely to occur (low probability) and will have little impact on the success of the new product development effort. Considered of low consequence, the NPD team may simply accept that the uncertainty exists and document the assumptions leading to the identification of the risk. A passive approach for some risks to an NPD project is necessary since the project team has limited resources to develop specific mitigation plans for every potential issue or uncertainty in the project.

Note that Risk G in Figure 41 is a risk event for which the consequences of the event are accepted. For example, a product may be planned to be completed for a commercial launch at a trade show in September. A risk to the project is that the schedule is delayed. The NPD team may choose to accept the schedule risk because there is another trade show in October reaching a similar audience. Uncertainties in the lower left hand corner can be addressed according to the specific nature of the innovation work, industry standards, and corporate policy.

Project risks requiring the most time and effort of the NPD team are those that fall within the midsection of Figure 41 (shaded orange). These uncertainties range from a low probability but high impact, to a high probability with low impact. Due to the wide range of potential outcomes, risk management responses may vary substantially among these mid-range risks.

For example, risks with low probability but high impact, such as Risk F in Figure 41, may require developing a contingency plan to mitigate the impacts of the risk should it occur. A *contingency plan* outlines a set of predetermined actions and steps to take if the identified risk occurs. An example of a contingency plan, as shown in Figure 42, is to add time to the project schedule to account for unknown quality variables in the manufacturing process. In this case, the schedule delay (contingency plan) will only be implemented if the specific trigger event for the risk is observed, such as greater than 15% quality defects counted in shipments from the factory.

Other medium-risk events (the orange area in Figure 41) may involve NPD project team personnel. For technology developments that require intimate product knowledge and experience, the NPD project leader may identify the transfer or resignation of key personnel as a medium-level risk (e.g. Risk D is Figure 41). Mitigation of the risk may be considered in general terms during risk assessment for the NPD project; however, a specific mitigation plan would not be developed until the event occurs.

Another example of a medium-level risk may involve the availability of certain parts and equipment necessary to manufacture the new product. This risk may be one of high probability but low impact, for instance, as in Risk L in Figure 41. An outcome of the risk management process will assign responsibility to one NPD team member to monitor the supplier's capability. If the equipment becomes unavailable due to external circumstances, then the team will implement the predetermined contingency plan to acquire equipment and parts from another qualified supplier.

Risk responses will vary widely depending on the risk tolerance of the firm and the objectives of each individual NPD project. Managing risk involves not only the new product development team, but also senior management and appointed risk management personnel at the firm. Cross-functional interactions among NPD team members are crucial in identifying and action on project risks.

Contingency Plans

Contingency plans are designed to offer responses to unexpected outcomes of a project. Normally, one element of the triple constraint – scope of work, schedule, or budget – is seriously impacted by the occurrence of a project uncertainty. Risk management plans for a project will identify mitigation steps for risk events, according to the company's standard practices and quantification of the risk as discussed above.

Schedule risk is a common uncertainty for new product development projects. For instance, the solar power system project (illustrated in Figures 39 and 40) requires completion of a task for the mounting subsystem. Assume that three components must be assembled for the mounting subsystem to be completed: mounting brackets, reinforcements, and hardware. Once these three components are assembled, the mounting subsystem will be tested, and then shipped for the final product installation.

Figure 42, below, illustrates several different schedule contingency plans for the mounting subsystem that the NPD team may consider. With the horizontal axis representing time, the schedule baseline plan is shown in Figure 42A in which the components are assembled, tested, and shipped.

If a risk trigger event is observed, the contingency plan is implemented. In this case, the quality of the mounting subsystem is impacted, so one contingency may be to add tasks. The assumption is that the mounting subsystem can be tested and adjusted prior to shipment in order to maintain quality. Figure 42B illustrates this contingency, with the initial test and adjustment activities highlighted. Overall, implementing this contingency plan will add time to the mounting subsystem task; however, the quality of the final part should be improved due to the extra steps from initial testing and adjustment.

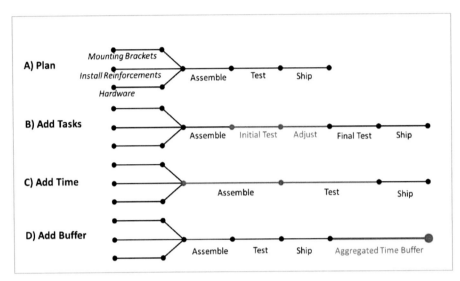

Figure 42 - Sample Schedule Contingency Plans

An alternative path to improving the quality of the mounting subsystem may be to increase the amount of time dedicated to each activity. Thus, with extra time, the components can be assembled and tested with a higher degree of quality. Such a contingency is shown in Figure 42C, in which the assembly and testing activities require twice the time to complete as in the original plan (Figure 42A). Again, the overall time to complete the mounting subsystem task has increased compared to the plan due to the need to mitigate an observed quality risk.

Finally, the contingency plan may allot additional time without assigning it to a specific task. This is shown in Figure 42D as an aggregated time buffer. Critical chain theory for scheduling (Goldratt, 1997) favors a contingency plan in which a buffer activity is considered but not yet assigned to a specific task. While the aggregated time buffer may be consumed by the most risky activity, project sponsors often balk at adding unknown time and expense to a development plan.

Note that in all cases, implementing the contingency plan for the mounting subsystem required additional time compared to the plan. It is not unusual for contingency plans to impact one or more elements of the triple constraint (scope, schedule, or budget). A priority for the NPD team is to document potential risks and closely monitor trigger events throughout the execution of the new product development effort.

Monitoring and Controlling Projects

Monitoring and controlling is a separate and iterative phase in project management (Project Management Institute, 2013). For new product development projects, the degree of monitoring and controlling of projects will vary depending on the firm, its processes, procedures, and policies. *Monitoring* refers to collecting project performance data and comparing the actual performance to the project plan. *Controlling*, on the other hand, denotes evaluating alternative actions based upon the comparison of actual project performance with the product development plan. Monitoring and controlling of an NPD project depends upon a well-considered project plan with an appropriately balanced scope, schedule, and budget in addition to consistent expectations throughout the structured NPD process.

Project Reports

Reports are often automatically generated by software used to monitor the structured NPD process and/or the portfolio management process. Such reports will contain a snapshot of data and information regarding the project's current status.

Depending on the complexity of the innovation work and corporate governance policies, project reports may be issued daily, weekly, monthly, or quarterly. Status reports will include the performance of the project relative to the scope of work specified, the time spent and time remaining on the project relative to the schedule, and the cost of the project relative to the planned budget. These triple constraint elements can be evaluated to determine impact on the commercialization of the new product. For instance, a delay in the project schedule for a critical path item in the development effort will translate to a delay in the market launch of the new product.

Most of the project management software on the market today will automatically generate project status reports that can be e-mailed to the NPD project leader and NPD team members. However, monitoring the performance status of a project is not sufficient to ensure that the NPD effort is completed successfully.

Project Reviews

The primary difference between *project status reports* and *project reviews* is that the latter involves an interactive meeting with all relevant project participants and stakeholders. Normally the data discussed at the meeting will be the same as provided in the project status reports; however, the proper managers are available at the review meeting to assist in decisions regarding the project. Furthermore, gate reviews are specific project reviews and are pre-determined activities required by the structured NPD process to approve and validate NPD project plans. Additional project reviews may be necessary for especially complex development work during Stage 4, for example.

Project reviews will not only assess information regarding the project status and performance relative to the project plan, but will also require decisions and actions to control the triple constraint. Suppose, for instance, that a project has fallen behind schedule with an anticipated launch date that is two months later than planned. During a project review, the project sponsor may authorize implementation of a schedule compression contingency plan that involves assigning additional staff to the NPD project. The NPD project leader will act on this decision by updating the project plan, including the additional budget required for the extra workers. Team members will also be advised of changes in their task assignments.

Because project reviews involve the same information that is included in a project status report, many firms do not differentiate between these monitoring and controlling activities. Risks and trigger events will be discussed on an ongoing basis and evaluated during the project reviews. More importantly, the NPD team must ensure that the project is meeting its performance goals and that the project plan is adjusted appropriately for each gate review in order to continue to advance the innovation effort.

Financial Analysis for NPD

New product development projects are generally designed to increase the profitability of a firm through increased sales or expanded market share. Thus, financial metrics are necessary to evaluate the success of an individual new product as well as to compare innovation ideas with one another.

Some financial tools that are commonly used in NPD have already been discussed in Chapter 3, Portfolio Management. Financial tools, such as net present value (NPV), return on investment (ROI), economic profit, and project payoff are used to evaluate the viability of individual projects. Other tools, such as the ATAR model (described below) are utilized in new product development to estimate future sales.

Net Present Value

Net present value (NPV) is a very common method used in financial analyses, and new product development practitioners should be familiar with formulating this metric. However, specific calculations for NPV are not included on the NPDP certification exam. Most financial experts will recommend an NPV calculation for all projects because it allows dissimilar projects with different time frames to be compared on a similar basis. Project prioritization using NPV was discussed previously in Chapter 3, Portfolio Management.

NPV is calculated by comparing future cash flows, both into the company as revenue and out of the company as expenses, on a discounted basis. Discounting is a typical financial treatment in which all future cash flows are reduced (discounted) to today's present value. Because inflation and interest work to increase future values, a discount factor is applied to future values in order to assess the value today. The core idea is that money today is worth more than money is in the future.

For example, assume that the price of a candy bar today is $1.00 (one dollar). Due to inflation, in three years, it will cost $1.30 to purchase the same candy bar (*future value*). Therefore, the discounted *present value* of a candy bar is $1.00 (consistent with current pricing). If we invest $1.00 in a savings account that pays an interest rate exactly equivalent to the inflation rate, in three years, we will have $1.30. In this case, the three-year *discount factor* is 1.30*.

Net present value takes into account both future revenues and expenses, discounting the *net* future value to today's dollars. Thus, the profitability of projects can be forecast and compared in present day terms. For different types of NPD projects with different life cycles and varying revenue and cost

---

* The formula to calculate present value (PV) is $PV = FV \times DF$, where FV is the future value and DF is the discount factor. In the simplified example for the candy bar, PV=1.00 and FV=1.30; therefore, DF=0.769. Additional details can be found in Appendix A.

streams, NPV can be used to evaluate the profitability of all projects on a consistent basis. (See Appendix A for some simple examples of NPV calculations typical for NPD projects.)

For instance, with limited cash flow, a decision must be made whether to invest in a future purchase of a candy bar or new pencils. Based on market research, a pencil is forecast to cost 30¢ in three years. Because there is a need for five pencils, the total future value is $1.50. Knowing that the discount factor is 0.769, today's investment is $1.15 in order to purchase five pencils in three years.

While the investment for a candy bar is less, the NPV analysis allows trade-offs to be evaluated. For instance, instead of purchasing five pencils, a decision could be made to purchase only four pencils in the future at a cost of $1.20. The present value to invest in four pencils is $0.92, an immediate cost savings of 8¢ today.

Of course, this example comparing candy bars and pencils is quite simplistic, yet the logic and reasoning are consistent with the financial evaluation for NPD projects. Trade-offs must be evaluated between current investment in specific new product development efforts, and future revenues from the products must be compared on a consistent basis. Certainly, the discount factor strongly influences the net present value of an innovation project, since the expected rate of inflation and predicted interest rates are key variables in the NPV calculation.

In addition, sales forecasts, in both volume and revenue terms, impact the NPV calculation. Sales that occur nearer in the future will offset current development costs to a higher degree than sales that occur farther in the future. Likewise, marketing and development costs that are planned in the near term will more strongly offset future revenues than expenses that occurring later in the project life cycle. Market research and additional tools, like the ATAR model described below, can strengthen the sales forecasts. Effective data analysis from post-launch reviews will help to validate product development costs for better estimating as well. Finally, a company's treasury or finance department will often offer specific guidance on recommended discount factors for project NPV calculations.

Note that NPV calculations can be easily automated with financial calculators. Many NPD project leaders will find that building an NPV model within a spreadsheet allows them to quickly and easily evaluate trade-off decisions for the new product development project. As indicated, the key elements in an NPV calculation are the discount factor and the life of the project. Such models also allow for easy adjustment of sales prices and volumes across the life cycle of the product in the marketing plan.

It is important to note that sunk costs (money already invested in the project) are not considered in the NPV calculation. The NPV calculation is used primarily to examine and evaluate go-forward decisions. For example, the past purchase cost of a car is irrelevant to the go-forward choice of repairing it or purchasing a different vehicle. In this case, the car owner would compare the present value of the repaired car to the present value of purchasing a new vehicle.

Net present value is amongst the most common financial metrics used for project evaluation. As indicated in Chapter 3, both NPD teams and senior management must use caution in applying this tool for early stage projects. However, almost every firm and every project will require a financial evaluation, like NPV, in order to demonstrate the product's viability and potential to generate a profit for the company.

Return on Investment

Another common financial metric utilized to evaluate the viability of a new product development project is *return on investment, or ROI*. Return on investment is a standard measure of project profitability, expressed as percentage showing the discounted profits over the life of the NPD project relative to the initial investment (development costs). More information on calculating ROI can be found in Appendix B.

In essence, ROI is an indication of how well assets are deployed at a firm. For the case of new product development, return on investment provides a consistent comparison among projects to evaluate which NPD efforts are most valuable based upon the investment in development resources (time, money, people, and equipment).

As a simple example, if a business invests $100 today and next year it is worth $110, the ROI is 10%. Most NPD projects will consider discounted costs and benefits since most projects extend many years into the future. In practice, all investment expenses are subtracted from the gain (benefits) of the project, then divided by the project investment. Because future revenues and costs are discounted to present values, similar cautions arise as with NPV. Appropriate discount factors and time periods for the ROI calculation must be applied consistently for comparison among NPD projects.

Often firms will use the return on investment as a hurdle rate in screening ideas or early stage projects. The *hurdle rate*, or required minimum rate of return, is a minimum acceptable ROI specified by the company for which a new product project must exceed in order to be considered as an active project. Firms will set the hurdle rate based on the rate of return (ROI) expected to be received elsewhere for an investment of comparable risk.

Economic Profit

Economic profit, also known as economic value added (EVA™), is an additional financial measure that simultaneously accounts for the value that a project adds to the organization and the opportunity cost of selecting one project over another. Thus, economic profit represents the value added by the project *above* the cost of money, where the money could have been spent on an alternate investment.

Similar to the interest rate (discount factor) used in NPV calculations, economic profit considers the opportunity cost of invested capital as a risk associated with the investment. However, unlike ROI which is a percentage measure of project returns, economic profit is a dollar metric, reflecting profitability and the size of the business. Sales growth attributed to the introduction of a new product nearly always requires additional investment in fixed assets or inventories. Economic profit helps to determine if such investments can be justified by the profit that is earned (Farris, et al., 2010).

For instance, an NPD project that contributes $10M in economic profit to the corporation will have (Boer, 1999):

EVA is a registered trademark of Stern Stewart in the United States.

- Paid for all cash outflows necessary to complete the project,
- Funded all cash outflows at the company's actual cost of capital, and
- Generated an additional $10M inflow for the corporation.

In one example, a new product project generates an after tax net profit of $12M but requires a capital expenditure of approximately $31M. Because the firm could otherwise invest this money at 6.5% interest, the cost of capital is $2M ($31M x 0.065). By deducting the cost of capital from the net profit after taxes, the value added to the corporation is only $10M.

Economic profit calculations are more complicated than NPV and ROI; therefore, the project team should consult the organization's project management office, finance, or treasurer's department for guidance. While somewhat more complex, economic profit can be a beneficial measure for NPD projects as it combines the concept of a return on investment with the volume of profits. In particular, economic profit, or EVA, is useful to assess trade-offs in innovation projects and other business activities.

Project Payoff

Project payoff, also known as payback, is another financial tool that is used to evaluate the simple return on a project. The *payoff period* is the amount of time it takes to recoup the development costs. Payoff is a simple return calculation and does not account for the time value of money; thus, financial experts generally prefer NPV and ROI over payoff period analysis. On the other hand, the simple relationship of project payoff is easily understood and can be useful in situations in which the revenues or profits from a current product are used to fund the next generation product.

Payoff analysis determines how much time (normally in months or years) will elapse before the accrued benefits (revenues and/or profits) from the new product will overtake the investment (development) costs. Figure 43 illustrates the payoff analysis for a new product development project. This graph is often called a *program return map* since it plots the cumulative returns of the project (y-axis) over time (x-axis).

Development costs for the new product are shown with the orange line in Figure 43. As the new product is launched at month 12, development costs decline substantially at this point in time; thus, the curve levels out with a total cumulative development cost of $36M spent during the previous twelve month period.

Immediately upon commercialization, revenues begin accruing for the new product (blue curve). A simple profit calculation subtracts the development cost from sales revenues (green curve). Note that at month 28, the profit from the new product is equal to the cumulative development costs ($36M). This point is commonly referred to as the *break-even point* or *break-even time*.

Program return maps can assist senior management and the portfolio management team in making project selection decisions. Additionally, many smaller firms will rely upon the cash flow from existing products to fund the next generation product development effort. Because the profit exceeds the costs any time after the break-even point, the timing to investigate the next generation effort can be optimized.

In other situations, senior management may establish an internal requirement on payoff period, often requiring a break-even point less than two years for simple product improvement projects. More complicated development efforts can expand the utility of the program return map by including discounted cash flows. Furthermore, other companies may feel secure investing in the next generation product when the revenues balance the development costs (month 22 in Figure 43 above).

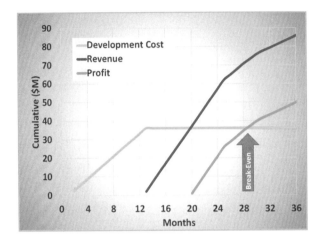

Figure 43 - Program Return Map

Certainly, the shorter the payoff period is, the better for the firm as it recovers development costs sooner. However, senior management must acknowledge the trade-off between simple product improvements with shorter payoff periods and more sophisticated, long-term development efforts that may lead to radical, market-changing innovations.

Sales Forecasting in NPD

Financial metrics described thus far (NPV, ROI, economic profit, and payoff period) all rely upon correct sales forecasts of the new product. However, budgets are normally far more accurate in predicting future costs than predicted sales can estimate future revenues. As described above, expenses can be estimated with a high degree of accuracy when using historical or parametric references. Sales of a new product, on the other hand, are less certain due to a variety of market factors.

Sales of new-to-the-world or new-to-the-company products may be estimated using market research methods. Forecasts will normally include a range of error to account for optimistic, average, and pessimistic sales estimates. As a product advances through the stages of the structured NPD process, the range of error for sales forecasts and costs to manufacture the product will both narrow.

Many new products are derivatives, enhancements, or improvements of existing products. Sales forecasting is straightforward in these cases as future sales can be extended based on existing data. This is similar to the historical cost estimating process described previously. For instance, an NPD team can estimate future sales to hold steady with a 5% price increase for an improved storage product offering larger capacity. In other cases, product sales will be forecast using a model based on actual sales figures from the market adoption of a similar product.

Diffusion of Innovation

Scientifically, the word *diffusion* means that a substance spreads from a single point. For example, an aerosol spray diffuses from the source throughout the room. Likewise, *diffusion of innovation* is defined as the process by which the use of an innovation is spread within a market group, over time, or through various categories of users adopting the product.

Sometimes called the *consumer adoption process*, diffusion of innovation was first introduced by Everett Rogers in 1962. Rogers identified four elements (Sahin, 2006) to spreading a new idea throughout a specific group:

- The innovation or idea itself,
- A communication pathway,
- Time, and
- A social system.

For new product development, these four elements are implemented through a consumer who is completely unaware of the existence of a product but is later converted into a regular user of the product. This transformation occurs when the consumer becomes aware of the product through communication channels in his or her social system, takes a risk to try the product when it is available to him or her, and then likes the product enough to purchase it again regularly.

New product marketing has shifted to include a consumer adoption process in which early adopters of the new product are targeted. This is in contrast to former marketing approaches in which heavy users with high degrees of brand loyalty or mass market approaches were used for new products (Kotler & Keller, 2006). The theory behind diffusion of innovation allows the marketing experts on the NPD team to identify the early adopters.

The most pertinent aspect of diffusion of innovation is how a new product moves through the marketplace. For example, Chapter 2 described disruptive innovation in which consumers in fringe markets will adopt a new product even with inferior performance on a standard measure because it offers more convenient features in other dimensions. Within the constructs of the theory of diffusion of innovation, these customers are identified as "*innovators*". Such consumers are willing to take a risk and personally value being the first to own a new product. The model indicates that innovators make up a small fraction (2.5%) of any market group or category.

Identified as *early adopters*, the next category of consumers make up about 13.5% of the market or category. Diffusion of innovation theory (Kotler & Keller, 2006) indicates that when about 15 to 20% of the market adopts a new product, the product will become a standard in the market and is accepted. At this tipping point, then, the *early majority* (approximately one-third of the total market group or category) assumes no substantial risk in adopting the new product for their own use. This early majority is then followed by the *late majority* (34% of the market) who wait until most of their peers have adopted the innovation.

Finally, a group called *laggards*, making up 16% of the market, demonstrate skepticism regarding the new product innovation. These consumers may never adopt the product or be very reluctant to do so. Laggards may not have the financial resources to purchase the product or the infrastructure in their communities to use the product. Additionally, this group of consumers requires a high degree of assurance that the product will work, and therefore, their decision period is very long. For example, when the touchtone telephone replaced the dial telephone, laggards in the United States often included elderly people who did not adopt the new technology because it was difficult for them to understand. On the other hand, countries with little infrastructure (geographical laggards) did not adopt the touchtone phone because the technology simply was not available to them.

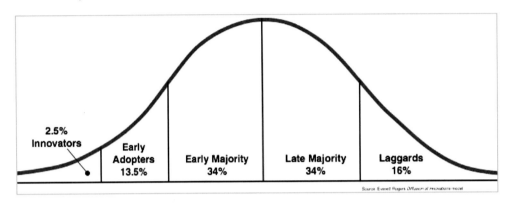

Figure 44 - Adopter Categories Based on Time of Adoption of Innovation[*]

It should be noted that many firms will stage the marketing of their new products based upon these different market segments identified in the diffusion of innovation model. Many products have a life cycle that follows a Gaussian distribution, similar to that presented in the diffusion of innovation model. Thus, an innovation may reach maturity congruent with the timing when late adopters finally become regular users of the product. Consequently, new product developers can use the model both for marketing purposes as well as planning for next generation product development projects.

ATAR Forecasting Model

Many firms will prepare and consider several different forecasts in order to converge on expected sales and profits from new products. In addition to the timing in which customers will adopt the new product, NPD teams will also approximate the profits from sales of new products. Costs and expenses to develop and manufacture the product are normally estimated with a higher degree of accuracy than are the sales. However, both sales volume and revenue can be forecast for many consumer goods, especially those with well-known target customer populations and similarly positioned products that have already been commercialized. A specific forecasting model that builds upon the theory of diffusion of innovation is the ATAR model.

The ATAR model, as illustrated in Figure 45, is based on expert assumptions estimating the percent of the target market that is *aware* of the new product, the percentage of these consumers who are willing to *try* the new product, the percent of these people who have the product *available* for purchase, and finally, the percent of customers who have tried the product and like it enough to *repeat* the purchase (Kahn, 2013). Thus, the acronym ATAR describes the chain model of adoption for a consumer who is initially ignorant of the existence of a new product to a loyal, repeat purchaser:

---

[*] Image courtesy of http://allinio.com/tag/diffusion-of-innovation/

- A – aware,
- T – trial (or try),
- A – available, and
- R – repeat purchase.

Using the ATAR model, the NPD team will first estimate the overall market size and then break down this target market to find a potential profit margin for the new product.

As shown in Figure 45, a company that is marketing a new liquid bath soap estimates the total market size for a geographical region of four million. Advertising and marketing campaigns are designed for magazines, radio, and television, contacting approximately 75% of the target market. Thus, awareness of the new product reduces the target market size to a potential market of three million customers. Based upon market research involving focus groups and free sample distribution at shopping malls, the NPD team estimates that 20% of consumers who are aware of the bath soap will try the product. Following the breakdown of the ATAR model, the potential market size is reduced to 600,000 potential consumers.

Further, distribution of the new bath soap is limited to partnerships with certain retail outlets, amounting to about half of the retailers in the geographic region stocking the new bath soap. Potential purchases of the new product are reduced to 300,000 based upon 50% availability. Finally, of consumers who are aware of the product, try the product, and have it available to them, 30% become loyal adopters and will make repeat purchases of the product. Again, following the breakdown of the ATAR model, the potential number of customers for the bath soap is 90,000.

Unit sales can then be estimated from the assumptions of the ATAR model, as illustrated in Figure 45. An average consumer will purchase a bottle of liquid bath soap every month. By combining the number of potential repeat purchasers (90,000) and the number of annual purchases (twelve), annual unit sales are predicted to be well over one million bottles of bath soap.

Next, with a retail price of $3 per bottle, the annual revenue for the new product can be estimated as $3,240,000. Profit is then forecast for the new bath soap by subtracting manufacturing costs ($0.50 per unit). Expected profits, then are $2,700,000 for the new product on an annual basis.

Benefits and Cautions of the ATAR Model

Unit sales and profit forecasts can be calculated with a high degree of accuracy using the ATAR model. While competition is not directly addressed within the model, understanding that market penetration is a factor of awareness, trial, and availability of the new product allows for the fact that a product will rarely gain 100% of the market to which it is targeted. Additionally, the ATAR model accounts for consumer behaviors based on market research (trial and repeat purchase rates) and it can be easily modified to frame products that may not have characteristics of consumer packaged goods (Kahn, 2011).

For instance, cars, appliances, and industrial equipment are not subject to frequent purchases, so elements regarding repeat purchases and number of units purchased per year can be removed from the model. Assumptions regarding market size, awareness, trial, and availability will then lead to predictions of unit sales and profit margin for such products or services.

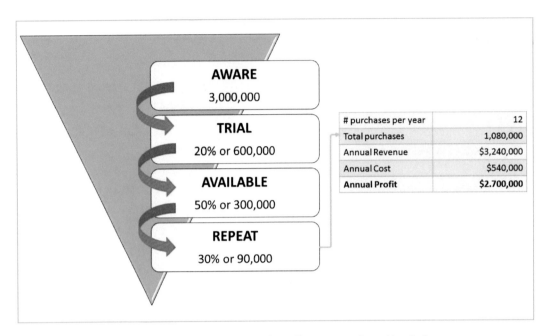

Figure 45 - ATAR Sales Forecasting Model

With any assumption based model in new product development, the output can be strongly influenced by the market size and breakdown expectations. For example, adjusting the trial rate in the bath soap example by just 5% (trial = 25% instead of 20%), the estimated profit will increase by over $500,000. To improve the accuracy of the sales forecast using the ATAR model, many companies will use historical market research data to populate the breakdown variables of awareness, trial, and repeat. A range of estimates can also provide valuable data to the NPD team. Thus, knowing that a similar product launched into the same geographical region one year earlier generated 23% trial rates would validate an optimistic sales forecast for the bath soap of $3,375,000 (trial = 25%) and a pessimistic forecast of $2,700,000 (trial = 20%).

Due to the amount of detail incorporated into the ATAR model, this forecasting tool is best applied at later stages of the NPD process. Outputs from the sales forecast and profit model may be incorporated for senior management decisions in portfolio management and the structured NPD processes. Pricing and cost assumptions will be validated as the product is commercialized, and actual sales data should be evaluated during the product post-launch reviews.

Summary of Innovation Tools

Innovation tools are wide-ranging and cover all aspects and stages of the NPD process. Idea generation tools can assist the NPD team during early stages of the NPD process to identify markets, technologies, and products. *Portfolio management* is also utilized during all stages of the NPD process to prioritize and rank new product ideas, including those that are generated from *brainstorming* or other *ideation* systems.

Likewise, portfolio management uses *financial analysis* tools (like NPV, ROI, economic profit, and payoff) to screen projects for the active portfolio and gatekeepers will evaluate financial attractiveness of each NPD project in order to advance it to the next stage of work. During development stages, engineers and designers will use a variety of innovation tools to add or improve the functionality of products.

Finally, market research data is incorporated into many of the NPD processes to assist with financial evaluations and commercialization forecasts. Diffusion of innovation and the ATAR model rely upon general market assessments as well as primary research data collected to evaluate each new product.

Senior management and NPD team leaders will evaluate NPD project decisions and strategic alignment by using a set of metrics. Many of the innovation tools lend themselves to further adoption as measures of innovation success.

Innovation Metrics

Metrics are needed to drive performance of innovation teams and to evaluate the results of new product initiatives. Innovation metrics are defined as a prescribed set of measurements to track product development and allow a firm to measure the impact of process improvements over time. While there is no one

> *Innovation metrics are a prescribed set of measurements to track product development.*

single set of specific metrics that will work for all organizations in all industries, innovation metrics are established to:

- Support the business and innovation strategies,
- Reinforce critical organizational capabilities,
- Evaluate the financial return on innovation efforts,
- Monitor industry best practices,
- Motivate continued learning among NPD teams, and
- Drive profitable business growth.

In addition, effective innovation metrics allow senior management to examine NPD efforts in support of the business strategy from a fact-based position, identify gaps in capabilities, and implement prioritized improvements as necessary.

Designing a Metrics Program

While most organizations use innovation metrics to review NPD project results, only 38% of firms utilize metrics to link strategy to individual goals and objectives (Chan, 2005). Firms must establish a balanced set of metrics to ensure quality decision-making to advance individual NPD projects as well as to prioritize the overall product portfolio. Metrics for innovation should be balanced across dimensions including historical performance; project, program, and portfolio; and productivity, timing, and cost. Furthermore, innovation metrics should not only measure the outputs and end results of a program establishing effectiveness of the NPD system, but should also measure inputs to the innovation efforts in order to drive preferred behaviors and capabilities within the organization.

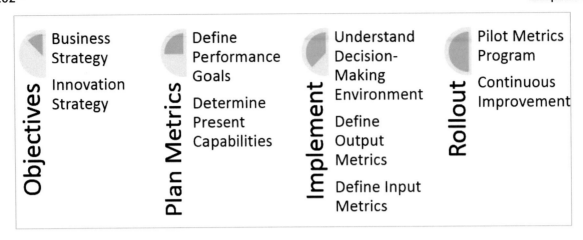

Figure 46 - Designing an Innovation Metrics Program

As shown in Figure 46, there are four steps to designing an effective metrics program for innovation:

1. Clarifying objectives,
2. Planning the metrics program,
3. Implementing innovation metrics, and
4. Rolling out the program across the business.

In addition, firms should consider metrics at four different levels:

- Corporate (or enterprise),
- Platform (or product),
- Program (or project), and
- Process.

A hierarchy of business metrics, from the corporate level to the process level, will allow an organization to balance interwoven new product development innovation objectives in support of the overall business and innovation strategies.

Objectives

Clarifying the objectives of the metrics program is perhaps the most important step in designing an innovation metrics system. Metrics must support the business and innovation strategies, yet tracking too many metrics can lead to unanticipated outcomes. Inappropriate metrics may encourage individuals and team members to focus on the metrics themselves, rather than driving behaviors and capabilities to grow and sustain the innovation system (Kerr, 1995).

Metrics for innovation must be tied to the strategy and linked to the performance of the new product development resources in support of the strategy. Factors that lead to innovation success differ by business and innovation strategies, yet different strategies can yield success for different companies competing within the same industry (Griffin & Page, 1996). For example, consider two fictional companies: ACME Corporation and Wiley Industries.

ACME Corporation follows a business strategy to produce leading edge products with an innovation strategy consistent with that of a prospector (see Chapter 1). To measure successful outcomes of their innovation programs, ACME will track the percent of sales derived from new-to-the-world products released in the previous three years. Additionally, ACME will use budget measures, such as percent of R&D spending relative to sales, to indicate performance and alignment of the innovation programs with their strategy.

Because metrics must also drive team behaviors, ACME will utilize measures such as time-to-market, NPD process life cycles (length of time to complete a stage of work), and number of new competencies. Capabilities and competencies for NPD team members may also be measured through the number or percentage of employees receiving technical and innovation training during a specific period as well as the effectiveness of the structured NPD program.

Wiley Industries, on the other hand, follows a classic cost leadership strategy (see Chapter 1). Wiley's innovation strategy closely resembles a defender; thus, success metrics will focus heavily on operational stability, such as the percent of components reused in a next generation product. You'll recall that a defender strategy involves maintaining an existing customer base with little investment in radical new product development. Wiley will also use performance metrics, such as ROI and break-even time, to encourage appropriate team behaviors that will lead to manufacturing excellence.

Corporate Metrics

At the highest level, a firm will evaluate its long-term effectiveness in undertaking research and development activities and in developing new products and services. *Corporate*, or enterprise, level metrics indicate the successful implementation of the company's business and innovation strategies. Corporate level metrics can be used to benchmark the firm's innovation performance against other companies. Moreover, corporate metrics provide feedback to senior management regarding growth and leadership capabilities within the organization.

Common corporate metrics may include the following:

- Capital investment in innovation activities,
- Percent of ideas from external vs. internal sources (open innovation),
- Product development cycle time,
- Current year percent of revenue from newly released products,
- Percent of new products capturing 50% or greater market share,
- R&D expense as a percent of sales,
- Number of new patents (including filed, pending, awarded),
- Innovation team headcount,
- Return on investment (ROI), and/or
- Break-even time (BET).

While many of these measures are common across various industries, senior management must consider the organizational value and utility of an individual metric in driving performance and team behaviors. For example, studies have *not* shown any direct correlation between R&D spending or number of patents granted and innovation performance (Jaruzelski, et al., 2005). However, such metrics do indicate visible commitment to new product development as a strategic goal for the firm and might be used to benchmark company performance against other industry competitors.

Strategic Alignment

As indicated, corporate metrics should align with the company's strategic objectives. Recall from Chapter 1 that innovation strategy types include *prospector* with a desire to be first to market, *analyzer* who is happy in a fast follower position, *defender* wishing to maintain stable operations but will innovate as necessary to protect its domain, and finally, *reactor* who may be struggling to concisely identify a consistent strategic direction for its innovation programs. Table 8 below illustrates some typical corporate level innovation metrics for each Miles and Snow strategy type (Griffin & Page, 1996).

Table 8 – Corporate Level Innovation Metrics by Strategy Type	
Strategy Type	**Suggested Innovation Metrics**
Prospector	• Degree that today's products offer future opportunities • % sales from products <N years old • % profits from products <N years old
Analyzer	• Degree that new products align with business strategy • Development program ROI • % profits from products <N years old • Success/failure rate
Defender	• Development program ROI • Program achieves 5-year objectives
Reactor	• Development program ROI • Success/failure rate • Degree that new products align with business strategy • Overall program success

Notice that metrics for a prospector strategy will primarily focus on growth and will assess how previous NPD efforts support future growth. Similarly, analyzer firms will include metrics related to growth from product development, while at the same time examining the productivity of the innovation programs. However, a defender strategy will utilize metrics aligned with the effectiveness and efficiency of a product development program because innovation is a necessary, but not a core, objective of the firm's operations. Finally, a firm with a reactor strategy will follow metrics that are generally subjective and may vary with each particular innovation project. Corporate level metrics for reactor firms, who are typically undergoing deep transformational change within their organizations, will subjectively track financial performance.

Corporate level innovation metrics drive both exploration and exploitation. That is, over the long run, innovation measures should increase the organization's capabilities in finding new ideas that are strategically aligned with the business as well as being successful in commercializing new opportunities.

Planning

An effective evaluation of innovation success requires understanding the objectives and then organizing the effort. *Planning the innovation metrics program* includes defining performance goals and identifying any gaps between current conditions and the future state. Companies that utilize metrics to drive their innovation systems are empowered to identify gaps in R&D and NPD capabilities, and then are able to initiate continuous improvement for long-term profitability and growth aligned with the business strategy.

Medium-term metrics are effective for innovation program planning and setting goals. Performance measures drive behaviors, help managers and team leaders select the right projects, and focus attention on the key innovation objectives. Senior management should plan an innovation metrics program that defines performance goals as well as determining present capabilities and competencies of the R&D organization. Goal-setting directs attention to what needs to be done, keeps creative people challenged, and provides a sense of purpose and urgency for the new product development efforts.

In planning innovation metrics and setting performance goals, NPD teams become motivated to achieve the strategic mission. People tend to accomplish more when striving for performance goals that are challenging or difficult, yet are clearly defined. Performance goals regulate behaviors by focusing attention on how hard and how long people work as well as encouraging diverse task strategies to facilitate accomplishing the goals.

Companies with the best performance measurement outcomes will choose metrics that balance productivity, quality, cost, and time to market (Chan, 2005). Firms will assess current innovation metrics to leverage them wherever possible, yet should also plan an innovation metrics program to measure appropriate variables that drive desired behaviors. Innovation performance metrics should be collected with accuracy and efficiency.

Platform Metrics

Sometimes called product metrics, *platform metrics* are medium-term, balanced measures to determine the effectiveness in meeting new product development project objectives. Often, these measures include technical performance, requirements specification, and/or product engineering and design constraints.

Furthermore, health of the overall innovation program can be assessed at the platform level by the number of employees who have received continuous training in innovation tools and systems. Maturity of the structured NPD process and portfolio management systems is also a leading indicator of innovation success.

Technical and design measures will be specific to the platform or product under development; however, some commonly utilized platform metrics may include:

- Number of customer needs identified,
- Cumulative number of changes in product requirements,
- Percent of specification deficiencies at different NPD stages,
- Number of mechanical design changes,
- Number of prototype revisions,
- Percent of post-design review changes,
- Product weight vs. plan / goal,
- Design range (lifetime) of the product,

- Mean time between failures, and
- Unit production costs.

Project Type Innovation Metrics

In balancing the product portfolio, companies will ensure that the project types are distributed according to the short- and long-term business goals. As indicated in Chapter 1, project types may be plotted on a graph similar to the product/market matrix. From a performance measurement perspective, a company may consider how new the product is in the marketplace as compared to how new the product is to the firm. Various recommended innovation platform level metrics are then recommended based upon project type as shown in Table 9.

New-to-the-World Products

Products that are *new to the world* will create an entirely new market. Such project types may be the primary focus of firms with a prospector strategy (Griffin & Page, 1996). New-to-the-world goods or services offer customers solutions to problems they had not previously been able to solve. Thus, new-to-the-world products will be gauged successful based primarily upon customer-based measures. Success may be indicated by the degree to which the product is accepted by consumers and end-users, and will spur the adoption of the product by others in the marketplace (see Figure 44).

New-to-the-Company Products

New-to-the-company products allow a firm to enter an established market. Products that are new to a firm are introduced by companies among all of the effective long-term innovation strategies: prospector, analyzer, and defender (Griffin & Page, 1996). Thus, useful innovation metrics will measure competitive performance, market share, and profits gained by the company. Customer-based metrics are important for these project types because customer satisfaction with the new product must be significant to gain market share for the firm. Product profitability is also important for a new-to-the-company product since the business case for the new product will identify additional revenue opportunities as a measure of success.

Line Extension Products

Additions to existing product lines (*line extensions*) are of moderate newness to both the market and to the firm. These type of products will supplement a company's established product lines. Product line extension projects are initiated for a variety of reasons, including:

- Reaching specific target markets and sub-categories of consumers,
- Defending the product line from competitive assault,
- Increasing frequency of use with new varieties, and/or
- Broadening the overall product appeal to additional markets or customers.

Line extension projects are initiated at the highest numbers within firms pursuing analyzer and defender strategies (Griffin & Page, 1996). In addition, reactor firms, undergoing a sea change in strategy and focus, will work on many new product development projects to extend the reach of existing product lines.

Table 9 – Common Platform Metrics by Project Type						
Suggested Innovation Metrics	New to the World	New to the Company	Line Extensions	Product Improvements	Repositioning	Cost Reductions
Newness to Market	High	Low	Medium	Low	Medium	Low
Newness to Firm	High	High	Medium	Medium	Low	Low
Competitive Advantage	✓	✓	✓	✓	✓	
Customer Acceptance	✓				✓	✓
Customer Satisfaction		✓		✓		✓
Market Share Goals		✓	✓	✓		
Met Profit Goals	✓	✓	✓	✓	✓	
Margin or ROI Goals	✓					✓
Revenue Growth		✓		✓		✓

As with the new-to-the-company project type, line extensions will utilize customer-based performance measures as well as financial metrics to gauge success. These metrics will include market share and profitability goals. Perhaps most useful to understand success of a line extension project is a measure of competitive advantage as the product line may be aging or susceptible to market erosion by new competitors.

Product Improvement Products

Product improvements are also of intermediate newness to the firm; although, the customers will generally view the improvement or revision to an existing product as low in newness. Projects of this type will offer improved performance or a greater value from the customer's perspective. Product improvement projects may completely replace an existing product already available from the company or other competitors with a "new and improved" version.

Firms within all of the Miles and Snow strategy types (see Chapter 1) are involved in developing and commercializing improved products (Griffin & Page, 1996). These projects offer the next generation performance for existing products and services. Henceforth, firms are concerned about maintaining market share and a competitive advantage, while at the same time, financial performance is important to sustain the product line.

Innovation success metrics for product improvement projects may depend upon the health and maturity of the overall industry. Revenue growth is an appropriate measure in a high-potential industry with many growth opportunities. However, customer satisfaction and market share may be adequate measures by themselves of platform level innovation success in the case of stagnating markets.

Repositioning Products

Repositioning existing products into new markets or market segments is a lesser practiced strategy (Griffin & Page, 1996). While the product is an existing technical offering from the firm, it may be of intermediate newness to a market. Such projects are undertaken to breathe new life into an existing product line which may be suffering from declining sales in the primary market.

Therefore, customer acceptance becomes a key success measure for the innovation project. As with a new-to-the-world product, consumers must not only accept the new product, but they also must be satisfied with the offering. Additionally, because the base product may be subject to increased competition or declining sales, meeting profitability goals is important in repositioning a product into a new market.

Cost Reduction Products

Cost reduction projects are low risk to a firm because they are not necessarily new to the firm nor to the market. These products will typically offer similar performance and benefits at a lower cost and are pursued by firms among all strategy types with the highest concentration of projects from companies with defender strategies (Griffin & Page, 1996). Cost reduction projects were also identified as support projects from a portfolio management standpoint (see Chapter 3).

Projects to reduce manufacturing costs of a new product may be undertaken throughout the life cycle of the product. Early in the NPD process, firms are learning how to streamline the manufacturing processes as well as building efficiencies into the distribution systems. As products mature, cost reduction projects can stimulate financial stability in the face of vigorous competition. Thus, many of the common measures of innovation success for a cost reduction project include financial goals, such as attaining profit margin, return on investment, and revenue growth.

Additional technical success metrics for a cost reduction project will include meeting quality standards and meeting performance specifications. These product requirements cannot be sacrificed in order to maintain the current market share and are necessary elements to continue to satisfy the existing customer base.

In planning innovation metrics, performance goals must be balanced against current capabilities. Matching the technical performance measures with platform level strategic initiatives can help a firm determine innovation success. While the project type innovation success measures presented in Table 8 are commonly used at both the platform and enterprise levels, many firms will focus the platform level metrics solely on the technical accomplishments of the new product.

Implementing

Devising an effective innovation metrics system requires clarifying objectives and aligning these goals with the strategy, and planning the metrics program by defining performance goals and evaluating gaps with the current measurement system. With this solid understanding of the background and reasons for assessing new product development program success, the next step is to *implement innovation metrics*. During the execution phase of an innovation metrics program, senior management and innovation leaders will need to fully understand the decision-making environment as well as to define the specific input and output measures.

In particular, many innovation measures are utilized to inform decisions regarding continuation of a new product development project or to halt those projects that are unattractive to pursue. Management should implement innovation metrics that move beyond simple financial measures and transform the capabilities of the organization. Innovation metrics should be balanced, transparent to the NPD teams, and flexible enough to provide continuous learning and growth. Furthermore, innovation metrics should support the decision-making processes for NPD.

Decisions are taken under many diverse circumstances in the life cycle of an innovation project. The structured NPD process (see Chapter 4) evaluates individual programs against a set of given strategic and tactical criteria. Many of these metrics blend medium-term platform (technical) goals with the overarching strategic direction of the firm. Portfolio management tools and techniques (see Chapter 3) also evaluate NPD projects by prioritizing all active projects within the constraints of available financial and human resources. Additional long-term corporate level metrics provide feedback to senior executives regarding the achievement of and appropriateness of the given business and innovation strategies. Finally, the ability to benchmark corporate and platform level innovation metrics alongside other industry competitors allows a firm to further gauge their level of success.

An effective innovation metrics system must identify *who* is responsible for reviewing the current performance of the new product development programs and *who* is responsible for initiating improvements. Often the NPD facilitator will play a key role in collecting and analyzing overall innovation metrics, especially those covering medium-term and long-term effectiveness. In addition, the NPD process owner will maintain ownership of many of the platform, program, and process level metrics. Both the NPD facilitator and process owner will review and revise gathering of innovation metrics in order to ensure consistency and relevancy in tracking new product development success measures.

Defining Output and Input Metrics

Many of the innovation metrics that indicate effectiveness of the innovation strategy tend to measure outputs of the innovation system; that is, gathering data retrospectively. NPD team behaviors and individual projects can be influenced by metrics that encourage innovative performance and balanced risk-taking (Kaplan, 2014).

Output metrics are typically lagging, measuring the outcomes of innovation efforts after the projects have been completed. These metrics describe the quantitative success of the business but do not necessarily drive innovation actions. Many of the corporate and platform level metrics are outputs of the innovation system: percent of revenue from products less than five years old, development program ROI, and percent of mechanical design changes.

Input metrics, on the other hand, establish and reinforce an innovation mindset. With leading indicators, managers can shape the environment and encourage NPD teams to convert nascent ideas into valuable business propositions. Input metrics demonstrate that innovation efforts are adequately staffed by the right people, appropriate budgets and guidance are provided through effective gatekeeping, and new product development is aligned with the overall strategy.

Examples of input metrics include percent of external ideas (open innovation), portfolio balance (breakthrough vs. incremental), and number of employees fully trained within the innovation systems.

Many of the medium-term metrics used to drive innovation performance are program level measures of innovation effectiveness.

Program Metrics

Program metrics evaluate the medium-term effectiveness in executing development projects and/or programs. Sometimes, program metrics are referred to as *project metrics*. Innovation metrics at the program level will assess organizational systems and processes in their ability to assist and streamline the innovation process. NPD process improvements may be initiated as a result of evaluating program metrics as well as implementing specific project management tools to drive continued performance and eliminate gaps between the current and ideal state of the innovation system.

In addition to measuring project performance with the traditional variables of the triple constraint (scope, schedule, and cost), program metrics will evaluate the productivity, development life cycle, and resource capabilities. The project post-launch review will provides a natural forum to discuss the medium-term effectiveness in implementing innovation programs at the firm. Recall that the post-launch review evaluates a project from a learning and growth perspective, asking what went well during the execution of the NPD project, what went wrong, and finally, what can be improved the next time.

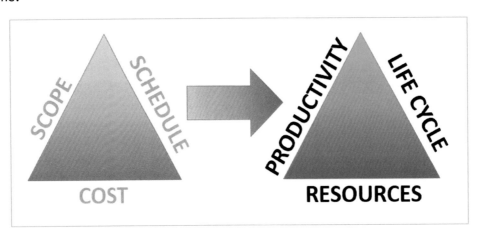

Figure 47 - Program Level Metrics

Additional program level metrics beyond the post-launch review may include:

- Schedule performance (actual vs. plan),
- Cost performance (actual vs. forecast), and/or
- Average number of innovation training hours per employee,
- Balanced scorecard.

Balanced Scorecard

A *balanced scorecard* is suggested as a program level metric to determine innovation success by examining financial and other measures that demonstrate effective implementation of the strategy. In utilizing a balanced scorecard, firms are able to bridge the gap between strategy development and strategy implementation within NPD teams. In addition to standard financial measures, a balanced scorecard will measure performance in three additional arenas designed to drive improved innovation behaviors. These four perspectives are (Kaplan & Norton, 1996):

- Financial dimension,
- Customer perspective,
- Internal business processes, and
- Learning and growth.

Financial Dimension

Businesses will always need to measure financial outcomes as they are the keys to survival. However, the advantage of the balanced scorecard is that financial metrics are incorporated across other strategic focus areas and are integrated with performance measures to drive continued improvements. Financial dimensions of the balanced scorecard will indicate whether the firm's chosen innovation strategy is contributing to the bottom line, and if not, allows for early course correction.

Some financial measures included on a balanced scorecard are percent of ideas selected for funding, return on R&D, and percent of R&D investment in new products. In general, a firm should select financial measures that reflect their strategic growth objectives, such as increased share in target markets or increased profits from new products. Financial metrics on the balanced scorecard help senior management and NPD teams understand value creation throughout the innovation life cycle.

Customer Perspective

While it is rather obvious that customer satisfaction is an expected outcome of innovation programs, many firms fail to specifically measure the results of new product development from the customer perspective. As described in Chapter 2, a business model includes application of a unique customer value proposition to a target market in order to improve the profitability of the company. A novel customer value proposition is measured within the balanced scorecard to ensure that product performance, quality, and service meet or exceed the customer's expectations.

Key benefits of including the customer perspective in a balanced scorecard is to focus the strategy implementation and to measure the perceived value from the customer's viewpoint. Consumer responses provide market insights and can yield new opportunities for innovation in next generation products.

Some customer measures that may be included on a balanced scorecard include product return rates, customer complaint levels, and return on R&D capital employed. Additional program level metrics on a balanced scorecard may include improved customer satisfaction and increased market share. A net promoter score is another commonly used customer perspective used within the framework of a balanced scorecard. In general, market metrics that detail customer profitability, growth, and satisfaction will guide senior management and NPD teams in understanding the effectiveness of implementing innovation strategies at the program level.

Internal Business Processes

A balanced scorecard will address whether internal business processes, procedures, and policies support the strategy through targeted innovation efforts. Organizational culture plays a large role in how decisions are made and in selecting active projects for new product development. Internal business processes, such as portfolio management and the structured NPD process, drive both management decision-making and NPD team behaviors. NPD teams will take actions consistent with policies and procedures, thus influencing the innovation value creation for the organization.

Internal business process metrics will focus on the operational side of the business and drive specific actions and team behaviors related to risk tolerance and decision-making for new product projects. Focus areas include operations management (R&D), customer integration, and regulatory impacts on innovation. Measures for the balanced scorecard within the internal business processes dimension may include development cycle time, NPD project costs, and pricing models.

Employee satisfaction may be included as a proxy or leading indicator of customer satisfaction, as well. Studies (Kaplan & Norton, 1996) have found strong correlations among employee satisfaction, number of product suggestions, and improved quality of work. Additional program level metrics included within a balanced scorecard may be coordination of activities, partner alliances, and influenced of external regulations on R&D programs. Moreover, a balanced scorecard approach to program innovation will allow integration of relevant business initiatives (e.g. total quality management) into a single management view describing successful strategy implementation.

Learning and Growth
Long-term, successful innovation depends upon continued organizational learning and knowledge transfer. The balanced scorecard measures learning and growth to ensure senior management focuses performance on internal skills and capabilities that support the value creation, delivery, and capture to customers through new product development.

While an organization can achieve short-term innovation success that is manifested through improved financial numbers, long-term, repeatable innovation success relies upon the systems and culture within the NPD teams and functions. Thus, learning and growth measures will detect gaps in employee performance and compare the firm to key competitors.

Some suggested measures for learning and growth within a balanced scorecard approach include NPD team member training and experience, competency or training needs, and employee attitudes and aptitude for innovation. Firms may also benchmark the number of patents, licenses, and technology transfer agreements to demonstrate learning and growth at the program level.

In general, a balanced scorecard approach is beneficial to a firm striving for innovation improvements. Because the measures integrate financial performance with key focus arenas on customers, internal business processes, and learning and growth, a firm can evaluate the effectiveness in the execution of its strategy at an operational level. In addition, the balanced scorecard offers early warning signs of trouble areas, such that gaps in performance or strategic direction can be identified and addressed.

Innovation Metrics Roll-Out
As with new products themselves, an innovation metrics system should be designed, tested, and adjusted for continuous improvement. As shown in Figure 46, designing an effective innovation metrics system involves clearly identifying the objectives, planning the metrics program, implementing innovation metrics, and rolling out the metrics plan across the business. Recall that

innovation metrics fall into several categories or levels: corporate, platform, program, and process metrics.

In previous steps of designing the innovation metrics system, senior management will have identified key measures to validate the innovation strategy as well as target levels for improvement. When the innovation metrics system is rolled out, this initial set of metrics will be tested along aspects such as:

- Availability of data,
- Ease of gathering data,
- Appropriate roles and responsibilities for data collection,
- Capacity of metrics to drive performance, and
- Establishment of continuous improvement opportunities.

Rolling out a metrics program should include a pilot program in which a single business unit or a small geographical division first tests and validates effectiveness of the innovation metrics. Senior management and innovation team members will solicit candid feedback from participants in the pilot program to identify improvement opportunities and to initiate any necessary corrective actions.

Once verified by a pilot program, the innovation metrics can be rolled out *en masse* across the corporation's business units and locations. As innovation metrics become accepted and standardized within the company culture, benefits will be apparent through the quality of the innovation projects that are initiated and selected, and NPD team performance will continuously improve to drive and support the strategy. Innovation metrics will include a balance of long-term, medium-term, and short-term measures of success.

Process Metrics

Process metrics are short-term measures to determine the effectiveness of the innovation process. Often process metrics are used to *predict* the performance of an individual NPD project or the product itself. Oftentimes, process metrics are evaluated during the first post-launch review to evaluate the effectiveness in applying the structured NPD process to the specific project. Such lessons learned reviews may be conducted throughout the life cycle of the NPD project in order to establish the current state of the project as compared to its plan. These intermediate project evaluations are a natural outgrowth of the project gate and milestone meetings.

Some example process metrics will include actual resource staffing as compared to the plan, cost and schedule performance (under- or over-runs), and quality measures (such as errors per 1000 lines of software code or number of design drawings issued). Like other innovation metrics, process measures are specific to the new product under development. However, a general rule of thumb regarding process metrics is that the measures should evaluate the current status of the project in order to predict performance of the product. Any actions necessary to bring the development effort back into line with the project plan, as determined in the product innovation charter (PIC) or specific gate deliverables, should be taken as a result of declining process metrics.

Pitfalls of Innovation Metrics

Because organizations use metrics to drive behaviors, it is important to be aware of some pitfalls in using innovation metrics. These include confusing or conflicting metrics, lack of transparency, and not supporting the business objectives.

First, as a firm is designing and implementing an innovation metrics system, it is best to start small with a few, transparent metrics. These measures should be simple and easily understood by the entire organization. Measures should be direct and lack confusion or conflict. For example, tracking both the percent of revenue *and* percent of profit from new products will be confusing to NPD team members. Actions to improve revenue performance may be quite different than actions to improve profitability. Team members will need to develop new products that are consistent with the innovation strategy, and thus, need clear, concise, and transparent metrics to drive and support performance and organizational learning.

Next, innovation metrics that are transparent are easy to understand and calculate. For example, the balanced scorecard financial measures should be kept simple, such as new product ROI, in order for team members to fully understand how their actions impact the performance measure. In addition, senior management needs to ensure that performance metrics are transparent so that team member behaviors are informed by input measures, and improvements in the innovation system are indisputable.

Finally, all innovation metrics must be tied to the business objectives. Often, when output performance measures are highly visible to an organization, workers will strive to improve their performance in the metric arenas alone. Instead, innovation metrics, both input and output measures, need to support the desired behaviors and actions that serve to close quality gaps in the innovation system. Therefore, all innovation metrics need to be closely tied to the business and innovation strategies, and provide clear linkages to actions that drive changes in the final measures.

Summary of Innovation Metrics

Innovation metrics are varied and specialized to accommodate a firm's particular innovation and business strategies. Measures of success for new product development span a wide range and need to accommodate many different circumstances. Innovation measures of success should support and drive the strategy.

Designing an innovation metrics system includes steps to clarify the objectives, plan the metrics program, implement the program, and rolling out innovation metrics across the business. Measures of new product development and R&D success will include output metrics by gathering and analyzing data on past performance. Firms with the most successful innovation programs also use input metrics that encourage and support team behaviors that sustain the innovation strategy, goals, and objectives. Metrics need to go beyond simple financial numbers to include customer focus, internal business processes, and learning and growth.

Four common levels of innovation metrics are *corporate*, *platform*, *program*, and *project*. These measures balance long-term, strategic opportunities with the performance of specific NPD projects and the firm's innovation systems. A hierarchy of these innovation metrics is illustrated in Figure 48.

Candidates for NPDP certification should be familiar with the four levels of innovation metrics as well as recommended measures of success in each category. Innovation metrics are supported by a variety of tools and techniques, yet are customized to match each firm's specific innovation goals and objectives.

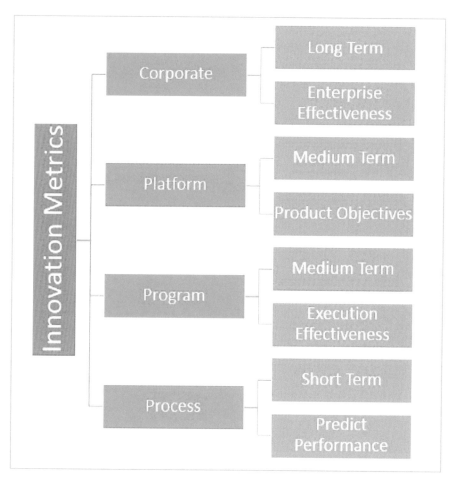

Figure 48 - Four Levels of Innovation Metrics

Chapter 8 – Hints and Tips for the Exam

New product development professional (NPDP) certification demonstrates mastery within the field of innovation. NPDP certification formally recognizes a commitment to process consistency and discipline in striving to improve products and services. Individuals with NPDP certification testify to their expertise of NPD principles and best practices, perform better on the job, and are recognized as leaders in the field.

Preparing for the NPDP Exam

As described in the Introduction and Overview, the NPDP certification exam covers six key topic areas supporting innovation best practices:

1. NPD Strategy,
2. Portfolio Management,
3. New Product Development (NPD) Processes,
4. Teams and Organization,
5. Market Research, and
6. Tools and Metrics.

Many candidates for the NPDP certification exam have experience in either technical product development or in marketing. Moreover, many candidates are mid-level managers and may not have had an opportunity in their career paths to participate in strategy development. Thus, the strategy section on the NPDP certification exam tends to be lower scoring than many other sections. Additionally, candidates should recognize that, in practice, the design and execution of an effective innovation strategy is interwoven throughout all arenas of a new product development professional's career.

Thus, experience plays a large role in preparation for the NPDP certification exam. However, there is no substitute for adequate study prior to the exam. In addition to reviewing the materials in this guide, candidates should be able to define common NPD vocabulary terms and apply NPD concepts to simple case scenarios. Knowing the material thoroughly is important to passing the NPDP exam, yet, candidates should not approach the exam through simple memorization of data. NPDP certification probes knowledge, application, and analysis of innovation principles and best practices.

Depending on one's learning style, a candidate for NPDP certification may prefer additional classroom study. Global NP Solutions offers affordable NPDP certification study options including a fully self-directed, self-study course; guided on-line training courses; and customized, face-to-face NPDP certification workshops.

Candidates should also practice answering test questions, especially if they are unfamiliar with the computerized exam format or have been away from a school environment for more than three to five years. Practice exams are available in a variety of formats. On-line practice exams often mimic the look and feel of the formal certification exam and can be found at www.globalnpsolutions.com.

Studies show that there is no advantage in cramming for an exam like the NPDP certification which relies upon deep knowledge and experience in the field. However, candidates must be careful to follow innovation best practices to pass the exam and not the typical procedures deployed at their own companies. While many firms follow the basic innovation principles outlined in this guide, many organizations have adapted shortcuts or use inadequate procedures that fail to encompass all six arenas of a successful new product development program.

Eight Tips for Taking the NPDP Certification Exam

1. The NPDP certification exam is computer based and will begin with a short tutorial on how to use the software at the testing facility. You will be able to mark questions for later review and this feature is convenient to give you a feel for how well you are progressing with the exam. Generally, candidates will proceed quickly through the entire exam while marking questions on which they later want to spend more time. Time management is an important skill in test-taking.

2. Visit the exam site prior to the day you are taking your exam. You'll want to know how long the commute is so that you arrive a few minutes early for your scheduled exam. Most people are "morning people," so it is generally recommended to take the NPDP certification exam in the morning when you are more alert. You also must manage stress appropriately and you cannot necessarily expect that the testing area will be quiet. You should prepare for personal comfort during the exam, such as bringing a sweater with you. Deep-breathing techniques help many candidates relax as they take the exam.

3. Although three-and-a-half hours seems like a lot of time for a multiple choice exam, remember that there are 200 questions on the NPDP certification exam. Each multiple choice question will have four possible answers. Candidates should answer all questions for which they have a high degree of confidence first, marking others for later review. There may appear to be more than one "correct" answer, but you must choose the *best* answer among the choices provided.

4. Do not try to read more into the question than what is stated. There are no trick questions on the exam, but some may be poorly worded or excessively lengthy. Many people are successful at reading the question, yet fail to read *every* possible answer. Choosing an answer on a multiple choice test before reading all of the options misleads candidates to select a "distractor" answer. Some people find it helpful to read the answers in reverse order (D to A instead of A to D) to ensure that they have thoroughly reviewed each answer choice.

5. To increase your odds in selecting the right answer, first eliminate the obviously wrong options, and then choose among the remaining options. Many questions will have only two plausible options. Do not be misled by negative words in the question or answer. Questions and responses may include words such as *not*, *none*, and *neither*. Sometimes these words are confusing to test-takers, but if you slow down and carefully read the question, you should be able to piece together the correct scenario and response.

6. You will be provided with blank paper and a pencil to use during the exam. Before you start the test, write down important items so that you do not have to rely later on your memory. If you have taken practice exams, you will want to jot down items for which you have struggled or been challenged to answer correctly. Remember that the NPDP certification exam is validating your knowledge of innovation best practices, and not what is typical at your company.

7. Be aware of answer choices with the words *always*, *never*, or *only*. These are considered extreme words and may indicate an incorrect answer because there are many exceptions to rules. Additionally, responses such as *all of the above* or *none of the above* may be distractors. Do not assume that these answers are correct and carefully review all of the answer choices.

8. Take a break after an hour or so. Many candidates will complete their first pass of the exam within an hour and a short break can clear your mind. A high protein snack may help you refocus on the exam, particularly in responding to the questions that you have previously marked for later review.

Final Words

New product development professional (NPDP) certification is an elite certification demonstrating mastery of innovation best practices. Completing your NPDP certification sets you apart as an expert and leader in the field. Again, congratulations on taking this step to advance your career!

Appendix A – NPV Example

Net present value (NPV) is a typical financial calculation used throughout business. Comparing the expected value of new product development (NPD) projects using NPV is a common practice within portfolio management. NPV is often used as a gate criteria in the structured NPD process as well.

NPV analysis is a method of calculating the expected monetary gain or loss by discounting the net value of all future cash inflows and outflows to the present time. Projects with a positive NPV indicate that the project payoffs will exceed the expense of developing the new product. Sometimes, however, NPD projects with zero or negative NPV will be considered as part of an overall development programs or for strategic reasons, even though the expected future costs are expected to exceed the revenues.

NPV Calculation Basics

At the foundation of net present value calculations is the assumption that future monetary values are less than they are at the present due to a combination of inflation and interest payments. Consider, for example, $100 deposited in a bank savings account that pays an effective interest rate of 5% per year. If there are no withdrawals, after one year the account will be credited with 5% interest, or $5, leaving a balance of $105. Holding this amount for another year, the account will grow to $110.25 since the interest on $105 is $5.25. Continuing to hold the balance in the savings account, with no withdrawals, the $100 can grow to $207.89 after 15 years, for example.

Mathematically, the future value is expressed as in equation [A-1] below.

$$[A\text{-}1] \qquad FV = PV\,(1+r)^n$$

In equation [A-1], FV represents the future value, PV is the present value, r is the effective annual interest rate, and n is the number of periods (years). Thus, a candy bar that costs $1.00 today will cost $1.30 in three years, as shown in equation [A-2] with an inflation (interest) rate of 9.1%.

$$[A\text{-}2] \qquad FV = \$1.00(1+0.091)^3 = \$1.30$$

Note that equation [A-1] can be rearranged to find the present value necessary to achieve an expected future value, as in equation [A-3] below.

$$[A\text{-}3] \qquad PV = \frac{FV}{(1+r)^n}$$

Thus, if the savings account balance must be $500 in 10 years with an assumed 6% effective annual interest rate, a deposit of $279.20 must be made today. This is shown in equation [A-4].

$$[A\text{-}4] \qquad PV = \frac{\$500}{(1+0.06)^{10}} = \frac{\$500}{1.791} = \$279.20$$

Taken as a variable, the factor of $1/(1+r)^n$ is called the *discount factor*. Tables of discount factors are published in many accounting and financial texts as well as on the internet. Sometimes called an interest rate table, these data tables will allow a user to look up a specific discount factor based on the interest rate and number of periods. Discount factor calculators are also readily available on the internet to provide future value estimates based on inputs of the present value, interest rate, and number of periods. Spreadsheet software is also utilized extensively to calculate future or present values.

Simple Project Comparison

Companies will use NPV to compare projects and to select active projects with the highest expected returns. NPD projects, like all other projects, are limited by resources and investment ability. Trade-offs among projects are necessary.

Instead of investing $1.00 today to buy a candy bar in three years, one could make an investment to purchase five pencils instead. Knowing that a pencil will cost 30¢ each in three years, the future value if $1.50 (5 x $0.30). Using equation [A-3], today's required investment is $1.15 as shown in equation [A-5] below.

$$[A-5] \qquad PV = \frac{\$1.50}{(1+0.091)^3} = \frac{\$1.50}{1.30} = \$1.15$$

Because the investment in the candy bar is less than pencils, the firm may choose to invest in snacks and to *not* invest in pencils. As a further example, let's assume that Company ABC is considering two new product development projects. However, there are only enough resources available to invest in one of the two projects. ABC can decide which NPD project to undertake based upon the NPV calculation.

Extension Project

First, Company ABC will consider an extension to an existing product. The extension is expected to cost $10,000 and complete development this year. Sales are not expected to occur for two years, at which point, the revenue will be $11,500. Equation [A-6] shows the details of the NPV calculation.

$$[A-6] \qquad NPV = -\$10,000 + \frac{\$11,500}{(1+0.05)^2} = -\$10,000 + \$10,430.84 = \$430.84$$

Thus, using a two-year basis, the extension project will have a net present value of $430.84.

Platform Project

Company ABC is also considering a new platform development project. In this case, the development costs are expected to be $8,000 this year. Revenue is expected to be $4,500 per year for the following two years.

Recurring payments or revenue streams are modeled by financial *annuity* calculation. Equation [A-7], below, shows the formula for an annuity, in which equally sized net monetary inflows and outflows occur on a regular basis. Annuity calculations are useful in predicting NPD project values when sales are forecast to be level over a long period of time. In equation [A-7], R represents this equally sized revenue stream.

$$[A-7] \qquad FV = R \left[\frac{1- (1+r)^{-n}}{r} \right]$$

Therefore, the platform project results in a net present value (NPV) of $367.35 as shown in equation [A-8].

$$[A-8] \qquad NPV = -\$8{,}000 + \$4{,}500 \left[\frac{1- (1+0.05)^{-2}}{0.05} \right] = -\$8{,}000 + \$8{,}367.35 = \$367.35$$

Project Comparison

Because the extension project and new platform project have different forecasts of future revenues, the NPV calculation provides a reasonable comparison of the value of the two projects. If Company ABC is only concerned with a two-year horizon and only financial innovation metrics, they will choose the extension project since the NPV is greater for it than for the platform project.

As indicated in Chapter 3, however, NPD projects should be compared on a life cycle basis rather than short-term horizons as given in this simple example. Moreover, factors other than NPV, such as strategic fit and market attractiveness, should be considered for all new product development projects.

Life Cycle Project Comparison

In contrast to the simple project comparison given above, most new product development projects will include complex sales forecasts over the product's expected life cycle. Both sales volumes and unit prices will vary over the lifetime of the product. In addition, the life cycle of one product may be somewhat shorter or longer than other products in the firm's portfolio. Thus, a life cycle NPD comparison is recommended, especially for project selection criteria within portfolio management functions.

Spreadsheet tools are extremely useful for life cycle NPV calculations of new product projects as well as for "what-if" scenarios. Using live spreadsheet analysis during portfolio management reviews can also address valuation questions that may arise from senior management. Microsoft Excel, for example, has simple built-in NPV functions and formulas that can be utilized in financial forecasting for new product development.

Derivative Project Example

In this case, Company XYZ is comparing a derivative project with a standalone new product. The derivative product has remaining development costs of $10,000. Sales forecasts have been completed and are shown in Table A-1 below. Thus, the net annual cash inflow and outflows can be estimated assuming an annual interest rate of 5%. Company XYZ expects to retire the derivative product after 12 years and completely replace the product line.

In Table A-1, the discount factor is calculated according to equation [A-3] above. The results of the net present value calculation are identical using the Microsoft Excel function "NPV". Note that the life cycle net present value of the derivative product is found by summing the net present value for each year. Moreover, the NPV formula accounts for varying sales volume and unit price forecasts over the lifetime of the product – forecast sales of 380 units at a price of $25.00 in Year 8 and forecast sales of 370 units at a price of $28.50 in Year 9. Even when sales volume and unit prices are higher, sales in later years are more heavily discounted than sales expected nearer to the present period. In summary, the overall expected NPV for the derivative product is approximately $55,000 over a 12 year life cycle with an assumed interest rate of 5%.

Year	Costs	Sales Volume	Unit Price	Annual	Discount Factor	Net
1	$10,000.00	0	$ -	$(10,000.00)	0.9524	$ (9,523.81)
2	$ -	200	$ 25.00	$ 5,000.00	0.9070	$ 4,535.15
3	$ -	250	$ 25.00	$ 6,250.00	0.8638	$ 5,398.98
4	$ -	300	$ 25.00	$ 7,500.00	0.8227	$ 6,170.27
5	$ -	325	$ 25.00	$ 8,125.00	0.7835	$ 6,366.15
6	$ -	350	$ 25.00	$ 8,750.00	0.7462	$ 6,529.38
7	$ -	370	$ 25.00	$ 9,250.00	0.7107	$ 6,573.80
8	$ -	380	$ 25.00	$ 9,500.00	0.6768	$ 6,429.97
9	$ -	370	$ 28.50	$ 10,545.00	0.6446	$ 6,797.40
10	$ -	350	$ 28.50	$ 9,975.00	0.6139	$ 6,123.78
11	$ -	300	$ 30.00	$ 9,000.00	0.5847	$ 5,262.11
12	$ -	260	$ 30.00	$ 7,800.00	0.5568	$ 4,343.33
TOTAL						$ 55,006.53

TABLE A-1: DERIVATIVE PRODUCT #1

Standalone New Product Example

As discussed above, Company XYZ is also considering a standalone new product development project. In order to commercialize Product #2, $8,000 is required to be spent this year and an additional $2,500 next year. (To simplify the calculations, we will assume that the entire expense occurs at the end of the period. A similar assumption is made that all sales occur at the end of the period.)

Sales data for the new product are forecast to vary in volume over the 18 year life cycle as shown below in Table A-2. Note that the unit sales price of Product #2 is about one-third lower ($16.00 per unit) than the initial price point of Product #1 ($25.00 per unit).

Year	Costs	Sales Volume	Unit Price	Annual	Discount Factor	Net
1	$ 8,000.00	0	$ -	$ (8,000.00)	0.9524	$ (7,619.05)
2	$ 2,500.00	330	$ 16.00	$ 2,780.00	0.9070	$ 2,521.54
3	$ -	380	$ 16.00	$ 6,072.00	0.8638	$ 5,245.22
4	$ -	436	$ 16.00	$ 6,982.80	0.8227	$ 5,744.77
5	$ -	502	$ 16.00	$ 8,030.22	0.7835	$ 6,291.89
6	$ -	577	$ 16.00	$ 9,234.75	0.7462	$ 6,891.11
7	$ -	664	$ 16.00	$ 10,619.97	0.7107	$ 7,547.41
8	$ -	763	$ 16.00	$ 12,212.96	0.6768	$ 8,266.21
9	$ -	878	$ 16.00	$ 14,044.90	0.6446	$ 9,053.47
10	$ -	1009	$ 16.00	$ 16,151.64	0.6139	$ 9,915.71
11	$ -	858	$ 16.00	$ 13,728.89	0.5847	$ 8,027.00
12	$ -	729	$ 16.00	$ 11,669.56	0.5568	$ 6,498.05
13	$ -	620	$ 16.00	$ 9,919.13	0.5303	$ 5,260.32
14	$ -	527	$ 16.00	$ 8,431.26	0.5051	$ 4,258.36
15	$ -	448	$ 16.00	$ 7,166.57	0.4810	$ 3,447.24
16	$ -	381	$ 16.00	$ 6,091.58	0.4581	$ 2,790.62
17	$ -	324	$ 16.00	$ 5,177.85	0.4363	$ 2,259.08
18	$ -	275	$ 16.00	$ 4,401.17	0.4155	$ 1,828.78
TOTAL						$ 88,227.74

TABLE A-2: STANDALONE PRODUCT #2

Project Comparison

After comparing the life cycle net present values of the derivative product #1 and the standalone product #2, Company XYZ will select the standalone product on its financial merits. Again, however, new product projects must be compared with other criteria, such as strategic fit and market attractiveness, since financial metrics alone do not comprise a full and complete innovation decision.

Benefits of NPV

Nearly every business uses net present value as a financial metric to inform decisions for new product development. The benefit of NPV is that NPD projects can be compared with different project characteristics, such as development costs, sales revenues, and life cycles.

In calculating the NPV of different NPD projects, the project leader should work with the sponsor, the project management office, and finance or treasurer's departments in order to follow corporate policies and procedures for assumed discount rates and time horizons for projects. Consistency among NPV calculations is a key to a complete portfolio evaluation as well as in advancing NPD projects at gate reviews.

Appendix B - ROI Example

Return on investment, ROI, is a standard measure of project profitability. ROI is expressed as a percentage and is calculated by subtracting the discounted project costs from future discounted benefits and dividing by the required investment. Equation [B-1] below represents the general formula for ROI.

$$[B-1] \qquad ROI = \frac{(Total\ discounted\ benefits - Total\ discounted\ costs)}{Discounted\ costs}$$

For a $100 investment today that will pay $110 in one year, the ROI is 10%, as shown in equation [B-2].

$$[B-2] \qquad ROI = \frac{(\$110 - \$100)}{\$100} = 0.10 = 10\%$$

NPD projects are often implemented over multi-year periods and the final product may sell at different prices throughout its life cycle. Thus, discounted monetary values are important to consider when comparing one project against another as in portfolio management.

For instance, consider a new product project that requires $500,000 to complete development prior to commercialization in the current year. Market research studies have forecast sales for several years in the future with introductory and mass market price points. The firm uses a four-year forecast. Estimated sales data is shown below in Table B-1 and is discounted according to the present value method described in Appendix A. Both expenses and revenues are expected to occur at the end of the period, and a 7% interest rate is applied.

TABLE B-1: NPD PROJECT						
Year	Costs	Sales Volume	Unit Price	Annual	Discount Factor	Net
1	$500,000.00	0	$ -	$ (500,000.00)	0.9346	$ (467,289.72)
2	$ -	1500	$85.00	$ 127,500.00	0.8734	$ 111,363.44
3	$ -	2500	$100.00	$ 250,000.00	0.8163	$ 204,074.47
4	$ -	3000	$105.00	$ 315,000.00	0.7629	$ 240,311.99
TOTAL						$ 88,460.18

Thus, the return on investment for the NPD project with the cost and benefit data shown in Table B-1 over a four-year period is 19%, as detailed in equation [B-3].

$$[B-3] \qquad ROI = \frac{[(\$111,363.44 + 204,074.47 + 240,311.99) - \$467,289.72]}{\$467,289.72} = \frac{\$88,460.18}{\$467,289.72} = 0.19 = 19\%$$

A company with a hurdle rate of 15% would approve this project to move forward. Meanwhile, a firm with a hurdle rate of 20% would need to also weigh non-financial factors, such as strategic fit, growth opportunities, and alternative investment opportunities, in order to advance this NPD project further.

Note that considering life cycle earnings, rather than a four-year period alone, can also impact the return on investment. For example, considering the new product may have a life cycle of six years, instead of four, can change the ROI calculation substantially, as illustrated in Table B-2 and equation [B-4] below.

TABLE B-2: NPD PROJECT						
Year	Costs	Sales Volume	Unit Price	Annual	Discount Factor	Net
1	$500,000.00	0	$ -	$ (500,000.00)	0.9346	$ (467,289.72)
2	$ -	1500	$85.00	$ 127,500.00	0.8734	$ 111,363.44
3	$ -	2500	$100.00	$ 250,000.00	0.8163	$ 204,074.47
4	$ -	3000	$105.00	$ 315,000.00	0.7629	$ 240,311.99
5	$ -	2500	$99.00	$ 247,500.00	0.7130	$ 176,464.08
6	$ -	1500	$75.00	$ 112,500.00	0.6663	$ 74,963.50
TOTAL						$ 339,887.76

$$[B-4] \qquad ROI = \frac{\$339,887.76}{\$467,289.72} = 0.73 = 73\%$$

Benefits of ROI

Return on investment is a common financial metric used to evaluate and compare NPD projects. Portfolio management selection criteria will often include a financial metric, such as NPV or ROI, in addition to other success metrics. ROI is also evaluated during project post-launch reviews to validate earlier project assumptions for continued learning and improvement within the structured NPD process.

Senior managers should be aware that the calculations for any time value of money financial metrics (NPV or ROI) can be easily manipulated by subtle adjustments in the selected interest rate and/or time period. However, ROI offers an additional metric to compare projects on a risk-adjusted basis, as shown in Table B-3, below.

TABLE B-3: RISK-ADJUSTED PROJECT ROI				
Project Name	Discounted Benefits	Discounted Costs	ROI	Probability	Risk-Adjusted ROI
Blue	$50,000	$35,000	43%	0.10	4%
Green	$100,000	$28,000	257%	0.50	129%
Orange	$75,000	$15,000	400%	0.25	100%
Purple	$28,500	$20,000	43%	0.50	21%
Red	$90,000	$12,000	650%	0.30	195%
Yellow	$115,000	$60,000	92%	0.60	55%

When probability of success is taken into account, the risk-adjusted ROI of Project Blue becomes far less attractive than Project Purple, both of which demonstrated similar returns. Likewise, Project Orange with a lower investment cost than Project Green results in a lower risk-adjusted ROI. These types of complications in evaluating a project portfolio are common across all industries working in new product development and emphasize the challenges that senior managers must overcome in selecting NPD projects to include in the active portfolio.

Related Metrics

Return on Assets (ROA)

Several other financial metrics are closely related to ROI, indicating measures of profitability relative to the investment. For example, *return on assets* (ROA) measures the return on assets for the firm. Whereas ROI is calculating the return on investment for a single project alone, ROA computes the ratio of net income for the company relative to the average assets deployed over the period. Assets include both debt and equity instruments. Return on assets is calculated as in equation [B-5].

$$[B\text{-}5] \qquad ROA = \frac{Net\ Income}{Total\ Average\ Assets\ in\ Period}$$

While ROA is a common business metric, it is typically utilized for operational performance rather than NPD project forecasts.

Return on Capital Employed (ROCE)

Return on capital employed, ROCE, is another frequently used business financial metric. Like ROA, however, ROCE, typically measures the overall business health and performance rather than the contribution from a specific innovation effort. Higher values of ROCE indicate that a firm is utilizing its capital efficiently.

ROCE calculations are somewhat more complicated that ROI or ROA since the ratio includes earnings before interest and tax because these variables are presumed outside the control of the business manager. A standard ROCE calculation is shown in equation [B-6].

$$[B\text{-}6] \qquad ROCE = \frac{Earnings\ Before\ Interest\ and\ Tax\ (EBIT)}{Capital\ Employed}$$

Note that operations with newer equipment will frequently have higher valued capital, skewing the ratio to lower numbers. As with all financial metrics, ROCE needs to be considered alongside other business and innovation performance measures. Like ROA, ROCE is primarily used to evaluate ongoing operational performance.

References

Ansoff, H. I., 1957. Strategies for Diversification. *Harvard Business Review,* Sept-Oct.pp. 113-124.

Barczak, G., Griffin, A. & Kahn, K. B., 2009. Trends and Drivers of Success in NPD Practices: Results of the 2003 PDMA Best Practices Study. *Journal of Product Innovation Management,* Volume 26, pp. 3-23.

Bergek, A., Berggren, C. & Tell, F., 2009. Do Technology Strategies Matter? A Comparison of Two Eletrical Engineering Corporations. *Technology Analysis and Strategic Management,* May, 21(4), pp. 445-470.

Boer, P. F., 1999. *The Valuation of Technology.* NY: John Wiley & Sons.

Carter, J. & Bradford, J., 2012. *Innovate Products Faster.* Menlo Park, CA: TCGen Press.

Chan, A., 2005. Using an Effective Metrics Program to Support Business Objectives. In: K. B. Kahn, ed. *The PDMA Handbook of New Product Development.* 2nd ed. Hoboken, NJ: Wiley, pp. 445-454.

Chesbrough, H. W., 2003. The Era of Open Innovation. *MIT Sloan Management,* Spring, 44(3), pp. 35-41.

Christensen, C. M., 1997. *The Innovator's Dilemma: When New Technologies Cause Great Firms to Fail.* Boston, MA: Harvard Business School Press.

Cooper, R. G., 2013. New Products - What Separates the Winners from the Losers and What Drives Success. In: K. B. Kahn, ed. *The PDMA Handbook of New Product Development.* 3rd ed. ed. Hoboken, NJ: John Wiley & Sons, pp. 3-34.

Cooper, R. G., Edgett, S. J. & Kleinschmidt, E. J., 2001. Portfolio Management Methods Used and Performance Results Achieved. In: *Portfolio Management for New Products.* 2nd ed. New York: Basic Books, pp. 145-171.

Dugal, S. S. & Morbey, G. K., 1995. Revisiting Corporate R&D Spending During a Recession. *Research Technology Management,* July-August.pp. 23-27.

Farris, P. W., Bendle, N. T., Pfeifer, P. E. & Reibstein, D. J., 2010. *Marketing Metrics.* 2nd ed. Upper Saddle River, NJ: Pearson Education.

Gallupe, R. B. & Cooper, W. H., 1993. Brainstorming Electronically. *MIT Sloan Management Review,* Fall, Volume 35, pp. 27-36.

Giang, V., 2013. *The 'Two Pizza Rule' is Jeff Bezos' Secret to Productive Meetings.* [Online] Available at: http://www.businessinsider.com/jeff-bezos-two-pizza-rule-for-productive-meetings-2013-10
[Accessed 12 Aug 2014].

Goldratt, E. M., 1997. *Critical Chain: A Business Novel.* s.l.:Amazon Digital Services, Inc..

Greenberg, J., 2010. *Managing Behavior in Organizations.* 5th ed. Boston: Prentice-Hall.

Griffin, A. & Page, A. L., 1996. PDMA Success Measurement Project: Recommended Measures for Product Development Success and Failure. *Journal Product Innovation Management,* Volume 13, pp. 478-496.

Hauser, J. R. & Clausing, D., 1988. The House of Quality. *Harvard Business Review,* Volume May-June, pp. 63-73.

Hoegl, M., Holger, E. & Luigi, P., 2007. How Teamwork Matters More as Team Member Dispersion Increases. *Journal of Product Innovation Management,* Volume 24, pp. 156-165.

Honan, M., 2013. *Remembering the Apple Newton's Prophetic Failure and Lasting Impact.* [Online] Available at: http://www.wired.com/design/2013/08/remembering-the-apple-newtons-prophetic-failure-and-lasting-ideals/
[Accessed 21 January 2014].

Jaruzelski, B., Dehoff, K. & Bordia, R., 2005. *Money Isn't Everything.* [Online] Available at: http://www.strategy-business.com/article/05406?gko=3705a
[Accessed 28 May 2013].

Johnson, M. W., Christensen, C. M. & Kagermann, H., 2008. Reinventing Your Business Model. *Harvard Business Review,* December, 86(12), pp. 50-59.

Jurgens-Kowal, T., 2012. *Product Development Innovation Teams: Organizing for Success in Product Development.* Dallas, TX: Get to the Point Books.

Kahn, K. B., 2011. *Product Planning Essentials, 2nd ed..* Armonk, NY: M.E. Sharpe, Inc..

Kahn, K. B., 2013. Forecasting New Products. In: K. B. Kahn, ed. *The PDMA Handbook of New Product Development.* 3rd ed. Hoboken, NJ: John Wiley & Sons, pp. 265-293.

Kaplan, R. S. & Norton, D. P., 1996. Using the Balanced Scorecard as a Strategic Management System. *Harvard Business Review,* Jan/Feb.pp. 75-85.

Kaplan, S., 2014. *How To Measure Innovation (To Get Real Results).* [Online] Available at: http://www.fastcodesign.com/3031788/how-to-measure-innovation-to-get-real-results
[Accessed 18 Feb 2015].

Kaplowitz, M. D., Hadlock, T. D. & Levine, R., 2004. A Comparison of Web and Mail Survey Response Rates. *Public Opinion Quarterly,* 68(1), pp. 94-110.

Kerr, S., 1995. On the Folly of Rewarding A, While Hoping for B. *Academy of Management Executive,* Feb, 9(1), pp. 7-14.

Kerzner, H. R., 2013. *Project Management: A Systems Approach to Planning, Scheduling, and Controlling.* 11th ed. New York: Wiley.

Kotler, P. & Keller, K. L., 2006. *Marketing Management*. 12th ed. ed. Upper Saddle River(NJ): Pearson Prentice Hall.

Lafley, A. & Charan, R., 2008. *The Game-Changer: How You Can Drive Revenue and Profit Growth with Innovation*. NY: Random House.

Markham, S. K. & Lee, H., 2013. Product Development and Management Association's 2012 Comparative Performance Assessment Study. *Journal of Product Innovation Management,* 30(3), pp. 408-429.

Markides, C. C., 1999. *All the Right Moves: A Guide to Crafting Breakthrough Strategy*. Boston, MA: Harvard Business Press Books.

Mascitelli, R., 2011. *Mastering Lean Product Development*. Northridge, CA: Technology Perspectives.

Mattimore, B. W., 2012. *Idea Stormers: How to Lead and Inspire Creative Breakthroughs*. San Francisco, CA: Jossy-Bass.

Miles, R. E. & Snow, C. C., 1978. *Organizational Strategy, Structure, and Process*. New York: McGraw-Hill.

Porter, M. E., 1985. *Competitive Advantage: Creating and Sustaining Superior Performance*. New York: The Free Press.

Project Management Institute, 2013. *A Guide to the Project Management Body of Knowledge (PMBOK Guide)*. Fifth ed. Newton, PA: Project Management Institute, Inc..

Rosenfeld, R. B., Wilhelmi, G. J. & Harrison, A., 2011. *The Invisible Element*. s.l.:Idea Connection Systems.

Sahin, I., 2006. Detailed Review of Rogers' Diffusion of Innovation Theory and Educational Technology-Related Studies Based on Rogers' Theory. *The Turkish Online Journal of Educational Technology*, April, 5(2), pp. 14-23.

Scneider, J. & Hall, J., 2011. Why Most Product Launches Fail. *Harvard Business Review,* April.pp. 21-23.

Smith, P. G., 2007. *Flexible Product Development*. San Francisco: John Wiley & Sons.

Smith, S., 2013. *Coca-Cola Lost Millions Because of This Market Research Mistake*. [Online] Available at: http://www.qualtrics.com/blog/coca-cola-market-research/ [Accessed 22 July 2015].

Thota, H. & Zunaira, M., 2011. *Key Concepts in Innovation*. New York: Palgrave Macmillan.

Tuckman, B. W., 2001. Devlopmental Sequence in Small Groups (reprint). *Group Facilitation: A Research and Applications Journal,* Spring.pp. 66-81.

Tuckman, B. W. & Jensen, M. A. C., 1977. Stages of Small-Group Development Revisited. *Group & Organization Management,* 2(4), pp. 419-427.

NPDP CERTIFICATION EXAM: *a 24-hour study guide*

Vishwanath, V. & Harding, D., 2000. The Starbucks Effect. *Harvard Business Review,* March-April.pp. 17-18.

Voigt, K., 2009. *Mergers fail more often than marriages.* [Online] Available at: http://edition.cnn.com/2009/BUSINESS/05/21/merger.marriage/index.html [Accessed 23 January 2012].

Walker, R., 2013. *Winning with Risk Management.* Singapore: World Scientific.

Wheelwright, S. C. & Clark, K. B., 1992. *Revolutionizing Product Development: Quantum Leaps in Speed, Efficiency, and Quality.* New York: The Free Press.

Index

3D printing, 177, 179

A

Active product portfolio, 56, 113
Affinity charts, 159
Affinity diagrams, 159, 170, 172
Alpha Test, 116, 127
Analyzer strategy, 20, 32, 65, 204-206
Ansoff matrix, 28
Anthropological research, 126, 169
Asynchronous communication, 145
ATAR model, 192, 198, 201
Autonomous team, 136, 139, 163

B

Balanced scorecard, 210, 214
Beta Test, 116, 127
Bottom-Up Approach, 68-69, 72
Bottom-Up Budgeting, 184
Brainstorming, 81, 83, 158, 163, 165-166, 172, 179, 200
Brainwriting, 168
Brand leverage, 106
Brand loyalty, 24
Break-even point, 195
Break-even time, 195, 203
Breakthrough, 38, 50, 51, 57, 63, 69 71, 136, 140, 145, 148, 152
Bubble Chart, 63
Budget, 80, 135, 139
Budgetary authority, 77
Bundle test, 125
Business case, 85-87, 125
Business model, 14, 36, 43, 211
Business Model Innovation, 35, 47
Business plan, 150, 155
Business strategy, 27, 31, 32, 37, 38, 53, 57, 58, 152, 201
Business-to-business, 106, 107, 108, 122, 123, 127, 128

C

Champion, 160, 163
Co-creation, 31, 49, 81, 116, 143
Commercialization, 76, 86-87, 96, 114, 122, 151
Competitive intelligence, 27, 37, 101
Computer aided design, 176, 178
Computer-aided engineering, 178
Computer-aided manufacturing, 177
Concept evaluation, 83, 85, 11, 151
Concept generation, 81, 151
Concept statement, 114
Concept test, 83, 90, 112-114, 124-125, 127

Concurrent engineering, 157, 177
Conditional gate pass, 74, 78
Confirmatory market research, 106, 109, 112
Conflict resolution, 157
Conjoint Analysis, 173
Conservative strategy, 17, 19, 32
Consumer adoption process, 197
Contingency plan, 189, 191
Continuous improvement, 89, 94
Controlled sale, 122, 126, 128
Convergent thinking, 166, 171
Cooper's strategy framework, 16, 32
Core team, 129, 130, 135, 156
Corporate level metrics, 203-204, 209, 214
Cost estimates, 90
cost leadership strategy, 13-15, 19, 32, 203
Cost reduction projects, 49-50, 63, 133,138, 208
Cost-cutting, 9
Crashing, 183
Critical chain theory, 190
Critical path, 183, 191
Critical success factors, 38
Cross-functional team, 22, 77, 86, 88, 104, 129-131, 135, 138, 157, 162, 175-177, 186
Customer needs, 9, 16, 19, 23, 78, 80, 83-85, 98, 107-108, 111, 165, 169, 172, 175, 205
Customer satisfaction, 39, 45, 85, 90, 96, 103, 110, 111, 117, 152, 173, 206, 207, 211, 212
Customer site visit, 106. 111, 127, 169
Customer value proposition, 16, 32, 36, 43, 45, 48, 88, 113, 211

D

Decision-making, 47, 52, 62, 69, 71, 73, 79, 106, 129, 135, 139, 142, 157, 163, 201, 208
Defender strategy, 19-20, 32, 39, 203, 204, 208
Deliverable, 76, 77, 130, 150, 155, 16181, 185
Delphi method, 159, 170
Derivative products, 22, 23, 25, 51, 52, 63, 69, 71, 139, 140, 144

Development stage, 85
Development plan, 155
Cifferentiated strategy, 15, 16, 32
Differentiation Strategy, 14, 32
Diffusion of innovation, 197, 198, 201
Direct marketing, 123, 126, 128
Direction setter, 49, 71
Discount factor, 192, 221
Dispersed teams, 153, 163
Disruptive innovation, 41-43, 45, 51, 197
Divergent thinking, 166, 169, 171, 172

Diversification Strategy, 30
    Horizontal diversification strategy, 30
    Lateral diversification, 30
    Vertical diversification strategy, 30
Down-market, 26, 29, 42, 43

E

Economic profit, 192, 194
Economic value added, 194
Emerging markets, 41, 43
Engineering analysis tools, 178
Engineering design tools, 176-179
Enhancement, 19, 49, 50, 51, 52, 140, 144, 152
Enterprise level metrics, 203, 208
Ethnographic research, 10, 106, 126, 169
Exit strategy, 7
Exploratory market research, 104, 106, 109

F

Failure mode and effects analysis, 177
Fast follower strategy, 20, 37, 122, 2014
Fast tracking, 183
Faux sale, 124, 125, 128
Features, 41, 52, 83, 114, 135, 138, 146, 170, 173, 175
Feedback, 90, 92, 94, 96
Financial analysis, 83, 192, 201
Financial metrics, 57
Financial scoring, 55, 61
Financial tools, 192
First-to-market, 19, 20, 32, 37, 65
Fixed costs, 13
Float, 183
Focus group, 104, 111, 124-125, 127, 170, 199
Fringe customers, 19, 42, 43, 45
Full Sale, 120, 124, 127
Functional department, 131
Functional manager, 132, 133, 136, 139
Functional work team, 52, 138, 140, 162

I

Innovation strategy, 40, 50, 54, 62, 69, 74, 78, 92, 143, 147, 161, 181, 209, 211, 214
Innovation tools, 165, 200
Intellectual property, 10, 14, 44, 45, 58, 75, 76, 86, 125, 146
Intellectual trust, 148
Issues log, 187
Iterative approach, 69

K

Kick-off meeting, 40, 130, 142, 147, 148, 153, 155, 157
Killer Variables, 80

L

Leadership, 21
Lean manufacturing, 73, 175, 179
Learning organization, 89

Lessons learned, 89, 90, 94, 96, 146, 152, 213
Life cycle management, 5, 7, 79
Lightweight team, 51, 134, 136, 138, 144, 149, 152, 162
Line extensions, 20, 49, 144, 206

M

Market assessment, 81
Market development, 29
Market opportunity assessment map, 81
Market penetration, 28, 39, 199
Market research, 5, 83, 90, 97, 112, 151, 165, 173, 199, 201
Market segment, 9, 10, 13, 14, 15, 25, 26, 27, 28, 32, 38, 111, 115, 123
Market share, 13, 19, 26, 39, 42, 207, 211
Market strategy, 27, 40
Market test, 87, 96, 120, 122-125, 127
Market vision, 27
Marketing collateral, 114, 121, 180
Marketing plan, 87, 88, 92, 120, 121, 122, 123, 124, 126, 127, 128, 193
Metrics, 165, 201
Miles and Snow strategy, 18, 32, 34, 35, 204, 207
Milestone, 76, 130, 150, 182
Mini-market, 123, 128
Mission, 11, 32, 67, 150, 152

N

Net present value (NPV), 55, 63, 192, 221
Net promoter score, 211
New product development (NPD), 7, 33, 43, 71, 74, 112, 129, 151, 192
New Product Introduction, 88
New-to-the-company, 49, 50, 65, 144, 196, 206, 207
New-to-the-world, 32, 49, 50, 65, 132, 137, 140, 196, 203, 208
next generation, 152
next generation product, 52, 137
No-go decision, 77, 79
Nominal Group Technique, 158, 167
Not in the Game Strategy, 17, 32
NPD process, 5, 27, 47, 53, 68, 73, 95, 106, 112, 119, 126, 127, 130, 133, 158, 162, 166, 172, 176, 180, 181, 186, 191, 196, 200, 203, 205, 208, 209, 212, 228
NPD process facilitator, 90, 91, 93, 94, 95, 96, 161, 163, 185, 209
NPD process owner, 53, 92, 94, 95, 96, 209
NPD team, 75, 77, 80, 147, 151, 162, 167, 187
NPDP certification, 1
NPDP certification exam, 7, 35, 47, 65, 73, 75, 79, 97, 129, 165, 176, 179, 192, 218

O

Open innovation, 35, 43, 45, 49, 143, 170, 203, 209
Opportunity Identification, 80
Organizational Culture, 74, 94, 143

Organizational Structure, 131, 140, 162

P

Parametric models, 184
Pass (gate pass), 158
Payback, 195
Payoff period, 195
Performance metrics, 38, 40
Platform product, 21, 39, 53, 63, 71, 134, 136, 139, 140, 144, 163, 205
Platform level innovation metrics, 205, 208, 209, 214
Platform projects, 51
platform strategy, 21, 33, 51
Porter's classical strategic framework, 32
Portfolio, 23, 32, 78, 171, 201, 228
Portfolio balance, 54, 62, 71
Portfolio management, 4, 47, 71, 78, 83, 165, 182, 186, 192, 200, 205, 208, 209, 212, 221, 223, 228
Portfolio management software, 63
Portfolio manager, 52, 53
portfolio reviews, 158
Portfolio value, 55, 71
Post-launch review, 76, 77, 84, 85, 89, 94, 96, 146, 152, 162, 185, 193, 200, 210, 213, 228
Preliminary Business Case, 82
Premarket testing, 124
Price-buyer, 27
Primary market research, 102, 106, 110, 111, 113, 126
Probability impact matrix, 187
Problem-based ideation, 169-171
Process metrics, 213
Product attributes, 83, 113-114, 146, 173
Product benefits 82-82, 114
Product concept 83, 88, 125, 172, 177, 179
Product concept statement, 82
Product development, 29
Product Development and Management Association (PDMA), 2, 73
Product family, 21, 26, 51, 52, 111
Product innovation charter (PIC), 36, 45, 76, 77, 78, 81, 92, 101, 130, 136, 139, 140, 142, 145, 147, 153, 155, 158, 161, 213
Product launch, 87, 88, 92, 117, 120, 152
product line, 26, 27, 29, 30, 51, 63
Product line architect, 50, 52, 71
Product policy, 37
Product positioning, 106, 114, 120
Product protocol, 37, 40, 83, 84, 85, 95, 113, 119, 130
Product roadmap, 23, 37, 81
Product use test, 85, 90, 106, 112, 115, 127, 145
Product/market matrix, 28, 33, 206
Profit margin, 13, 43, 81, 208
Profitability, 16, 20, 42, 92, 192, 194, 206, 207, 227
Program metrics, 210, 214
Program return map, 195
Project leader, 143

Project management, 47, 80, 85, 95, 165, 180, 210
Project management office (PMO), 48, 93, 186, 195, 225
Project management plan, 84
Project manager, 131, 134
Project metrics, 210, 214
Project payoff, 192, 195
Project reports, 191
Project resourcing, 85
Prospector strategy, 18, 32, 50, 203, 204, 206
Prototype, 85, 95, 105, 125, 128, 176, 179, 205
Proven product prototype, 86
Pseudo Sale, 124, 125, 128

Q

Qualitative market research, 104, 108, 111, 126
Quality function deployment (QFD), 83, 102, 172
Quality management, 175
Quantitative market research, 110, 111, 127

R

RACI Chart, 155
Radical innovation, 35, 37, 49, 51, 152
Rapid inch-up, 31
Rapid prototyping, 179
Reactor Strategy, 20, 32, 204
Recycle (gate), 78
Redirect (gate), 78
Repositioning, 208
Resource allocation, 54, 55, 56, 69
Resource productivity, 70
Return on assets (ROA), 228
Return on Capital Employed (ROCE), 229
Return on investment (ROI), 49, 55, 192, 194, 195, 203, 208, 227
Risk management, 87, 165, 186, 189
Risk mitigation, 188
Risk register, 187
Risk tolerance, 50, 54, 63, 187, 189
    Risk-averse, 187
    Risk-neutral, 187
    Risk-seeking, 187
Roles and responsibilities, 131, 156, 157, 159
Rollout, 120-122, 126, 127

S

Sales forecast, 82, 83, 84, 109, 113, 124, 125, 193, 196, 200
Scenario analysis, 170
Schedule, 80, 139
Schedule compression, 183, 191
Schedule Compression, 183
Scope of work, 37, 47, 80, 131, 136, 146, 154, 157, 159, 181
Scope creep, 37, 89
Scoring methods, 54, 58, 62, 71
Secondary market research, 99, 111, 126
Secondary wave strategy, 24
Segmentation strategy, 15, 17, 19, 23, 26, 32

Semi-structured interview, 111
Senior management, 8, 32, 39, 47, 49, 50, 52, 66, 67, 69, 77, 80, 92, 95, 143, 147, 151, 159, 163, 187, 195
Senior Management Influence, 162
Sequential development, 132, 157
Shareholder value, 8, 9, 11
Showstopper, 79, 80
Simulated market testing, 124
Simulation, 179
Six Sigma, 175
Slack time, 183
Social media, 10, 88, 122, 170
Span of responsibility, 144
Speculative sale, 125, 128
Sponsor, 145, 148, 158, 160, 161, 163, 191, 225
Stage 1, 76, 80
Stage 2, 81, 166
Stage 3, 80, 83, 106, 112, 113, 119, 127, 169, 172
Stage 4, 80, 85, 106, 112, 113, 120, 180
Stage 5, 87, 106, 113, 117, 118, 120, 127, 151
Stage-Gate™ process, 73
Stages, 75, 76, 79
Stakeholders, 141, 170, 191
Strategic alignment, 52, 58, 66, 67, 68, 71, 91, 93, 204
Strategic Bucket Approach, 67, 68
Strategic launch plan, 86, 87, 88, 91, 120, 148
Strategy, 71, 76, 80, 129, 150, 170, 213
    see also *Innovation strategy*
    see also *Business strategy*
Subject matter experts, 133, 136, 137, 158, 166, 167, 176
Sunk costs, 193
Supply chain, 13
Support projects, 52, 63, 71, 208
Surveys, 109, 111, 127
Sustaining innovation, 41, 42, 43, 45
SWOT analysis, 169-171
Synchronous communication, 145

T
Task dependencies, 183
Team charter, 37, 149, 154
Team contract book, 149, 150, 153, 154, 155, 157, 158, 161, 163
Team development, 146
Team leader, 131, 147, 154
Team values, 152
Technical development, 151
Technology push strategy, 17, 18, 32, 38, 41, 132
Technology roadmap, 11, 22, 69
Technology strategy, 27, 30, 33, 40
Test Market, 120, 127
Tiered marketing, 121
Tiger team, 136
Time value of money, 58
Time-to-market, 14, 62, 74, 161, 203

Time-to-market, 14
Top-down approach, 67, 72
Traditional innovation, 44
Triple constraint, 180, 182, 183, 189, 190, 191, 210
Trust, 89, 148, 152, 153

V
Values, 12, 32, 67
    Team Values, 152
Venture team, 50, 136, 139, 140, 151, 163
Virtual teams, 153
Vision, 11, 32, 67
Voice of customer, 83, 107, 102, 111, 127, 173

W
Work breakdown structure (WBS), 181, 184

About the Author

Teresa Jurgens-Kowal is an inspired coach and mentor, guiding strategy and innovation development. As a trusted educator, Teresa provides guidance for candidates of the New Product Development Professional (NPDP) and Project Management Professional (PMP©) certifications. After 13 years of experience in the chemical industry, she founded Global NP Solutions, LLC. Since 2009, dozens of candidates have successfully completed their NPDP requirements under her coaching.

In addition to NPDP and PMP certifications, Teresa holds degrees in chemical engineering from the University of Washington (PhD) and University of Idaho (BS) as well as an MBA from West Texas A&M University. She is an active member of and book review editor for the Product Development and Management Association (PDMA). Teresa currently lives in Houston, Texas, and relaxes by scrapbooking and bicycling.

Made in the USA
Middletown, DE
10 March 2019